DAY TRIPS®
FROM INDIANAPOLIS

"A valuable edition for prowling Indiana and finding its treasures."

—David Mannweiler, Travel Editor, *Indianapolis Star*

"Day Trips from Indianapolis is a well-researched book that doesn't just tell you where to go and how to get there, but why you'd want to go in the first place. . . . great for anyone with a day to spare here and there."

—Donna Mullinix, Editor-in-Chief, *WHERE Indianapolis* and *Indianapolis Woman*

Help Us Keep This Guide Up to Date

Every effort has been made by the author and editors to make this guide as accurate and useful as possible. However, many things can change after a guide is published—establishments close, phone numbers change, facilities come under new management, and so on.

We would love to hear from you concerning your experiences with this guide and how you feel it could be improved and be kept up to date. While we may not be able to respond to all comments and suggestions, we'll take them to heart and we'll also make certain to share them with the author. Please send your comments and suggestions to the following address:

The Globe Pequot Press
Reader Response/Editorial Department
P.O. Box 480
Guilford, CT 06437

Or you may e-mail us at:

editorial@globe-pequot.com

Thanks for your input, and happy travels!

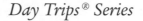

Day Trips® Series

GETAWAYS ABOUT TWO HOURS AWAY

DAY TRIPS®
FROM INDIANAPOLIS

by
Helen W. O'Guinn

The
Globe
Pequot
Press

GUILFORD, CONNECTICUT

Copyright © 2001 by The Globe Pequot Press

Cover image: Dubé Studio
Text design: M. A. Dubé
Maps: William Nelson and M. A. Dubé

Day Trips is a registered trademark.

Library of Congress Cataloging-in-Publication Data
O'Guinn, Helen W.
    Day trips from Indianapolis : getaways about two hours away / by Helen
W. O'Guinn.--1st ed.
        p. cm. -- (Day trips series)
    ISBN 0-7627-0838-7
        1. Indianapolis Region (Ind.)--Tours. I. Title. II. Day trips series (Guil-
ford, Conn.)

    F534.I33 O48 2001
    917.72'520444.dc21

                                                      2001023621

Manufactured in the United States of America
First Edition/First Printing

I dedicate this book
to my parents,
who taught me the art of traveling.

CONTENTS

NORTHWEST

WEST

SOUTH

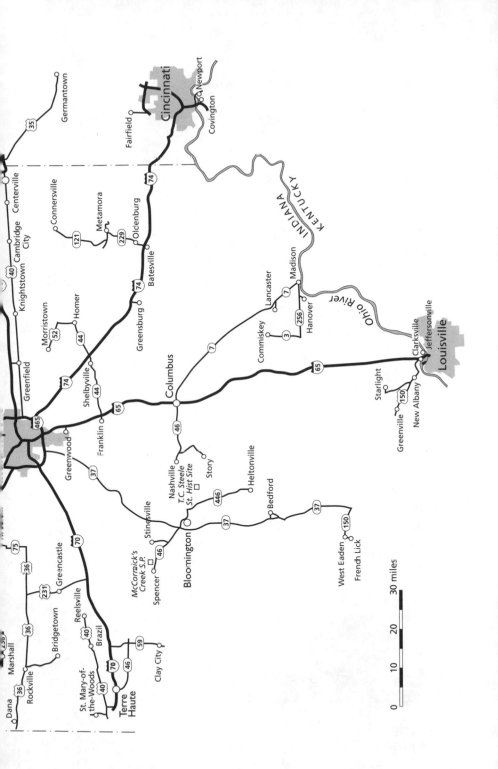

ACKNOWLEDGMENTS

I am grateful for the assistance of so many people in Indiana, Kentucky, and Ohio. In particular I owe special thanks to Megan Alexander, Barb Barnhard, Laurie Bowman, Ellen Crabb, Kate Drane, Susan Dallas, Mark Dollase, James Fadely, Alison Grant, Cari Grant, Amy Hwilka, Tanya Lenko, Jackson Mahaney, Tim Meyers, Nancy Sartain, Marilyn Smith, and my supportive husband, Dave O'Guinn.

PREFACE

Compiling this book of day trips—getaways less than two hours away—has been a delight. Those clever planners who, in 1820, chose to plop the capital in the center of Indiana made it possible for today's travelers to reach much of the state in two hours or less and to zip across the borders as well. Admittedly, a few trips do stretch the two-hour limit.

As my odometer ticked upward, I rolled up and down hills, through the majestic Hoosier National Forest, and across miles and miles of farmland. I have been to Indiana towns called Deputy, Mexico, Ceylon, and Monrovia. I have been to the Green towns: Greenwood, Greenfield, Greentown, Greencastle, Greensburg, and Greendale. I have taken wrong turns, but I have never felt lost. And I have passed turnoffs that I regret not taking, such as Groomsville and Hazelrigg.

Some states might be neatly divided into natural travel pockets. Indiana is not. In slicing up the state into day trips, I tried to consider not only those destinations that are clumped together geographically but also about how one might logically do a trip. For instance, while Cincinnati has a host of attractions and could be divided into separate Cincinnati and Northern Kentucky trips, Indianapolites are more likely to make it a single trip, including a night or two. On the other hand, Hamilton County, which is a skip away, is divided into two day trips to cover all the attractions.

I have discovered some passions in the Hoosier travelscape. For a state that has plotted its capital around a war memorial, it comes perhaps as no surprise that Hoosier cities make much of their war heroes and histories. Markers, statues, historic homes, and more abound. We also seem to have a lingering romance with trains. Although Amtrak's service barely casts a shadow in the state's transportation constellation, there are small excursion trains that enthusiasts refuse to let rust on the rails. In Corydon, French Lick,

Noblesville, and many other places, trains still run—erratically, perhaps; slowly, definitely—but run nonetheless. On a newer note, Indiana has developed a bubbling wine industry, beginning with the Oliver Winery in the 1970s. These wineries usually have tastings and dandy little gift shops.

The state's cuisine runs the gamut. Many restaurants thrive on the old standbys: biscuits and gravy, fried chicken, pork tenderloins, and green beans cooked forever with bacon. Yet innovative chefs are taking the region's best ingredients—fresh tomatoes, squash, pork, corn, and more—and creating their own distinctive dishes.

I confess two weaknesses: On the lofty end, I love historic sites. I cannot go to a town without searching for a historic marker, home, or building. Fortunately, Indiana has one of the strongest preservation organizations in the country, Historic Landmarks Foundation of Indiana. As a result, wonderful places, including the awesome West Baden Springs Hotel, are not only spared the ravages of time or the wrecking ball but are also revitalized. Most county seats have historical museums, but the quality of these varies widely. In general the museums are stuffed with interesting items representing local histories, but display is more problematic. Some displays are cohesive and well labeled; others leave too much to the visitor's imagination. Too few are interactive, inviting questions and helping the visitor understand the time. The ones listed here are among the state's best.

As you travel you'll develop a sense of styles of the past: decades-old little gas stations with overhangs supported by pillars, often antiques shops today; tall-windowed farmhouses with sweeping porches; and small downtowns with three-story brick buildings with wedding-cake touches. You may even come to recognize different barn styles.

My other weakness is not nearly as educational. I can shop anywhere: an art gallery, an electronics store, a bookshop—it doesn't matter. On the positive side, I've nearly perfected the art and know what to look for and where to find it. In each town I've let my nose lead me straight to the shops that sell the local specialties—mugs depicting the courthouse, note cards picturing historic local homes, or the jelly made from local currants. Antiques stores proliferate; I cannot remember cruising through a small town without at least one. Antiques shops dot the countryside as well.

USING THIS TRAVEL GUIDE

Maps and road designations: Maps are included that will generally show you the routes, and you can easily see how trips might be mixed together. You should, however, pick up a detailed state map. You can obtain a free one from EnjoyIndiana.com or at local tourism offices throughout the state.

For anyone getting off the main roads exploring the back roads of Indiana, knowing how the county roads are numbered is essential. County road numbers represent the number of miles from the county seat. So in Montgomery County, a road numbered 900 South would run east/west 9 miles south of Crawfordsville, the county seat. A road numbered 300 West would run north/south and be 3 miles west of Crawfordsville.

Time zones: Central Indiana is all in the same time zone, which does not observe Daylight Saving Time. As you get to the eastern edges of the state and head across the border, however, you'll find that the time zones change. The counties closest to Cincinnati, for instance, observe Eastern Daylight Saving Time.

Where to eat: The restaurants listed here are local stops, excluding national and regional chains, which are widely recognized. At least one dining spot is listed in every day trip, but some cities, such as Fort Wayne, Louisville, and Cincinnati, are packed with great dining choices; there simply isn't room to list them all. The price designations are as follows: $ (inexpensive, $7.00 and under for an entree); $$ (moderate, $8.00–17.00); $$$ (expensive, $18.00 and over).

Where to stay: With few exceptions, lodgings listed, like restaurants, are local spots, with many bed-and-breakfast inns included. In some cases an inn's restaurant is so widely touted that it is listed separately under Where To Eat. Price designations are as follows: $ (inexpensive, $74 and under per night for a standard room); $$ (moderate, $75–$134); $$$ (expensive, $135 and up).

Call ahead: Small-town attractions can be relaxed about adherence to posted hours. Hours of operation can change with the departure or addition of an employee, and restaurants may change the meals they offer. Often smaller attractions are open only in the afternoon. It is wise to call ahead to confirm that the places you are especially interested in are really open.

The prices and rates listed in this guidebook were confirmed at press time. We recommend, however, that you call establishments before traveling to obtain current information.

Northwest Day Trip 1

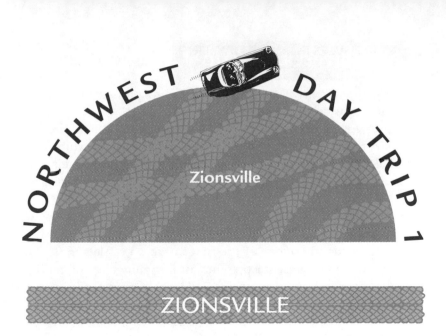

ZIONSVILLE

Settled in 1823 and platted in 1852 by William Zion, Zionsville is about 8 miles northwest of Indianapolis, reached by taking U.S. 421 (Michigan Road) north to State Road 334 and going west, until you reach the village's famed brick street. Rigorous local enforcement has kept Zionsville quaint, when so many other once-sweet small towns have gotten ticky-tackied up and pocked with all-night gas station/minimarkets. The quaintness is no accident. In the 1950s and 1960s the town reinvented itself in the fashion of an early American village, leading to the restoration of old homes and an influx of tourists. Historic homes and commercial ventures coexist on peaceful, tree-lined streets, and the town is a mecca for antiques lovers, who know that shops here are packed with treasures. The outskirts are home to horse farms and, to the west, suburban megahouses. Zionsville annually hosts the prestigious Traders Point Hunt Charity Horse Show.

WHERE TO GO

Lincoln Memorial Park. Corner of Cedar and First Streets. A railroad station once stood where this snippet of park sits today. The place is embedded in local lore because the train carrying Abraham Lincoln to his first inauguration stopped here, and the President-elect gave a speech to the citizenry. The park's gazebo figures prominently in local literature and is the focal point for local events.

Munce Art Center. 205 West Hawthorne Street, Zionsville, IN 46077. A small gallery, the Munce Art Center presents exhibits by regional artists, which change six to eight times a year; one room always includes Zionsville artists. Open Tuesday through Saturday. Free. (317) 873-6862.

P. H. Sullivan Museum and Genealogy Library. 225 West Hawthorne Street, Zionsville, IN 46077. Founded in the 1970s by the great-granddaughter of one of the first European settlers in Boone County, this small museum presents an intriguing mix of county heritage: furniture, quilts, costumes, old photographs, and even a Victorian hair wreath. The genealogy section contains more than 4,000 volumes and 70,000 surname cards. Open Tuesday through Saturday. Free. (317) 873-4900.

Walking Tour. Stop by the Greater Zionsville Chamber of Commerce, 135 South Elm Street (317-873-3836), for a visitor's guide and a walking-tour brochure, called *This Old Zionsville House.* (Some local merchants have this brochure as well.) The tour clearly marks a 2¼-mile route along tree-lined streets, past charming residences and commercial buildings. Diagrams distinguish house styles and their periods. Forty-nine separate sites are described in the brochure, along with details about history and architecture. For instance, you'll learn that Abraham Lincoln spoke at Lincoln Park, #39 on your tour, and that the home at 510 Pine Street, #43, is an example of vernacular architecture with an early-Victorian porch. Using the map you can slice up this tour to suit your own needs; there's hardly a more pleasant way to spend a sunny day.

WHERE TO SHOP

Altum's Horticultural Center & Gardens. 11335 North Michigan Road, Zionsville, IN 46077. Okay, it may seem more like Indianapolis, but there are some people who have not discovered this gardener's paradise on Michigan Road. Here there are acres and acres of plants and trees, along with a huge garden store filled with books; necessities, such as gloves and tools; and almost-necessities, such as garden art. Open seven days a week, except January and February, when Altum's is closed on Sundays; also closed on major holidays. (317) 733-4769; www.altums.com.

Brown's Antiques. 315 North Fifth Street, Zionsville, IN 46077. Out of the cluster of downtown shops, Brown's can be reached by heading north on Main to Walnut. Turn left and go 4 blocks to Fifth Street; turn right, and you'll see Brown's just 2 blocks up on the right. Two houses and additional buildings clustered around a pretty garden hold an array of antiques and gifts. One building contains almost exclusively lamps and lamp shades. The shop, which has been in this location for sixty-plus years, draws customers from throughout central Indiana. Open daily. (317) 873-2284.

Butler's Pantry. 213 South Main Street, Zionsville, IN 46077. A home and hearth store, the Butler's Pantry will inspire you to culinary greatness. Here you'll find precious teapots, scone mixes, lovely table linens, and all the decorative touches that turn a house into a home. Open Monday through Saturday. (317) 873-0911.

Firehouse Antique Mall. 85 East Cedar Street, Zionsville, IN 46077. The old fire station has been turned into an antiques mall and lighting center, with a nice selection of items, including some new accessories. It's all on one floor, not too large, and easy to navigate and find just what you'd like. Open daily. (317) 733-1073.

Harold's Haberdashery. 140 South Main Street, Zionsville, IN 46077. For men Harold has a wide range of clothing from casual to dress, including suits, blazers, golf wear, and fun Tommy Bahama clothing. Although the name might suggest a men's-only shop, the store now sells women's casual wear, which you'll find in a separate room in the back of the store. Open Monday through Saturday. (317) 873-2308.

Kogan's Antiques and Lighting. 195 South Main Street, Zionsville, IN 46077. One of the joys here is just walking through the pleasant little yard and garden to get to the front door. It's a second-generation business and has been in this spot for thirty years. Inside the old home you'll feel a little closer to New England as you survey the attractive array of items, many old American antiques included. There's a lovely selection of traditional interior and exterior lighting. Open Monday through Saturday. (317) 873-4208.

Lilly's Boutique. 40 West Pine Street, Zionsville, IN 46077. Upscale, one-of-a-kind clothing and accessories fill Lilly's, where the owner strives for "fun and sophistication." You might find a hand-painted jacket, a fancifully beaded bag, a garden smock, or a gauze cocktail dress. Open Monday through Saturday. (317) 873-0323.

My Mother's Doll Shop. 10 North Main Street, Zionsville, IN 46077. No doll lover can resist this charming shop, filled with beautiful collectible dolls and their furniture and accessories. Open Monday through Saturday. (317) 873-4338.

Stacy LaBolt's Fine Women's Apparel. 125 West Sycamore Street, Zionsville, IN 46077. Classic ladies fashions, including that lake-cottage look, are for sale here. Shoppers stock up on styles that don't go out of style. Open Monday through Saturday. (317) 873-2087.

WHERE TO EAT

Adams' Rib and Seafood House. 40 South Main Street, Zionsville, IN 46077. Located in a nineteenth-century building on the brick street, Adam's Rib has been a popular fixture since the 1970s. You can try an alligator appetizer and then move on to a rich variety of main dishes, such as homemade chicken potpie, fresh Boston scrod, filet mignon, or barbecued ribs. Open for lunch and dinner Tuesday through Saturday. $$-$$$. (317) 873-3301.

Friendly Tavern. 290 South Main Street, Zionsville, IN 46077. The Friendly, as it's called, is where Zionsville locals hang out. Always a place to hear gossip and meet your neighbors, this restaurant has a rustic atmosphere and consistently tasty, simple meals, including catfish, burgers, and filets. Open for lunch and dinner Monday through Saturday. $$. (317) 873-5772.

Gisela's Kaffeekranzchen. 112 South Main Street, Zionsville, IN 46077. German through and through, this upstairs restaurant offers sauerkraut, bratwurst, schnitzel, and mouthwatering Black Forest torte. Regulars flock to the "Grand Buffet" each Wednesday and Saturday night. Open for lunch and dinner Tuesday through Saturday; brunch served on Sunday. Not wheelchair accessible. $$-$$$. (317) 873-5523.

Silver Spoon Tea Room. 211 South Main Street, Zionsville, IN 46077. Located adjacent to the Butler's Pantry, a gourmet food and accessories shop, this tearoom serves lunch and afternoon tea. Soups and desserts are particularly tasty. Reservations are essential for tea. Open Monday through Saturday for lunch and Wednesday through Saturday for tea. $. (317) 873-0911.

WHERE TO STAY

Brick Street Inn. 175 South Main Street, Zionsville, IN 46077. Built in 1865, this cozy inn has five warm, welcoming, and spotlessly clean old-fashioned suites, three of which have a private sitting room and bath. In cool weather guests gather in the living room around a grand piano and fireplace; in summer there's a hot tub and garden in back. Breakfast is included in the price of the stay. $$. (317) 873-9177.

    Country Gables. 9302 State Road 334, Zionsville, IN 46077. West of downtown and past the intersection of Ford Road, Country Gables is the fifth driveway past the Catholic church at the intersection of County Road 950 on the north side of 334. With an old Victorian farmhouse at the inn's heart and a beautifully matched new addition, innkeepers Garland and Jean Elmore have created a haven in the country. All three suites are well furnished, including private baths and such extras as board games and VCRs; one has a kitchen. The common areas are inviting, and home-baked goods are a breakfast specialty. $$. (317) 873-5382; www.countrygables.com.

FOR MORE INFORMATION

Greater Zionsville Chamber of Commerce. 135 South Elm Street, Zionsville, IN 46077; (317) 873-3836; www.brem.com/zionsville.

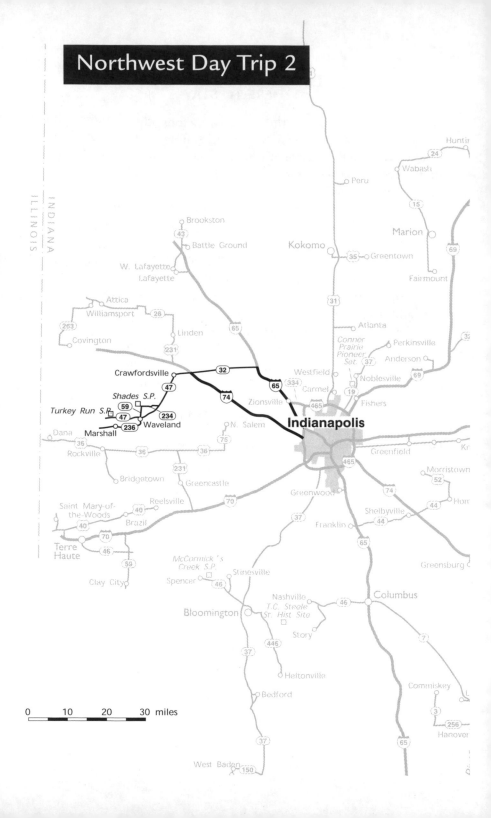

Visiting this section of Indiana combines history and natural beauty. Two of Indiana's most dramatic state parks lie within twenty minutes of each other, both a short distance south of Crawfordsville along a picturesque route. That city has three interesting historical sites, rare for a small town, as well as a variety of places to shop.

CRAWFORDSVILLE

There are two routes from Indianapolis to Crawfordsville: I-65 North toward Chicago to the third Lebanon exit, labeled State Road 32 and the Crawfordsville exit. At the top of the exit ramp turn left, or west, for a 21-mile drive on a two-lane road, curving through farm country and passing through small towns with antiques shops. The other route is I-74 West, interstate all the way to State Road 32, where you turn west at the top of the ramp for a short jaunt into town. State Road 32 T's into Market Street, where you turn right toward the center of downtown.

Crawfordsville is rich in Hoosier heritage and history and has been home to notables past, including Henry S. Lane, a prominent figure in Abraham Lincoln's political life, and Lew Wallace, author of *Ben Hur,* and notables present, including Will Shortz, editor of the *New York Times* crossword puzzle, and Eleanor Lambert, grand dame of the New York fashion scene. Wabash College, fertile farmland, and a hearty industrial base have combined to create a diverse, culturally rich community, which once called itself the Athens of Indiana.

Like many other small Indiana towns, Crawfordsville has lost many fine old buildings over the years, leaving a less cohesive downtown business district. Vigilant preservations have, however, saved the Ben Hur Building, the town's only remaining five-story building. The old high school is now a spiffy residence for seniors; and a group is working to restore the dome on the courthouse, de-domed during World War II. While modern dream homes have sprouted out of the cornfields on the outskirts of town, other families have turned their hearts and efforts to restoring beautiful old homes along the town's tree-lined streets. Make sure to include a drive along West Wabash Avenue and West Main Street for a picture of middle America.

The town draws crowds for its softball tournaments and for its annual Strawberry Festival.

WHAT TO DO

Ben Hur Museum. Pike Street and Wallace Avenue, Crawfordsville, IN 47933. Although you can drive into the museum parking lot on the far east side of the museum, you will get the best feel for this lovely property if you park along Wallace Street and walk in through the western gate, which winds up to the museum, once the study of General Lew Wallace. The name of Lew Wallace is little known today, but he was celebrated in his lifetime as a true Renaissance man: statesman, warrior, author, artist, and sportsman. He wrote the famed novel *Ben Hur;* patented an aluminum fishing rod; was a major general in the Civil War; served as ambassador to Turkey; and crafted his own violins. As an architect, he designed this study, which is now much as it was in his day, surrounded by beautiful grounds. There's a movie about Wallace, a knowledgeable curator, and scores of artifacts from Wallace's time as well as from the various productions of *Ben Hur.* At the gift counter you'll find old and new copies of Wallace's books, items carved from wood on the property, and more. Seasonal hours; closed Mondays and December through February. Longer hours in June, July, and August. Fee. (800) 866-3973 or (765) 362-5769; www.ben-hur.com.

Clements Canoes. 613 Lafayette Avenue, Crawfordsville, IN 47933. Sugar Creek threads together some of the loveliest scenery in this part of the state, including the Shades State Park and Turkey Run. Clements, a major canoe livery, will rent all the equipment (and can provide lunches) and steer canoeists on one of several journeys, ranging from about 1 mile to as far as 29 miles, at the far end of Turkey Run State Park. There are several guided canoe and kayak trips to choose from as well. Daily May though October. Fee. (765) 362–2781; www.clementscanoes.com.

Lane Place. 218 East Pike Street, Crawfordsville, IN 47933. This antebellum Greek Revival mansion sits like a gem in Indiana's crown of historic homes. In 1845 young widower Henry S. Lane married the girl across the street, nineteen-year-old Joanna Elston, and the pair set to work creating Lane Place, furnishing the home with pieces from Cincinnati, New Orleans, New York, and Paris. From the kitchen to the parlor to the bedrooms, you'll see furnishings (most of which are original to the home) and artifacts, including a funeral wreath from President Lincoln's funeral, for which Lane was a pall-bearer. A cabin that once served as a stop on the Underground Railroad stands on the beautiful lawns. Regular tours are in the afternoons, Tuesday through Saturday; closed holidays. Call to schedule tours at other times. Fee. (765) 362–3416.

Old Jail Museum. 225 North Washington Street, Crawfordsville, IN 47933. An engineering wonder, one of seven rotary jails known to have been built in America, the Old Jail remains the only one in operating condition. Two floors of pie-shaped cells were built on a turntable and were rotated to let prisoners in and out of the one stationary door. Built in 1882 the jail was used until 1973, although the turntable, declared a fire hazard, was immobilized in 1939. The museum has changing exhibits but sparse artifacts beyond that. Explore all four floors to understand the ingenuity of this creation; ask about the prisoner who escaped. Among other items, the gift shop sells, naturally, toy handcuffs. Donation requested. Open Wednesday through Sunday April through October; open Tuesday through Sunday June, July, and August. (765) 362–5222.

Wabash College. West Wabash Avenue, Crawfordsville, IN 47933. One of few all men's colleges left in the country, Wabash lays claim to a lovely campus—worth a drive through and, perhaps, a walk to see a few sites. Enter through the circular drive on West Wabash Avenue. To the right you will see Forest Hall, Hovey Cottage, and the Caleb Mills Home, three buildings built in the 1830s, making them among the oldest in town. The Fuller Arboretum, home to virtually all native tree species in Indiana, comprises one of the most impressive stands of trees in the state. The Eric Dean Gallery in the Fine

Arts Center, on Grant Avenue, mounts interesting exhibits, bringing in works from all over the country, and the bookstore in the Campus Center is a good spot to browse. You can pick up a campus map at the Public Affairs office, which is in the Hays Center (open weekdays only) on West Wabash Avenue opposite the main entrance to the campus. Free. (765) 361–6100; www.wabash.edu.

Walking Tour of Elston Grove. The Montgomery County Visitors and Convention Bureau at 218 East Pike Street has a brochure delineating this walk, which is about 1½ miles long. Of particular note, beyond the Lane Place and Ben Hur Study listed above, are the Elston Homestead on Pike Street (now home to the president of Wabash College), St. John's Episcopal Church on Green Street, and the Daughters of the American Revolution house (a Queen Anne Victorian, unaltered since it was built by one of the Elston family) on Wabash Avenue. The entire district is on the National Register of Historic Places.

WHERE TO SHOP

Earthworks. 114 North Grant Avenue, Crawfordsville, IN 47933. Slightly west of the main business district, this shop sits at the corner of Grant Avenue and Market Street, with the parking lot entrance on Grant. The focus is on florals, with wonderful live and silk arrangements, but there are rooms of gifts as well, including home decor and seasonal items. Open Monday through Saturday. (765) 362–9154.

Heathcliff. 101 North Washington Street, Crawfordsville, IN 47933. The owner of this shop has an eye for fashion, drawing smart shoppers from miles around. Classic, casual, and elegant clothes, along with a good selection of shoes, lingerie, and accessories, fill several rooms in a nineteenth-century building. The shop also carries a complete line of Estee Lauder products. Sale items pack a second-floor balcony. Open Monday through Saturday. (765) 362–0888.

The Homestead. 111 North Washington Street, Crawfordsville, IN 47933. For gifts of all sorts, the Homestead is the place to shop. The array includes candles, china, chintz lingerie bags, pottery, and paper goods, as well as Crawfordsville-exclusive items, such as afghans with local landmarks and stationery featuring Wabash

College. Open Monday through Saturday; closed holidays. (765) 364-0696.

Milligan's Flowers & Gifts. 115 East Main Street, Crawfordsville, IN 47933. In business for more than forty years, Milligan's has just moved to a new location right downtown, where it has expanded its offering of gifts and collectibles. There is an extensive array of Department 56—those charming lit decorative houses—as well as figurines in period costumes, cards, live and silk flowers, and Hadley Pottery. Open Monday through Saturday year-round. (765) 362-3496.

WHERE TO EAT

The Bungalow & The Cellar. 210 East Pike Street, Crawfordsville, IN 47933. This Arts and Crafts-style bungalow is rooted firmly in the town's historic district. You can dine on the main floor as well as in the bar area in the basement. The Bungalow has earned devoted diners in part because they grill hamburgers and steaks outside year-round. In addition to those menu items they serve a tasty spinach melt at lunch, big salads, and seafood. Chocolate fondue is a popular dessert. Open for lunch Monday through Friday and for dinner Monday and Wednesday through Saturday. $-$$ for lunch and $$-$$$ for dinner. (765) 362-2596.

Little Mexico. 211 East Main Street, Crawfordsville, IN 47933. Located right downtown, Little Mexico offers authentic Mexican cooking. Fajitas, of which there are seven varieties on the menu, are one of the most popular dishes. For those who can't make up their minds, two different combination platters let you sample a variety of foods. The restaurant also has a selection of domestic and imported beers. Open daily for lunch and dinner; closed Thanksgiving, Christmas Day, and July 4. $-$$. (765) 361-1042.

WHERE TO STAY AND EAT

The Maples Bed and Breakfast. 4814 State Road 47 South, Crawfordsville, IN 47933. Once a private residence to the south of town, the Maples is now a relaxing spot for lunch or dinner, as well as a bed-and-breakfast. Luncheon favorites include chicken salad and homemade soups. At dinner and at noon on Sunday, pork roast with dressing, Swiss steak, and fried chicken are popular. For lodgers the rooms are decorated with a mix of antiques and reproduction furniture, accented with crisp linens and quilts; all have private baths and views of the surrounding rolling farmland. Open for lunch Tuesday through Friday and Sunday; open for dinner Tuesday through Saturday. Reservations are advisable for Sunday noon. $$ for lodging (breakfast included) and restaurant. (765) 866–8095.

WAVELAND

If you are coming straight from Crawfordsville, the easiest route is south on State Road 47 and west on State Road 234.

WHERE TO GO

Shades State Park. State Road 234, Route 1, Box 72, Waveland, IN 47989. Slip back to primeval Indiana with a trip to this spectacular park. While the glaciers plowed northern Indiana flat, they stopped about midway down, leaving gorges, gullies, streams, and waterfalls that take those who have never explored the state by surprise. Once called the Shades of Death (many legends strive to explain that name), the park is now known by its shortened name, apropos for the deep shades in its forests. Geared to hikers, the park has few amenities but great sites, including Kickapoo Ravine, Devil's Punchbowl, and Lover's Leap. Less than a mile north on 234 lies **Pine Hills Nature Preserve,** a favorite with hikers and cross-country skiers, known for its four narrow ridges, or backbones. Free. (765) 435–2810.

MARSHALL

Although Turkey Run's address is listed as Marshall, the park is actually north of town, with its main entrance on the north side of State Road 47. Follow State Road 59 south from Shades State Park then take State Road 47 west to get to Turkey Run.

WHERE TO GO

Sugar Valley Canoe Trips. State Road 47, Rural Route 1, Marshall, IN 47859. Situated directly across the street from the Turkey Run campground, Sugar Valley offers canoe trips along Sugar Creek, covering the Shades, Turkey Run, and more. The company also rents kayaks and tubes. Trips can range in length from an hour to overnight. Open May through October. Fee. (800) 422-6638 or (765) 597-2364; www.sugarvalleycanoes.com.

Turkey Run State Park. State Road 47, Route 1, P.O. Box 164, Marshall, IN 47859. Nearly 2,400 acres of hardwood forest, cut in two by Sugar Creek, make up this pristine park. The south side contains the tamed features: Turkey Run Inn, a nature center, saddle barn, shelters, and playground equipment. Cross the suspension bridge into the wilderness, laced with about 13 miles of trails, some of them quite rugged, leading through sandstone canyons, up cliffs, and into deep ravines. The combination of visitor amenities and varied grades of hiking make this an exceptional park. Free. (765) 597-2635.

WHERE TO STAY AND EAT

Turkey Run Inn. State Road 47, Rural Route 1, Box 444, Marshall, IN 47859. This pleasant old inn is situated amidst some of Indiana's loveliest vistas and has an open, second-floor veranda designed just for surveying the scenery. Built in 1919, the inn has been altered and updated many times over the years. Third-floor rooms were redecorated in 2000; all the cabins, which are essentially freestanding rooms, were redecorated in 1999. An indoor pool draws crowds, particularly on rainy days. The main floor houses a restaurant, which serves traditional Indiana cooking: pork, mashed potatoes, fried chicken, green beans, steaks, and more. There's a well-stocked gift shop. Lodgings and restaurant, $-$$ (877) 500-6151 or (765) 597-2211; www.state.in.us/dnr.

FOR MORE INFORMATION

Montgomery County Visitors and Convention Bureau. 218 East Pike Street, Crawfordsville, IN 47933. (800) 866-3973 or (765) 362-5200; www.crawfordsville.org.

Putnam County Visitor Center. 2 South Jackson Street, Greencastle, IN 46135. (800) 829-4639 or (765) 635-8743.

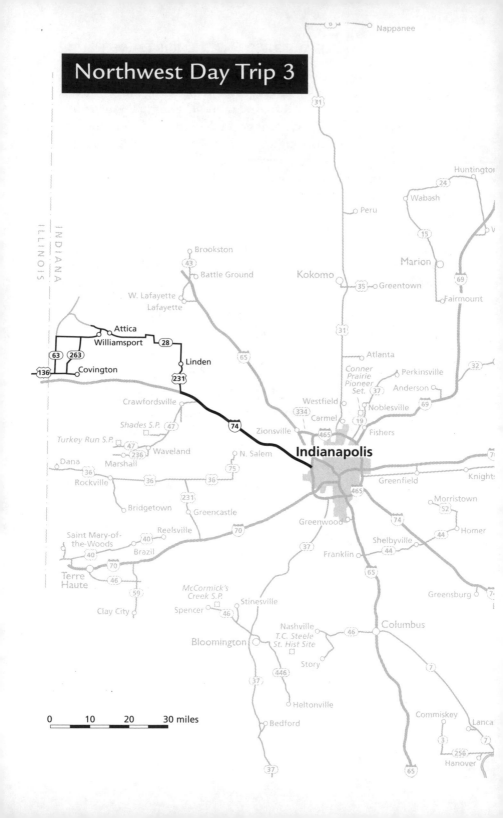

Linden · Attica
Williamsport · Covington

A day traveling to these places is a day chiefly spent looking at old homes, appreciating historic districts, and shopping for antiques. Tiny Linden is home to a good train museum, and there are two notable restaurants on this route. You can actually visit most of the places listed here in a single day.

LINDEN

To reach Linden take I–74 west to U.S. 231, where you turn north and travel about ten minutes to this dot of town. The museum is on the west side of the street.

WHERE TO GO

Linden Railroad Museum. 520 North Main Street, Linden, IN 47955. Just as many other Midwestern train depots have been put to new use, so has this one in Linden. Built in 1907, it bears the distinction of being the oldest junction depot in the state and is listed on the National Register of Historic Places. Model railroads and memorabilia and artifacts, mainly from the Monon and the Nickel Plate, which stopped at this station, fill the various rooms. A caboose is on display outside and train souvenirs are available in the gift shop. Open Friday through Sunday, May through September, and other times by appointment. Fee. (765) 339–7245; www.tctc.com/~weaver/depot.htm.

ATTICA

Platted along the Wabash River in 1825, Attica's fortunes have waxed and waned over the years: rising during the state's canal years in the 1830s and 1840s and up until the Civil War, surging again in the late 1800s and early 1900s with industry, and then falling flat during the Depression. Fortunately, unlike some other towns, Attica's population didn't decrease during the Depression, keeping up the demand for housing. Because the economy wasn't good, however, the old houses were maintained rather than new ones built. Similarly, new businesses didn't seek sites in the community, tearing down old buildings and replacing them with new, larger structures. As a result Attica has a remarkable cache of intact historic districts, four of which are listed on the National Register of Historic Places. While homes are not open to the public, it is nonetheless a delight to drive or walk around and gaze at these places, so cherished and well preserved today.

WHERE TO GO

Many of the sites listed below are covered in some detail in *Historic Attica,* a booklet produced in the early 1990s and available at a variety of local businesses, including the Sam Newmark Store. Although some of the information in the book is dated, the historical information gives readers a deeper appreciation of the town.

Brady Street Historic District. Bounded by East Jackson (State Road 28) on the north, Perry Street on the West, New Street on the south, and Council Street (U.S. 41) on the east. The largest of the historic districts, the Brady Street area contains homes, businesses, churches, and the town's 1904 Carnegie Library. You can go in the Schlosser home—today a shop, the Antiquer, at 401 South Perry Street. One of the state's best examples of Greek Revival architecture is the home at 305 South Brady Street, built around 1850. The home at 403 South Brady was originally owned by a cabinetmaker, and it is believed that he designed and built the intricate porch himself.

Cottrell Village. At the intersection of Main and Council Streets. Although it isn't exactly a village, this trio of buildings have taken on a life their own since designer John Cottrell transformed them.

Cottrell grew up in Attica and considers himself a Hoosier, although he made his fortune in California. Deeply committed to historic preservation, Cottrell purchased the Old Church—built as a Presbyterian church 1849–50 and later used as a Christian Science church—and restored it. Cottrell subsequently purchased and renovated two homes adjacent to the church, both built in the mid-1800s by Norman Brown. Both homes are furnished and are occasionally open for tours. Check at the Sam Newmark Store to find out about upcoming tours.

Downtown Business District. This most scenic section runs along Perry Street, north from Council Street clear to Vine Street. The lack of modern facades gives this downtown district its charm, despite a number of vacant storefronts. The pride of the street is the Devon Theater, which has been restored and now shows first-run movies.

Old East Historic District. Bounded by East Washington Street on the north, Council Street on the west, East Monroe on the south, and Oak Street on the east. Note the house at 404 East Washington Street, which was built around 1866 and remains little changed since 1869. Many interior features, including square-head nails and plank floors, remain. Another interesting home stands at 400 East Washington, an Italianate from the 1870s.

WHERE TO SHOP

Antiquer. 401 South Perry Street, Attica, IN 47918. Set in an 1850 Italianate home, the Antiquer has a carefully selected collection of antiques for sale, along with utterly charming American folk art. Folk art pieces include painted gourd baskets and decorations, dolls, imaginative animals, and garden decor. You'll also find upscale soaps and candles. In warmer weather you can stroll through the garden. Open daily year-round; closed major holidays. (765) 762–3273.

Sam Newmark Store. 107 South Perry Street, Attica, IN 47918. Although the fashions have changed, this shop has been selling clothing and accessories since 1927. The shop is also a source of information about historic Attica, selling the booklet entitled *Historic Attica,* which contains full details about many sites in town, as well as postcards and other souvenirs. Open Monday through Saturday; closed holidays. (765) 764–4228.

Wolf's Homemade Candies. 503 South Council Street, U.S. 41, Attica, IN 47918. This local purveyor of treats is an ideal place to stop to satisfy your sweet tooth or get a memorable souvenir of Attica. Chocolates and other candies are made on site. The shop also sells ornaments, pictures, frames, and other small decorative items. Open daily; closed holidays. (888) 982–2639 or (765) 762–6707; www.wolfshomemadecandies.com.

WHERE TO STAY

Apple Inn. 604 South Brad Street, Attica, IN 47918. Featured twice in *Midwest Living* magazine, the Apple Inn has eleven rooms: five in the old family home built in 1903 and six in a carriage house built in 1998. The two structures are connected by an enclosed courtyard with two fountains and a hot tub. Each rooms is themed (for example, the Train Room has a Lionel train in it), some have their own balconies, some have fireplaces, and one has a Jacuzzi. All the rooms in the carriage house have their own baths, but there are some shared baths in the original house. In warm weather flowers spill out of the flower boxes lining the broad front porch. $–$$. (765) 762–6574; www.appleinninc.com.

WILLIAMSPORT

Known as a good spot for antiquing, Williamsport is a skip west and slightly south of Attica. You reach it by following U.S. 41/State Road 28 West; make sure to watch for the point where State Road 28 splits from U.S. 41, heading south to Williamsport. Just as you come into town, the beautiful residence on your left is another home restored by John Cottrell and one he uses from time to time. To see the town's interesting buildings, follow SR 28 to Monroe Street, turn right, and go across the bridge to where the road splits. Take the right split, Grant Street, which leads past an 1890 Presbyterian church. Follow Grant down to Washington Street, turn left and go over to Lincoln Street, where you turn left again. At 303 Lincoln Street you'll see a Tuscan-style brick mansion built in 1854. Lincoln dead ends into Monroe; you turn left again to return to the main business district.

WHERE TO GO

Williamsport Falls. To reach the falls follow State Road 28 into town and turn south on Monroe Street, which is at the courthouse. Go across the railroad tracks. The falls are behind the block of buildings to your left and can be reached by a narrow drive at the end of that block. The falls are most spectacular in the spring when water rushes down Fall Branch and cascades down the full 67-foot drop.

COVINGTON

The swifter route from Williamsport to Covington follows State Road 28 west to State Road 63, a smooth-sailing highway that will quickly convey you south to U.S. 136, which leads directly east into downtown Covington. But the more scenic route follows State Road 28 west to State Road 263 south, which follows the curves of the Wabash River. This route, too, leads to U.S. 136 and east into Covington.

The seat of Fountain County, Covington has a number of attractive older homes, which you can see by driving up and down the streets east of town, and is noted for its distinctive courthouse murals. Astonishingly, the town, which has fewer than 3,000 residents, has two restaurants that can each seat more than 500 persons!

WHERE TO GO

Fountain County Courthouse. Courthouse Square, Covington, IN 47932. Neither Italianate nor Federal, the Fountain County Courthouse is remarkably unlike other Indiana courthouses. Built in the 1930s with Works Progress Administration funds, it has a distinctly Art Deco look. Its interior portrays the history of the people of the Wabash Valley in murals, designed by and painted under the direction of Eugene Savage. A 1930s realist artist, Savage was originally from Covington and gained renown as professor of art at Yale University. These murals, which depict scenes such as the arrival of pioneers and the county during the Civil War, were restored in the 1980s. Open Monday through Friday; closed government holidays. Free. Fountain County Clerk's office, (765) 793-2192.

WHERE TO SHOP

House with Lions. 602 East Washington Street, Covington, IN 47932. Founded in a smaller space, the House with Lions now occupies a large storefront on the courthouse square. Owners eschew ticky-tacky and flea market merchandise, opting for quality antiques and collectibles. This is an easy place to browse. Open daily; closed major holidays. (765) 793-2710.

WHERE TO EAT

Covington Beef House. 16501 North State Road 63, Covington, IN 47932. Get off I-74 at the exit for State Road 63 (Newport/Covington); turn right at the bottom of the exit; you'll see the restaurant at the top of a hill on your left. A classic in this part of the state, the Beef House has been drawing crowds—huge crowds—since it opened in 1963. Beef in many permutations is the specialty and steak dinners are the biggest sellers, but chicken and fish dinners are just as good. Soups are especially tasty, and large rolls come piping hot. The restaurant seats hundreds in several airy rooms decorated with plates and sports memorabilia. Open for breakfast, lunch, and dinner Monday through Friday; for dinner on Saturday; and for lunch and dinner on Sunday. (765) 793-3947.

Maple Corner Restaurant. 1126 Liberty Street, Covington, IN 47932. Begun in a home in 1931, Maple Corner today occupies a large enough space to seat more than 600. Popular choices include combination dinners, such as catfish and steak or fried shrimp and filet mignon. Apple pie topped with a slice of cheddar cheese in the shape of a maple leaf is the classic dessert. Open for dinner daily and for lunch on Sunday. $$. (765) 793-2224.

FOR MORE INFORMATION

Fountain-Warren Chamber of Commerce. 100 South Brady Street, Attica, IN 47918; (765) 762-2511.

Beyond the chamber of commerce, the unofficial source of information on historic sites in these two counties is the Sam Newmark Store (listed above), which keeps a supply of brochures and information and where one of the owners is president of Historic Landmarks of Fountain County.

Montgomery County Visitors and Convention Bureau. 218 East Pike Street, Crawfordsville, IN 47933. (800) 866-3973 or (765) 362-5200; www.crawfordsville.org.

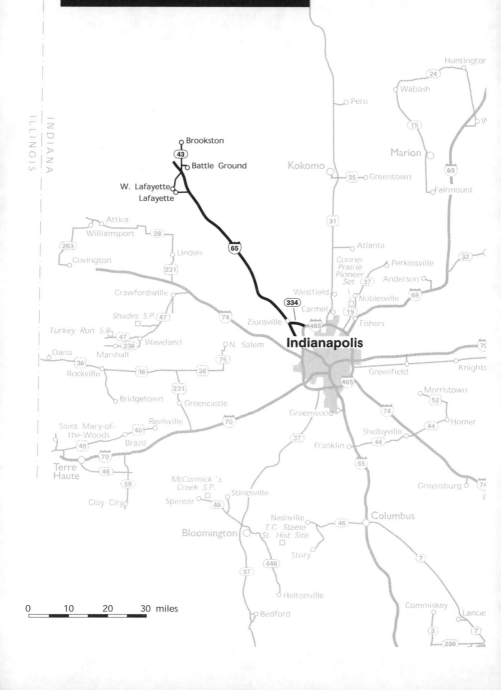

Northwest Day Trip 4

Before the city of Lafayette was established, Indian settlements thrived and French traders settled here along the Wabash River throughout today's Tippecanoe County. In 1811 a confederation of tribes—led by Tenskwatawa, the Shawnee Prophet, and his half brother, Tecumseh—attacked U.S. soldiers under the command of William Henry Harrison in what is now known as the Battle of Tippecanoe. The soldiers defeated the Indians, and ultimately the tribes were driven farther westward. The victory helped Harrison win the presidency in 1840. The Wabash Heritage Trail, a new 13-mile path, connects several historic sites, beginning at the Tippecanoe Battlefield Park in Battle Ground, winding south through Riehle Plaza in downtown Lafayette, and ending at Tapawingo Park in West Lafayette. Plans call for an extension to Fort Ouiatenon, site of an early fort and the city's best-known festival, Feast of the Hunters' Moon.

LAFAYETTE

To reach downtown Lafayette, take I-65 north to State Road 26 West. In the past two decades, this city has gone from dull to dazzling with the revitalization of its downtown, including waterfront improvements and the creation of greenways. Historic neighborhoods, notably those east of downtown, are being restored in style. In the Ninth Street Hill Neighborhood, note the Ball House,

402 South Ninth, situated high on a hill and still owned by descendants of Cyrus Ball, who began the home in 1864. Just around the corner is the William S. Potter House at 920 State Street, which was built in 1904 to house the State of Connecticut exhibit at the St. Louis World's Fair, dismantled after the fair, and reassembled here by a wealthy businessman. In the heart of downtown, the Tippecanoe County Courthouse received a $15 million facelift, completed in 1993, and the Long Center for the Performing Arts (opened in 1921) glitters from a $2 million renovation, completed in 1999. Beyond restoration, the city has an increasing number of interesting shops and restaurants. One not-so-small traffic warning: Trains creep through downtown Lafayette at all hours, tying up traffic. However, as long as you don't get cut off from your car, you can usually find a clear intersection.

WHERE TO GO

Columbian Park. 1915 Scott Street, Lafayette, IN 47904. Just east of downtown, Columbian Park sprawls across forty-three acres, including a newly created playground and Tropicanoe Cove, a family aquatic center with a huge water slide and water playground. At the heart of the park stands Memorial Island, the city's tribute to its veterans. Names of every fallen veteran from the Civil War to the present, including two local men who died during the Berlin Airlift, are inscribed here. Partake in a local tradition by scooting across the street to Frozen Custard (2319 Wallace Avenue) for a treat. Park, free and open year-round; waterpark, fee and open daily from Memorial Day weekend through Labor Day. (765) 771–2220; www.lafayetteparks.org.

    Fowler House. 909 South Street, Lafayette, IN 47901. Moses Fowler, a prosperous merchant and John Purdue's business partner, completed this house in 1852. Fowler had a vision and directed a builder, without any blueprints, in creating this Gothic Revival masterpiece. Designed to awe, the entryway has a magnificently carved staircase and high ceilings. Woodwork throughout is intricate. Little of the furniture comes from the Fowler family, but there are fine period pieces nonetheless. Open Tuesday through Sunday. Free. (765) 476–8417; www.tcha.mus.in.us/fowler.htm.

Museum of Art of Great Lafayette. 101 South Ninth Street, Lafayette, IN 47901. The permanent collection focuses on nineteenth- and twentieth-century Indiana artists, such as T. C. Steele, and includes a selection of pottery, notably Rookwood. At least two special exhibitions are going on at any given time; most rotate out in about two months. Open Tuesday through Sunday. Fee requested. (765) 742–1128; www.glmart.org.

Imagination Station. 600 North Fourth Street, Lafayette, IN 47902. Although the address is Fourth Street, the parking lot entrance is off Cincinnati Street. Want to compare your weight on earth to that on the moon and Mars? Weigh in by the front door and find out. This small museum has a number of clever areas to keep youngsters thinking. At one table children dissect derelict computers, figuring out how they were assembled. Elsewhere, children sit in a fire engine or the cockpit of a jet. There's a small gift shop with mostly mind-challenging toys. Open Friday through Sunday. Fee. (765) 420–7780; http://users.nlci.com/imagination.

Red Crown Mini-Museum. 605 South Street, Lafayette, IN 47901. For those who want to fit a museum into a trip but haven't time, this walk-by spot at the corner of Sixth and South Streets fits the bill. You can't enter; you don't pay. You simply walk up and gaze in the windows at old cars, attendant uniforms, and other paraphernalia from the days when a gas station was a full-service operation. Free. (765) 742–0280.

Tippecanoe County Courthouse. 20 North Third Street, Lafayette, IN 47901. An elegant mishmash of no fewer than seven architectural styles, this courthouse, completed in 1884, contains a range of interesting features. Exterior features include a hundred columns and a cast-iron dome, topped by a statue of the Goddess of Liberty, inexplicably holding the scales of justice. The walnut doors at the main entrances are estimated to weigh 500 pounds each. During the $15 million renovation, scores of improvements were made in the building, such as restoring stenciling dating back to 1885 and uncovering the skylights. On the second floor, there's a mural depicting the Battle of Tippecanoe. A free self-guided-tour brochure is available from the Greater Lafayette Convention & Visitors Bureau (listed below); the County Clerk's Office might have copies as well. Open Monday through Friday; closed government holidays. Free. County Commissioners Office, (765) 423–9215.

WHERE TO SHOP

Flower Mill. 1530 Kossuth Street, Lafayette, IN 47905. From downtown head east on Main Street; turn right, or south, on Ninth Street, and take that until you reach Kossuth. Turn east again and travel 6 blocks to the shop. The Flower Mill has made a name for itself through its superb silk flower arrangements. The shop also sells giftware, mirrors, prints, and lamps, choosing lines that are not found in other area stores. Styles range from contemporary to traditional and include the French Revival look. Open Monday through Saturday year-round and on Sunday from Thanksgiving until Christmas. (765) 742–9054.

Hawkins Rail Services. 903 Main Street, Lafayette, IN 47901. With one of the best selections of HO merchandise in the country, this shop sells all manner of cars, parts, books, videos, and model train paraphernalia, including the decals for the local Monon line. A 117-car model train zips along a layout that runs about 90 feet from the front window to the back of the store. Open Monday through Saturday; closed major holidays. (765) 742–5577.

Mainstreet Mercantile. 1000 Main Street, Lafayette, IN 47901. Fine antiques, folk art, and curiosities fill this shop. You might find a carousel animal, a life-size wooden Indian or Santa Claus, a pier mirror, or a desk. A small room on the second floor is filled chiefly with uniforms: baseball, bowling, military, and more. For treasures, gifts, and gawking, this is a one-stop shop. Open Monday through Saturday. (765) 742–8667.

One Earth Gallery and Gifts. 1022 Main Street, Lafayette, IN 47901. Located just west of the railroad tracks, One Earth specializes in handmade American Indian art and artifacts, including jewelry, baskets, dream catchers, and pottery. The owner travels throughout the United States looking for authentic Indian pieces and tries to find those representative of the Woodland Indians who once populated this area. There's a selection of items from Africa and Asia. Open Monday through Saturday and the two Sundays before Christmas. (765) 742–7564; www.oneearthgallery.com; www.americantreasures.com.

O'Rears Pastry Shop. 321 North Ninth Street, Lafayette, IN 47901. If you just must have a petit four that really tastes as good as it looks, this is your stop. There are also doughnuts, cookies, cakes, and pies, ready to give you a shot of sugar for the drive home. Open daily; closed holidays. (765) 742–2280.

Project Bike Shop. 676 Main Street, Lafayette, IN 47901. Need a custom bike? John Cherry will make one for you, measuring you and creating a bicycle frame to suit your human frame; it's rather like going to a tailor and having a suit made. Dedicated to cycling, the store also sells many lines of bicycles and accessories in addition to handling maintenance and being a source of information for cyclist events. Open Monday through Saturday; closed holidays. (800) 263–9254 or (765) 423–4488; cherry.dcwi.com.

Salzburg Haus. 140 Frontage Road, Lafayette, IN 47909. From I-65 take exit 172 and turn east, getting immediately into the left lane. Turn north on Frontage Road. Salzburg Haus bedazzles year-round with Christmas decorations. Santas, ornaments, lighted villages, creches, stockings, and all manner of festive accessories fill every corner of this large store. Open daily; closed holidays. (765) 446–8800.

Two Tulips. 846 Main Street, Lafayette, IN 47901. Two Tulips specializes in personalized gifts, mainly stationery, but there are other things as well, including linens and baby gifts. Personalized piggy banks are a big seller. There's a selection of unusual and upscale paper goods, including placecards and napkins. (765) 420–8990.

WHERE TO EAT

Bistro 501. 501 East Main Street, Lafayette, IN 47901. You can't miss this golden yellow and blue building, where the color scheme carries through to the inside. Bright and light, the restaurant's decor is instantly appealing and clearly upscale. Salmon, sea bass, duck breast, and prime rib are among a long list of dinner entrees. The luncheon menu is somewhat shorter but includes many tasty sandwiches and salads. Bisques are delicious. Open for lunch Monday through Friday and for dinner Tuesday through Saturday. $$–$$$. (765) 423–4501.

Maize, An American Grill. 112 North Third Street, Lafayette, IN 47901. This restaurant has many enticing entrees for both lunch and dinner: pecan-crusted catfish, roasted pork loin, and cranberry-glazed chicken, among many others. Pasta is made on the premises daily, as are desserts. A polished addition to the Lafayette restaurant scene, Maize is in a restored Italianate building directly west of the courthouse. Open for lunch Tuesday through Friday and for dinner Tuesday through Saturday. $$–$$$. (765) 429–6125; www.maizer-estaurant.com.

McCord Candies. 536 Main Street, Lafayette, IN 47901. The candy shop, opened in 1912, has evolved into a restaurant, serving breakfast and lunch into the late afternoon. Here things are done the old-fashioned way, using stoves and scales installed here when the store opened; McCord's didn't even replace its rotary phones until 2000. The menu includes homemade soups, sandwiches, banana splits, milk shakes, and fountain drinks. Once inside, you may find the candy counter irresistible. All the candies are made here, including candy canes, made by hand from creme de menthe, which makes them softer than other candy canes. Open for breakfast and lunch Monday through Saturday. $. (765) 742–4441.

Sarah's Oaks. 4545 West 660 South, Lafayette, IN 47909. From Lafayette take State Road 25 south to County Road 375 West; turn left and proceed to County Road 660 South, where there is a cemetery on the corner. Turn right and go a mile to the restaurant, which is on the left. Farm-style meals, such as roast pork loin, baked steak, pot roast, and pan-fried chicken, are served family-style, meaning that each table must choose a single entree. The building itself was built circa 1860 and retains much of its charm. Rooms are lit by kerosene lanterns. Other diversions include a flower and butterfly garden and a gift shop. Open by reservation only Tuesday through Sunday for breakfast, lunch, afternoon tea, and dinner. $$–$$$. (765) 538–3880.

Sarge Oak on Main. 721 Main Street, Lafayette, IN 47901. Founded more than sixty years ago, this steakhouse retains its mid-twentieth-century atmosphere, complete with period lighting and old photographs. The specialties here are steaks and seafood; spaghetti is offered with every meal. For lunch you can order an eight-ounce or a sixteen-ounce burger, among other choices. Sarge Oak's is also noted for its pies, which are baked on site daily. Open Tuesday through Friday for lunch and Tuesday through Saturday for dinner. $$$. (765) 742–5230.

WHERE TO STAY

Loeb House Inn. 708 Cincinnati Street, Lafayette, IN 47901. A sophisticated bed-and-breakfast, Loeb House Inn pampers its guests with elegant rooms and turndown service. Set in a fashionable older neighborhood, the home was completed in 1882 and became a B&B in 1996. Rooms are beautifully decorated, all with private baths and cable television; some have fireplaces and whirlpool tubs. The downstairs parlor and dining rooms allow you to relax and dine in style. $$-$$$. (765) 420-7737; www.loebhouseinn.com.

WEST LAFAYETTE

From Lafayette follow Columbia Street west across the Wabash River, where it becomes West Lafayette State Street. Established in 1866 as Chauncey, this town, synonymous with Purdue University, was renamed West Lafayette in 1888. In 1862 the federal government enacted a law granting each state public lands to establish an agricultural college. John Purdue, a successful businessman, offered $150,000 if the school were located in Tippecanoe County, and the deal was sealed. The town has other landmarks. At 210 West State Street stands Bank One in a building designed by renowned architect Louis Sullivan; note the terra-cotta design details. At 1301 Woodland Avenue, there's a picture-perfect Usonian home, Samara, designed by Frank Lloyd Wright. It's occasionally open for tours; visit www.hort.purdue.edu/arch/samara for more information.

WHERE TO GO

Celery Bog Nature Area. 1620 Lindberg Road 47906. To reach the bog, take the bypass, go left on Yeager Road and left again on Northwestern, which leads south to Lindberg, where you turn right. The entrance is just past the Purdue golf course. This bog, part of a wetland, presents a rare opportunity for bird- and animal-watching. Hawks, woodpeckers, orioles, deer, cottontail rabbits, and coyotes are among the creatures you may spy. Cattails, dogwood, wild black cherry trees, sunflowers, and asters decorate the landscape. There are trails and a nature center. Open Wednesday through Sunday year-round; closed major holidays. (765) 775-5172; www.eas. purdue.edu/geomorph/celerybog; West Lafayette Parks and Recreation, (765) 775-5110.

Purdue University. Visitor Information Center, 504 Northwestern Avenue, West Lafayette, IN 47907. This center is a good place to launch your tour of Purdue, although there is also a guest information kiosk in the Great Hall of Memorial Union. For a quick driving tour, enter the campus from State Street onto Oval Drive. Memorial Union is to your right as soon as you enter. Inside, there are several places to eat and shop, an inn, and, in the Great Hall, a full-scale model of the campus. At the top of the oval there's a fountain, a popular spot for students to splash in warm weather. University Hall, the campus's oldest building is on the west side of the drive, almost opposite John Purdue's grave, where there is a flag and marker. Ross-Ade Stadium and Mackey Arena are north of the oval. As you tour the campus, note the symmetry among the buildings. While Indiana University buildings are chiefly limestone, here at Purdue the structures are predominately brick. Visitor Information Center, (765) 494–4636; www.purdue.edu/vic.

WHERE TO STAY

Commandant's Home Bed & Breakfast. 3848 State Road 43 North, West Lafayette, IN 47906. This B&B is perched high on a hill overlooking the Wabash River about 2 miles south of the State Road 43 exit off I–65 and about 5 miles north of the Purdue campus. On the grounds of the Indiana Veterans' Home, this historic 1895 mansion was once the residence of the commandant in charge of the home, and each of the six guest rooms is named after a commandant. Rooms are decorated in Victorian reproductions. The entrance, with is columns and statues of Civil War soldiers, is magnificent. $$. (877) 319–2783 or (765) 463–5980; www.commhomb-b.com.

BATTLE GROUND

To reach Battle Ground, travel north on State Road 43. Just past the Tippecanoe County Amphitheater, but before the entrance to I–65, turn right on Burnetts Road. Follow that road to Ninth Street and turn left, which will take you into town.

WHERE TO GO

Museums at Prophetstown, 3549 Prophetstown Trail, Battle Ground, IN 47920. Currently you reach the museum entrance from Swisher Road. The Museums at Prophetstown, about 300 acres, and Indiana's newest state park, the 3,000-acre Prophetstown State Park, are in their nascence. Neither will be completed for several years, but the beginnings are promising. The farmhouse of the Living History Farm—a re-created 1920s Sears & Roebuck house—and the Council House of the Native American Village are open now. Eventually there will be an entire Woodland Native American Cultural Complex, with a museum, an Indian village as William Henry Harrison would have known it, and a precontact village, showing life prior to European exploration. At presstime, tours were scheduled Monday, Wednesday, and Friday through Sunday from June through October and Saturday and Sunday the remainder of the year; call to confirm. (800) 872-6648 or (765) 567-4700; www.prophetstown.org.

Tippecanoe Battlefield. State Road 43 North, Battle Ground, IN 47920. On this site in 1811, a three-hour battle crushed Indian hopes of establishing a Native American confederation and dealing as equals with the white army and settlers. Today hiking trails lead through the former battlefield and an obelisk commemorates the conflict. Inside the museum there are a variety of exhibits, artifacts, and a light show, which lasts about eight minutes. Open daily during warm weather; call for winter hours. Grounds, free; museum, fee. (765) 567-2147.

Wolf Park. 4012 East 800 North, Battle Ground, IN 47920. Arriving in town on State Road 225, head east across the railroad tracks, stay to the left for 1 long block to Jefferson Street; turn left again and travel about 1½ miles along a winding road until you see the signs for the park. Wolf Park is a research and education center focusing on wolves, although there are bison, foxes, and a coyote on the property as well. The most popular time to visit the park is for Wolf Howl Nights (weather permitting, held Saturday year-round and Friday May to October), when visitors hear the wolves howling and are encouraged to join in. The gift shop sells all manner of wolf-related merchandise. Open Tuesday through Sunday May through November. Fee. (765) 567-2265; www.wolf park.org.

WHERE TO SHOP

Crossroad Pottery. 104 Main Street, Battle Ground, IN 47920. The pottery shop is just to the east of the railroad tracks in downtown Battle Ground. Scott Frankenberger has been working as a potter and artist for more than twenty-five years and has works exhibited in collections nationwide. A vivid red characterizes much of his pottery, most of which is made from porcelain clay. Vases, bowls, and dinner-ware are among the many objects Frankenberger creates and sells here. Open Tuesday through Sunday afternoons year-round, but because this is a one-man operation, it is best to call ahead to check on hours. (765) 567–2678; www.dcwi.com/~dscottf.

BROOKSTON

Take I-65 north to the West Lafayette-Brookston exit and turn north on State Road 43. Brookston, a one-stoplight town, is about ten minutes up the road.

WHERE TO SHOP

Twinrocker Handmade Paper. 100 East Third Street, Brookston, IN 47923. At Brookston's light, take a right onto State Road 18. As soon as you cross the railroad tracks, you'll see Twinrocker. Founded in 1971, Twinrocker has established a name worldwide for its exquisite art papers and custom-made papers, all from cotton and linen rag. The shop contains a wide range of these beautiful papers and stationery along with supplies for making paper, including kits for amateurs. Open Monday through Friday year-round; closed holidays. Early Tuesday afternoon, tours of the facility are offered for a fee. (800) 757–8946 or (765) 563–3119; www.twinrocker.com.

WHERE TO EAT

Klein Brot Haus. 106 East Third Street, Brookston, IN 47923. This European-style bakery is known first and foremost for its delicious breads, such as challah and cinnamon. Its deli serves breakfast and lunch; sandwiches include ham, turkey, roast beef, and chicken salad. The soup bar usually features two soups a daily—one broth and one cream. Tuesday through Friday, specials, such as casseroles, are offered. For breakfast, try French toast made with cinnamon bread. Hardwood floors and a hundred-year-old bar from an Indianapolis tavern set the scene. Open for breakfast and lunch Tuesday through Saturday and for dinner on Friday night during the spring and fall. (765) 563-3788; www.kleinbrothaus.com.

FOR MORE INFORMATION

Greater Lafayette Convention & Visitors Bureau. 301 Frontage Road, Lafayette, IN 47905. Among other brochures, the CVB offers a number of self-guided tours, including an audio-tour of the historic downtown. (800) 872-6648 or (765) 447-9999; www.lafayette-in.com.

 Tippecanoe County Historical Association. 1001 South Street, Lafayette, IN 47901. In addition to operating the Wetherill Historical Resource Center for genealogy and historical research and the Tippecanoe Battlefield Museum, this group organizes many programs, including the Feast of the Hunters' Moon, one of Indiana's most popular festivals. (765) 497-6440; www.tcha.mus.in.us.

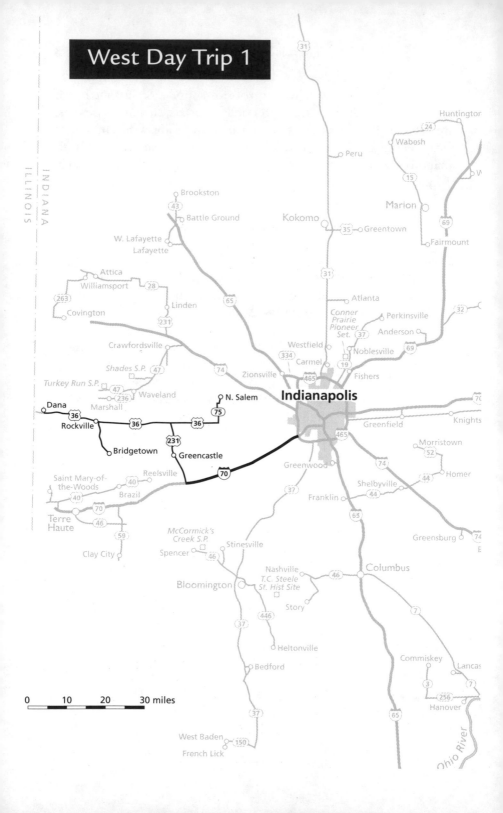

Scooping up tracts of western Indiana, this trip covers diverse sites, including the home of World War II journalist Ernie Pyle and Parke County's famous covered bridges. There's gourmet cuisine at A Different Drummer in Greencastle and home cookin' at Apple Annie's in little North Salem.

GREENCASTLE

From Indianapolis take I-70 west to U.S. 231 North, following that numbered road into the courthouse square in Greencastle. As in so many other county seats, the courthouse square sits in the center of town. The building itself is a Greek Revival style, built in 1904. At one corner a doughboy commemorates World War I; at another a German buzz bomb is mounted—one of two on display in America; the other is in the Smithsonian. Future drug giant Eli Lilly got his start here before the Civil War, opening a drugstore. John Dillinger made his single biggest haul—about $75,000—when he robbed the bank at 20-24 West Washington Street. DePauw University is just south of the square.

WHERE TO GO

DePauw University. Office of Admission, 101 East Seminary Street, Greencastle, IN 46135. Founded in 1837 as Indiana Asbury College, DePauw was renamed in 1884 after businessman Washington

Charles DePauw, who saved the school from financial ruin. Today it ranks among the finest small liberal arts colleges in the country. Begun in 1868, East College, the oldest building on campus, stands at the corner of Locust and Simpson Streets. Inside, an old chapel has been restored and services are still held here. Memorial Student Union Building has been renovated and is a good stop, particularly to pick up something in the bookstore. Eugene S. Pulliam Center for Contemporary Media stands out among the university's newer facilities. A number of attractive older homes, fraternities, and sororities ring the periphery of the campus. Visitor's coordinator, (765) 658-4113; www.depauw.edu.

WHERE TO SHOP

Anne's Fashion Corner. 8 West Washington Street, Greencastle, IN 46135. Anne's has a loyal clientele, drawing women from nearby counties for its broad selection of clothes that can suit work, leisure, and dressier occasions. Clothes lean toward classics, such as Susan Bristol, that won't go out of fashion next season. Open Monday through Saturday; open daily between Thanksgiving and Christmas; closed holidays. (765) 653-9470.

Fine Print Book Store. 6 East Washington Street, Greencastle, IN 46135. Small-town bookstores are such a rarity that when you find one with a nice mix of best sellers, classic, and children's books it is well worth pointing out. This bookstore thrives in part because it serves DePauw students during the school year, but it also carries board games and art supplies. The building was built in 1876 and has an oak parquet floor. Open Monday through Saturday; open daily between Thanksgiving and Christmas. (765) 653-2665.

WHERE TO EAT

Almost Home. 17 West Franklin Street, Greencastle, IN 46135. On the north side of the courthouse square, this tearoom and gift shop has a pleasantly interesting menu, featuring sandwiches (the turkey melt is one of the most popular), soups, and salads at lunch and pastas and other entrees at dinner. Desserts are all homemade and change daily; pies are scrumptious. Because it is also a gift shop, Almost Home sells most of the attractive art and flower arrangements hanging on the walls; you'll see price tags peeping out and dangling down. There are also tea-related items, such as cups, saucers, tea-themed notecards, and decorative items. Having run out of room here, Almost Home has opened a shop just two doors down that carries candles, antiques, stationery, linens, Beanies, and more. It's the kind of spot where you can pop in and buy a just-right gift for a friend. $$. (765) 653–5788.

A Different Drummer. The Walden Inn, 2 Seminary Square, Greencastle, IN 46135. The Walden Inn's restaurant has proved to be a popular dining spot, drawing people from nearby counties. The fare changes regularly, but you can count on fish, such as grilled halibut; a vegetarian dish like roasted eggplant with spinach; filet mignon; and some sort of bird, such as grilled chicken breast. The dining room is warm and inviting with large windows. Open for breakfast, lunch, and dinner daily except Christmas Day. $$$. (800) 225–8655 or (765) 653–2761; www.waldeninn.com.

WHERE TO STAY

Walden Inn. 2 Seminary Square, Greencastle, IN 46135. An elegant pied-à-terre describes the rooms here. The decor hints of Colonial America, with each room decorated a little differently. You might find a fluffy quilt and a four poster, along with a wing-back chair. The inn was built in 1986 in large part to accommodate DePauw University alumni and parents of students. $$–$$$. (800) 225–8655 or (765) 653–2761; www.waldeninn.com.

ROCKVILLE

From Greencastle continue north on U.S. 231 and turn west on U.S. 360. You will be in Indiana farm country at its best. No single business here employs more than 250 people; there's no McDonald's and no Wal-Mart. But Parke County produces more maple syrup than any other county in Indiana and lays claim to thirty-two covered bridges. County seat of Parke County, Rockville activities swirl around those celebrated covered bridges. There's a map showing you how to reach all of them, a journey that would take some time and lead through picturesque farmland and along gravel roads. During Covered Bridge Festival in October, the state's largest festival, this county is packed with visitors. To spread out the crowds, the county has inaugurated Covered Bridge Christmas and the Maple Syrup Festival. And why were the bridges covered? To protect the wooden timbers from the weather, thus preserving the bridge.

WHERE TO GO

Billie Creek Village. U.S. 36, Rural Route 2, Rockville, IN 47872. Billie Creek Village was begun in 1964 by county preservationists who saw a way to preserve historic buildings and create a local attraction. One by one, an 1830 log cabin, a 1913 schoolhouse, an antebellum doctor's office, an 1859 church, and many other buildings were moved to a site east of Rockville that included the 1895 Billie Creek Covered Bridge. Two other bridges were eventually added to the site. This village thrives on special events—such as its Civil War Days, antique car show, tractor and engine show, and Halloween Fright Nights—and demonstrations where you can see cider and molasses made, weaving, quilting, and pottery throwing. You might go on a bird walk or listen to a master gardener explain how to grow herbs. An old-fashioned wagon ride, which includes clip-clopping across a stream, is a favorite any time. The General Store contains a variety of items, including folk art and locally made Amish crafts and foodstuffs. The General Store and some buildings are open daily except Thanksgiving, Christmas Eve, Christmas Day, and New Year's Day. When the village is in full operation there is a fee; when operation is limited, it is free. Call to find out if the village will be in full operation when you wish to visit. (765) 569-3430.

Covered Bridges Driving Tour. The self-proclaimed Covered Bridge Capital of the World, Parke County lays claim to thirty-two covered bridges, some of which you can still drive through. Local tourism officials have designed five separate routes that guide you to all of them, although, frankly, seeing them all is overkill. Pick up a map at the Tourist Information Center (address below) or from a Rockville merchant and choose a route or routes. A southern route including Bridgeton and Mansfield is a good choice. Remember to relax and review how county roads are labeled (explained in the Using this Travel Guide section). You'll be on narrow roads; you might even end up on a gravel one. Once you've spied your first bridge, you'll want to see more. The scenery is icing. Many routes make good bicycle paths as well.

WHERE TO SHOP

Beiler's Bakery. Nyesville Road, Rockville, IN 47872. To find this bakery, which is in a home, turn northeast on Nyesville Road, directly opposite the entrance to Billie Creek Village, and travel about 2 miles. You'll see a white house, with a sign in the yard advertising home-baked goods, on your right. (If you see the marker commemorating Chicago Cubs player Three Fingers Brown, you've gone too far.) The specialty here is scrumptious raisin bread, liberally doused with icing. Cookies and other goods are delicious as well. Open Monday through Saturday when the light is on in the window. No phone.

Covered Bridge Art Association Art Gallery. 124 West Ohio Street, Rockville, IN 47872. Having snaked all through Parke County seeking covered bridges, some people feel they must go home with more than just a postcard of one. Many area artists who spend hours painting those very bridges display their works in this gallery. You can find a picture of almost any bridge, and you're apt to find it in more than one season. Open daily; closed major holidays. (765) 569–9422.

G&M Variety. 108 West Ohio Street, Rockville, IN 47872. Astonishingly, there is an old-fashioned variety store in downtown Rockville, occupying the space Murphy's abandoned. There's a bit of everything from food to a huge collection of wind chimes to fishing supplies and souvenirs and spices. With reasonable prices and a huge sale (20 percent off everything in the store) the Sunday before Thanksgiving each year, this store has kept Wal-Mart at bay. Open daily year-round. (765) 569–3154.

Harriet's. 102 West Ohio Street, Rockville, IN 47872. Just across from the courthouse, Harriet's carries a broad selection of souvenirs and home decor items, including wreaths, collectible plush toys, garden decorations, and ornaments. There's a selection of covered bridge souvenirs, including wind chimes. Open daily year-round; closed holidays. (765) 569–5402.

The Villagers. 112 East Ohio Street, Rockville, IN 47872. Beanie Babies, enamelware, dolls and accessories, unfinished wooden pieces, and antiques fill this shop just off the square. Open daily year-round; closed major holidays. (765) 569-5977.

WHERE TO EAT

Herb Garden Restaurant. 114 South Market Street, Rockville, IN 47872. Located on the west side of the square, this restaurant's entrance is through the Country Grapevine, the adjacent gift shop. Typically the menu includes three kinds of quiche, sandwiches, and soups; there's also a salad bar. Homemade desserts, at least a half-dozen different ones each day, are made using the owner's own recipes. The decor suggests a garden and trimmings change seasonally. Open for lunch Tuesday through Saturday. $. (765) 569-6055.

WHERE TO STAY

Billie Creek Inn. U.S. 36 East at Billie Creek Village, Rockville, IN 47872. The exterior is boxy and not particularly promising, but this hotel has its own charms. No cookie-cutter pictures here; walls are lined with photos of local sites and events. Rooms are spotless and nicely decorated; some have whirlpool tubs. There's an outdoor swimming pool and a breakfast bar, where snacks are available all day long. $-$$. (765) 569-3430.

BRIDGETON

Bridgeton is on the Red Route of the covered bridge route map and can be reached by taking County Road 80 East, heading out of town to the south. The road curves and spurs shoot off, but if you stay on the main road you will reach Bridgeton at County Road 780 South. The town is nearly 8 miles south of Rockville—but about a hundred years back in time. While there are several shops and places to visit in town, most of them are open only during the Covered Bridge Festival and at other selected times.

WHERE TO GO

Walking Tour. The town's drawing card is its big covered bridge, spanning Raccoon Creek, and the adjacent Bridgeton Mill, a three-and-a-half-story operating mill, the oldest continuously operating mill west of the Alleghenies. The first 2 blocks of town south of the mill are on the National Register of Historic Places. You can find a map in one of the shops in town or on the county's Web site that tells what the buildings are.

WHERE TO SHOP

Although there are many shops in town, most of them are open only during the Covered Bridge Festival and other special events.

1878 Bridgeton House. Main Street, Bridgeton, IN 47836. Just a couple of doors south of the bridge, this house contains a large selection of collectibles and homespun merchandise including quilts, rusty tinware, candles, pottery, and wooden board games. Reasonable prices lead city folks to gobble up the goods. Open Thursday through Sunday from the last week of April through the first weekend in December and during Covered Bridge Festival and other special events. (765) 548–2136.

DANA

To reach Dana, take U.S. 36 west from Parke County, turning north on State Road 71 and traveling for another mile to downtown Dana.

WHERE TO GO

Ernie Pyle State Historic Site. 120 Briarwood, Dana, IN 47847. This trim home is located at the corner of Maple Street and Briarwood Avenue. Birthplace of World War II journalist Ernie Pyle, the site features a spectrum of items spanning his life. You'll see samples of his newspaper articles chronicling the war, as well as personal letters. Newly upgraded, the visitor center has multimedia exhibits. Veterans and anyone interested in World War II will genuinely appre-

ciate this site, illuminating the life of the journalist who put a human side to the war, winning the Purple Heart and a Pulitzer prize before being killed on a small island near Okinawa in the final days of the war. (765) 665-3633; www.state.in.us/ism/sites/erniepyle.

NORTH SALEM

North Salem, established in 1835, is about 5 miles north of U.S. 36 on State Road 75 where it intersects with State Road 236. There are several attractive older homes and buildings downtown.

WHERE TO EAT AND SHOP

Apple Annie's. North Salem, IN 46165. This little town is a wink in the road, but the restaurant and its gift shop are popular. Once a furniture store and factory, the building flows over much of a block, with rustic interiors. Chicken and pork are good; bread, baked and served in little flowerpots, is delicious. Delicate bisque dolls, beautifully attired and handmade by a woman in a nearby town, are the highlight of the gift shop. Open for dinner Thursday through Saturday. $$. (765) 676-5805.

FOR MORE INFORMATION

Parke County Tourist Information Center. 401 East Ohio Street, Rockville, IN 47872. The center is situated in a Victorian train station. (765) 569-5226; www.coveredbridges.com.

Putnam County Visitor Center. 2 South Jackson Street, Greencastle, IN 46135. (800) 829-4639 or (765) 635-8743; www. coveredbridgecountry.com.

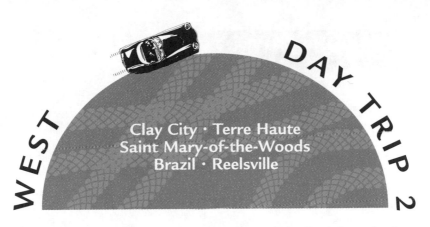

It is easy to shoot southwest on I-70 to reach all of these destinations; you can hit the major sites and easily return in one day. Your dilemma will be in trying to decide where to eat, since there are several good restaurants. The two stops in Clay City are worth the drive, and Terre Haute will be particularly appealing to those who attended or are interested in the three universities—Rose-Hulman, Indiana State, and Saint Mary-of-the-Woods. Taking U.S. 40 home through Brazil makes a pleasant alternative to the interstate.

CLAY CITY

Clay City, which is on State Road 59 south of I-70 (exit 23), has two interesting home-grown enterprises.

WHERE TO SHOP

Yegerlehner Farm. 1087 East County Road 550 South, Clay City, IN 47841. County Road 550 South is about 11 miles south of I-70, just on the south side of a bridge spanning a cornfield. Turn left (east), and follow the road about a mile to the farm, which sits on the left. You'll see an old water pump and a flagpole in the front yard. Although the process for making cheese is neatly outlined above the glass windows looking in upon the production facility, the real attraction is tasting and buying these cheeses, all made from the milk of cows who are fed on grass. The farm doesn't use synthetic hormones or pesticides. Ice cream is made on the premises as well,

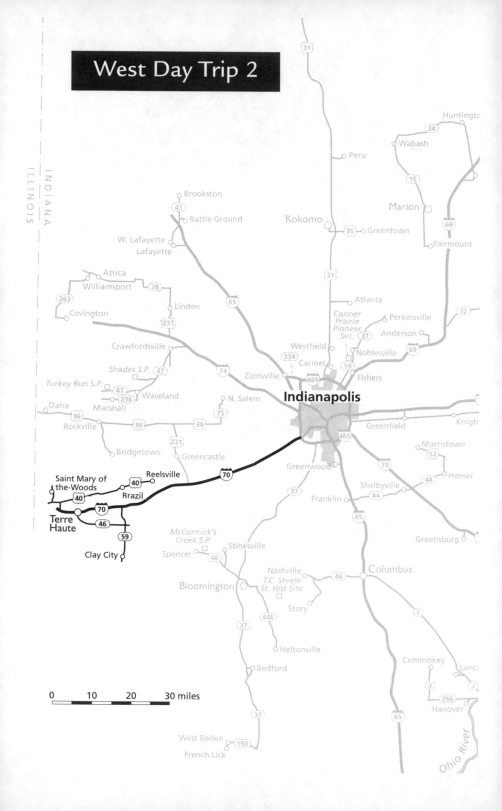

West Day Trip 2

ILLINOIS
INDIANA

31

Huntingto
24
Wabash

Peru

Marion

Brookston
43
Battle Ground
Kokomo
35
Greentown
15
69
Fairmount

W. Lafayette
Lafayette

Attica
Williamsport
28
263
Covington
Linden
231
65
31
Atlanta
32
Perkinsville
Conner
Prairie
Pioneer
Set. 37
Anderson
69

Crawfordsville
Westfield
334
Carmel
19
Noblesville
Fishers

Shades S.P.
47
74
Zionsville

Turkey Run S.P.
47
236 Waveland
N. Salem
Indianapolis

Dana
36
Marshall
Rockville
36
36
75
231
Greencastle
465
Greenfield
Knigh

Bridgetown
Morristown
52
Homer
44

Saint Mary of
the-Woods
40 Reelsville
70
Greenwood
Brazil
74
Shelbyville
44
Terre
Haute
70
40
46
37
Franklin
44
59
65
Clay City
McCormick's
Creek S.P.
Greensburg
Spencer
46
Stinesville
Columbus
Nashville
T.C. Steele
St. Hist Site
46
Bloomington
Story
7

446
Heltonville
Commiskey
Lanc

Bedford
3
256
Hanover
65
Ohio River

0   10   20   30 miles

West Baden
150
French Lick

but from milk brought in. Open Monday through Saturday, April through December, with shortened days January through March. (812) 939-2813.

Clay City Pottery. 510 East Fourteenth Street, Clay City, IN 47841. Once you get to the main block of buildings in Clay City, follow State Road 157, which makes three 90-degree curves; the factory and shop are on the third curve on the right side. Back in the late 1800s the Griffith family began creating pottery, and the same family is still running the company. You can purchase pitchers, dishes, plates, and many other pieces in a variety of colors and designs. Cobalt blue pottery and spongeware seem to be the most popular, although there are cheery holiday lines as well. Amazing finds await careful shoppers in the seconds room. You can also tour the facility, which takes thirty to forty-five minutes. Open Monday through Saturday year-round; however, there is no production on Saturday. (800) 776-2596 or (812) 939-2596.

TERRE HAUTE

From Clay City take State Route 59 north to State Road 46 west and north, skirting the eastern edge of town and crossing most major east-west streets. Although Terre Haute (meaning high ground in French) has a number of interesting sites, they are spread out. At press time the tourism office has no easily portable map that clearly shows streets and pinpoints the attractions.

Founded in 1816, Terre Haute thrived for more than a century, in part as a transportation hub—first with packet boats and later with trains and automobile routes, which allowed farmers to get their livestock and produce to market. Later the city developed a large industrial base, including breweries and ironworks, and became a strong union town. Eugene Debs, labor organizer and Socialist Party founder and leader, hailed from Terre Haute. His home from 1890 until 1926, 451 North Eighth Street, commemorates Debs and the labor movement.

Beyond Debs, the city claims a number of early luminaries, including Paul Dresser, author of "On the Banks of the Wabash Far Away," and his brother, Theodore Dreiser, author of *Look Homeward*

Angel; Max Ehrmann, author of "Desiderata"; entertainer Scatman Crothers; and Tony Hulman of Indianapolis 500 fame.

Farrington's Grove Historic Residential District, listed on the National Register of Historic Places, showcases many lovely old homes in a range of styles. Some are businesses; others, sororities and fraternities for Indiana State students. Another stellar site is the Indiana Theatre, 683 Ohio, just south of the Swope Art Museum. It is one of only a handful of theaters remaining nationwide that were designed by architect John Eberson. Eberson, born in Romania in 1875, became famous for his "atmospheric" theater, incorporating European styling with arches and domes and creating ornate interiors.

A number of small museums can add interest to a visit: Fire and Police Museum (Eighth and Idaho Streets), C.A.N.D.L.E.S. Holocaust Museum (1532 West Third Street), and the Children's Science and Technology Museum (523 Wabash Avenue). The city is also home to Inland Aquatics (10 Ohio Street, near the courthouse), which is a saltwater fish hatchery with many exotic fish; open for tours and sales.

WHERE TO GO

Fowler Park Pioneer Village. 3000 East Oregon Church Road, Terre Haute, IN 47802. Traveling south of Terre Haute on U.S. 41, you'll see the sign for this park in about 6 miles; get into the left lane and then the turn lane immediately. The road is not labeled. The park is about ¾ mile east on the left, or north, side. Once you've entered the park, follow the road to the left, back around a small lake (a great spot for swimming in the summer) to the village. Pioneer life is re-created here with a blacksmith shop, general store, covered bridge, and more. Each October during Pioneer Days the village comes alive with costumed interpreters. Structures open weekends Memorial Day through Labor Day, although you can wander around the building exteriors any time. Free. Vigo County Parks Department, (812) 462–3391.

Historical Museum of the Wabash Valley. 1411 South Sixth Street, Terre Haute, IN 47802. Confectioner William Sage built this Italiante home in 1868. It became a museum in 1958, where three floors are given over to exhibits. The upstairs re-creates rooms of the Victorian period; the basement has a number of displays showing period implements, including washtubs and other items; and the first floor has a drugstore, gift shop, and Coca-Cola display. This is, after all, the city where the Coke bottle was created. Open afternoons Tuesday through Sunday; closed January. Free. (812) 235-9717; www.indstate.du/community/vchs.

Swope Art Museum. 25 South Seventh Street, Terre Haute, IN 47907. The Swope's fine collection of nineteenth- and twentieth-century American artists earns it a prominent place in the Indiana art scene. The collection includes Terre Haute artists; Indiana artists such as William Merritt Chase and T. C. Steele; and national greats such as Robert Motherwell and Edward Hopper. A renovation begun in 1999 has given the museum a new, more sophisticated look, enhancing all the exhibition space and restoring the building's limestone exterior. The museum's symbol, a statue entitled *Diana* by Paul Manship (who also created *Prometheus* at Rockefeller Center in New York), greets visitors. There's a small gift shop. Open Tuesday through Sunday; closed holidays. Free. (812) 238-1676; www.swope.org.

WHERE TO SHOP

Meme's Boutique. 121 McCallister Drive, Terre Haute, IN 47802. South of I-70, McCallister shoots off on the east side of U.S. 41. A tidy dress shop with an assortment of women's clothing and accessories, Meme's carries clothing that can take you from casual to formal. There are also some children's things. Open Monday through Saturday; closed holidays. (812) 235-1888.

WHERE TO EAT

Magdy's. 1000 South Sixth Street, Terre Haute, IN 47807. Situated at the corner of Farrington and Sixth in Farrington's Grove, a historic district south of downtown and east of U.S. 41, this restaurant was built as a doctor's office and home in 1873. The staff is exceptionally helpful, and the food is good. The entryway provides a cheerful welcome, with a long staircase and 12-foot-high ceilings. The menu is small but mighty: Fish, pasta, lamb, and steak are offered, along with such appetizers as crab cakes. Lunch features sandwiches (Magdy's Favorite—with chicken, eggplant, mozzarella, and roasted red peppers—is delicious) and heavier dishes, such as an entree portion of crab cakes. Open for lunch Monday through

Friday, for dinner Monday through Saturday, and for brunch on Sunday. $$. (812) 238-5500.

M. Mogger's Brewery, Restaurant and Pub. 908 Poplar Street, Terre Haute, IN 47807. Located in the Bleemel Building, which predates the Civil War, this site first housed a brewery in 1848. The menu has an array of hearty sandwiches and other items, along with more than one hundred beers. Beef items, the barbecue pork loin sandwich, and pastas are popular. There is live jazz on Wednesday and Thursday evenings. Open for lunch and dinner daily; closed on holidays. $$. (812) 234-9202.

Pino's "Il Sonetto" Restaurant. 4200 South Seventh Street, Terre Haute, IN 47802. Seventh Street runs parallel to and east of U.S. 41; the restaurant is south of I-70, near the hospital. Around for about fifty years, Pino's is Italian to the core, with an extensive dinner menu based on the Sicilian style of cooking. There are a wide variety of seafood dishes from appetizers to pastas to main course items, as well as an entire page of choices for the vegetarian. Open for dinner Monday through Saturday. $$-$$$. (812) 299-9255.

WHERE TO EAT AND STAY

Sycamore Farm. 5001 East Poplar, Terre Haute, IN 47803. Headed east on Poplar Street, you'll see Sycamore Farm on the south side of the road just past Deming Park. Built in the early 1860s, this farmhouse has five guest rooms, four with private baths. The Sunrise Room is cheerful and decorated in blue and yellow; the Master's Room has its own porch overlooking the property. Some furnishing are antiques. Lunch is hosted in one of several rooms on the first floor, including the cozy front parlor and a sunny porch. Chicken salad, quiche, and homemade soup are some of the popular entrees, all served in a relaxing atmosphere. Lunch, $-$$; lodgings, $$. (812) 877-9288.

WHERE TO STAY

Butternut Hill. 4230 Wabash Avenue, Terre Haute, IN 47803. Wicker rockers sit on the broad front porch, giving guests a sweeping view of the wooded property and the lane that leads up to this bed-and-breakfast, built in the 1830s. Inside, rooms are light and airy with simple white lace curtains in all the windows. The five guest rooms are decorated with period pieces; honeymooners favor the Rose Room. There are only three baths, but the innkeepers ensure that baths are shared only with family or friends. Hearty country breakfasts with plenty of coffee are served each morning in the dining room. $. (812) 234-4352; members.aol.com/bttrnthll.

SAINT MARY-OF-THE-WOODS

The school is the town, which can be reached by following U.S. 40/150 into West Terre Haute, where U.S. 150 splits and heads north. Follow that route to St. Mary's Road, where you turn west. The school is at the top of the hill; use the second entrance.

WHERE TO GO

Saint Mary-of-the-Woods College.　Saint Mary-of-the-Woods, IN 47876. Another of Indiana's inviting college campuses, Saint Mary's welcomes visitors at its Providence Center, which is at the end of the main drive into the campus. The center contains a small museum and a gift shop. You will pass a diorama chronicling the establishment of the Sisters of Providence here in the 1840s as you stroll an indoor walkway connecting the Providence Center to the Church of the Immaculate Conception. The church and its Blessed Sacrament Chapel are stunningly beautiful, rich in marble, gilt, carvings, stained glass, and other details. There's a cafeteria on site. Open daily. Free. (812) 535-3131; www.smwc.edu.

BRAZIL

Although none remain, at the beginning of the twentieth century, Brazil, seat of Clay County, boasted thirty clay factories. This important part of the county's history is chronicled in the county museum, located in the old post office building (a neoclassical gem built between 1911 and 1913), 100 East National Avenue. Notables hailing from Brazil include rock star Henry Lee Summer and popcorn king Orville Redenbacher. The city lies squarely on U.S. 40, the National Road, east from West Terre Haute.

WHERE TO EAT

Company's Coming. 303 North Forest Avenue, Brazil, IN 47834. Forest Avenue is also State Road 59. Cheese-and-chicken casserole and homemade bread are just two of the mouthwatering items at this restaurant, situated in a trim Victorian home. Simple sandwiches, such as egg salad, and soups, including tomato herb, are popular as well. Diners sit in various rooms on the main floor of an attractively decorated old home. Open for lunch Tuesday through Saturday and for dinner by reservation only. $-$$. (812) 443-7963.

REELSVILLE

Reelsville lies on U.S. 40; however, this site is actually closer to Manhattan, which is about 2 miles east of Reelsville.

WHERE TO SHOP

Leatherwood Hill Candles. 8995 County Road 375 West, Reelsville, IN 46171. Past Reelsville, you will see Woods Market on the right. Beyond that, you'll see the sign for the town of Manhattan and past that you will see County Road 445 West. Turn south and follow that road, which veers left. When you come to the Y, follow the main road, which bends to the right. Then you will come onto 375 west. You will cross a bridge, which will take you over Leatherwood Creek. At the top of the hill, take the first driveway on the left. Candles and candlemaking supplies—wax, scents, additives, and wicks—draw craftspeople to this shop, despite its out-of-the-way location. There's also primitive folk art, including dolls, wood, and rusty tin; some antiques; and handmade soaps and bath and body products. Leatherwood Hill has been in business for three years, making candles for two years before that. Open Wednesday through Sunday and on Monday and Tuesday during December and the Covered Bridge Festival. (765) 672-4922.

FOR MORE INFORMATION

Clay County Chamber of Commerce. 12 North Walnut Street, Brazil, IN 47834. (812) 448-8457.

Terre Haute Convention & Visitors Bureau. 643 Wabash Avenue, Terre Haute, IN 47807. (800) 366–3043 or (812) 234–5555; www.terrehaute.com/thcvb.

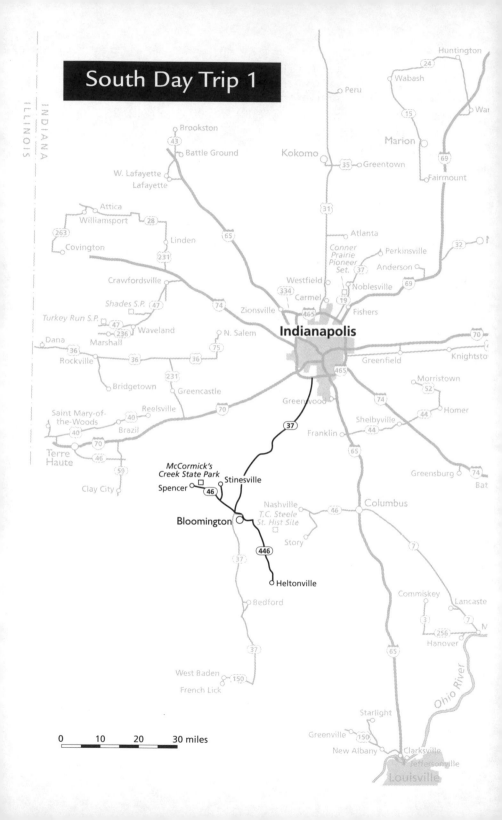

South Day Trip 1

Home to Indiana University, Bloomington exudes diversity and sophistication. The community offers the most accessible gateway to Lake Monroe and its recreational resources, along with access to a hunk of the Hoosier National Forest and, to the west, McCormick's Creek State Park. The nearby communities of Heltonville to the south and Stinesville to the west have solo attractions worth the side trips.

BLOOMINGTON

To reach Bloomington, take State Road 37 South. Bloomington blends small-town charm with the sophistication and diversity concomitant with a large university. You can't escape the pro-I.U. feel of this town. For instance, on the northwest corner of Indiana and Seventh Streets, there's a house with the I.U. logo shingled into the roof. To drink in the town's atmosphere, walk along Kirkwood Avenue from Indiana University's Sample Gates to the courthouse square. The town was once known for its limestone, which dominates local architecture. Bloomington hosts a number of splashy festivals, including the nationally known Little 500 and the Fourth Street Festival of the Arts and Crafts, held Labor Day weekend. Parking anywhere near campus can be a problem. Your best best is to get a temporary parking permit, which you can purchase from the hotel desk at the Indiana University Memorial Union (812–855–1245), allowing you to park in designated areas without risking a ticket.

WHERE TO GO

Indiana University/Indiana Memorial Union. 900 East Seventh Street, Bloomington, IN 47405. The largest student union in the country makes a great starting point for a visit to the campus. Inside there's a bowling ally, bookstore/gift shop, bakery, hotel, and several dining spots. Outside are walks leading through the university's wooded campus. You can stroll to Jordan Hall Greenhouse, view the Hoagy Carmichael memorabilia in Morrison Hall, wander up Seventh Street to the circular fountain, or take in a performance at the I.U. Auditorium or the Musical Arts Center. For basketball fans a peek in Assembly Hall is a must. (812) 856-6381; www.indiana.edu.

Indiana University Art Museum. 1133 East Seventh Street, Bloomington, IN 47405. Encyclopedic in nature, this collection holds samples of works from every culture and many eras, all housed in a building designed by renowned architect I. M. Pei. The first floor is a walk through Western art, including Rembrandt and Picasso. The second floor contains works from the pre-Christian Western world, such as Roman busts, as well as Asian works spanning centuries. The third floor displays what is widely considered one of the country's finest collections of art from Africa, Oceania, and the Americas. Open Tuesday through Sunday; closed major holidays. The building's atrium is open daily; the gift shop, Tuesday through Saturday; and the coffee bar, Monday through Friday. Free. (812) 855-5445; www.indiana.edu/~iuam.

Lake Monroe. Lake Monroe was created by the damming of Salt Creek and the area comprises many pieces. Morgan-Monroe State Forest occupies a chunk, the Hoosier National Forest sweeps around it, and the Charles C. Deam Wilderness edges the southeast. The scenic route from Bloomington is south on State Road 446, which leads directly past the Paynetown Visitors Center (812-837-9546), where you can pick up literature and read about the rules that govern use of the park. There is fishing, boating, and hiking year-round. For a panoramic view, climb the fire tower in the Deam Wilderness, just north of Tower Ridge Road near the third parking area. Fee to enter some areas.

Lilly Library. 1200 East Seventh Street, Bloomington, IN 47405. Lilly Library is Indiana University's repository of rare books, manuscripts (about seven million), and objects. The main gallery contains a portion of the Gutenberg Bible, James Audubon's giant *Birds of America* (a page is turned weekly, revealing a new bird; it takes eight and a half years to go cover to cover), and portraits of George Washington, Booth Tarkington, Julia Ward Howe, and others. The Lincoln Room features a desk used by Lincoln in his Springfield law office, a bust of Lincoln, thousands of books, and green damask wall covering, which replicates the covering in his White House office. You may not simply grab a book off the shelves. You register, request materials, and then read them in the library's reading room. Open Monday through Saturday, with shortened hours during academic breaks; closed major holidays. Free. (812) 855-2452; www.indiana.edu/~liblilly.

Mathers Museum of World Cultures. 416 North Indiana Avenue, Bloomington, IN 47405. At this diverse museum, you can find a West African xylophone gourd and an automobile made in Bloomington in the late 1800s. There is an exceptionally strong selection of Native American artifacts and photographs of Native Americans. A children's area has changing exhibits. The offerings in the gift shop are as diverse as those in the museum. Open Tuesday through Sunday; closed major holidays and during semester breaks. Free. (812) 855-6873; www.indiana.edu/~mathers.

Monroe County Historical Society, Inc. 202 East Sixth Street, Bloomington, IN 47408. In this county historical museum, imaginative displays crossing about two centuries make local history interesting to outsiders. Of note are the old schoolroom, complete with slates and desks, and a log cabin built of massive timbers, unlike any available today and filled with artifacts of the time. Historical quotes help bring the history to life. There's a genealogy library and a bookstore/gift shop. Museum is open Tuesday through Sunday; genealogy library is open Tuesday through Saturday, with more-limited hours than the museum. Free. (812) 332-2517; www.kiva.net/~mchm/museum.htm.

Oliver Winery. 8024 North State Road 37, Bloomington, IN 47404. The winery is on the east side of State Road 37, about 7 miles north of Bloomington. Since its founding in 1972, the winery has grown into a bucolic haven, as well as the state's largest winery. There are acres of wooded property, a lake, picnic tables, and limestone sculptures. There are usually more than fifteen different wines to taste daily. Here's a secret: In Indiana you can buy packaged alcohol on Sunday from a winery that produces it. Open daily. Tours run Friday through Sunday afternoons and last thirty minutes. Free. (800) 258-2783 or (812) 876-5800; www.oliverwinery.com.

Tibetan Cultural Center. 3655 Snoddy Road, Bloomington, IN 47402. Take Walnut Street south to Winslow Road (also called Country Club Road) and turn east. Go through the roundabout to Snoddy Road, which is a four-way stop, and turn south. The center will be on your left, marked only by a generic church sign on the right. Grab a map from the mailbox at the front of the drive; it will be your only guide to the property. Thought to be the only Tibetan cultural center in the United States, this peaceful retreat was established by a professor emeritus of Indiana University, who also happens to be the brother of the Dalai Lama. There are two stupas, which you may walk into, along with a main building with some exhibits, all geared to familiarize visitors with Tibetan people, history, and culture. Free. (812) 334-7046; www.tibetancc.com.

Walking Tours. The Monroe County Historical Museum has eight separate walking tours, covering various areas of Bloomington. The guides are divided geographically, so you might choose to stroll the courthouse square, which is on the National Register of Historic Places; visit the west side, Bloomington's original residential district; or meander through the Vinegar Hill Historic Limestone District, built when mining limestone was bringing prosperity to the county. The guides have good maps, along with pictures and vital information about the notable sites. You can pick up the free maps at the Monroe County Convention & Visitors Bureau, the Monroe County Museum, and Bloomington Restorations, Inc. (812-336-0909), which has an office on the lower level of the mall on the west quadrant of the courthouse square.

WonderLab. 116 West Sixth Street, Bloomington, IN 47404. On the north side of the courthouse square, WonderLab temporarily occupies an old department store. Here kids can dig for fossils, get measured by a talking dinosaur, freeze their shadow, and build a robot. Totally hands-on, the museum helps children learn about the world around them. In 2002 WonderLab will move to permanent quarters west of the square at Fourth and Morton Streets, where it will have regular museum hours and about six times as much display space. Open Tuesday and Thursday afternoons and all day Saturday. Fee. (812) 337-1337; www.wonderlab.org.

Wylie House Museum. 307 East Second Street, Bloomington, IN 47401. As historic homes go, Wylie House will appeal chiefly to Indiana graduates and to gardeners. The former will appreciate the old home, residence of Indiana University's first president. The rooms are decorated and furnished to reflect the 1830s and 1840s, when the Wylies occupied it; at least one item in each room actually belonged to the family. Gardeners will appreciate the gardens, which are planted using heirloom seeds rather than hybrid ones. Open Tuesday through Saturday March through November. Free. (812) 855-6224.

WHERE TO SHOP

Baseline Shop. Carmichael Center, corner of Kirkwood and Indiana, Bloomington, IN 47401. If you see a bad call during an I.U. game, what do you do? Throw a brick at the TV—a foam brick emblazoned with the I.U. logo and available here. You can also buy a thick sweatshirt, T-shirts for tots, an I.U. Barbie doll, and a piece of the old Assembly Hall floor. Indiana graduates and fans will find it hard to get out the door without a souvenir. Open daily; closed holidays. (812) 856-4388.

By Hand Gallery. 106 Fountain Square, Bloomington, IN 47408. An artists' cooperative, this shop is where you will find a sampling of local work, such as hand-woven scarves, glass, vases, cloth dolls, leather purses, and wooden carvings. Open daily; closed major holidays. (812) 334-3255; www.byhandgallery.com.

Classical Film & Music. 108 Fountain Square, Bloomington, IN 47404. Bloomington has long nurtured musical talent, and this is one of many stores in which you will find a good selection of tunes. The specialty is jazz, but there is a range of other music types, as well. You can also purchase or rent classical films here. Open daily; closed major holidays. (812) 333-8828; www.filmandmusic.com.

Elegant Options. 403 North Walnut Street, Bloomington, IN 47404. When you are shopping here you are also visiting a site of local historical note. Built in 1845 for a daughter of I.U.'s first president, the house is the city's only surviving example of brick Italianate architecture. Appropriately enough, the home now houses an antiques store, with a nice smattering of new items to complement the old. You might find a French armoire, an Italian garden statue, or a vintage chandelier. Open Monday though Saturday; closed major holidays. (812) 332-5662.

Goods. 117 North College Avenue, Bloomington, IN 47404. Located in the mall on the west side of the courthouse square, Goods features culinary tools and accessories, including teapots, cocktail napkins, aprons, pans, knives, and coasters. The selection is geared toward gourmets and those who love beautiful things for the kitchen. Open Monday through Saturday; closed holidays. (812) 339-2200.

Grant Street. 213 South Rogers Street, Bloomington, IN 47404. Once on Grant Street, this store now occupies the northeast corner of Rogers and Third. The owners describe it best when they call Grant Street "an arty department store." The department store concept may be old, but this take on it is decidedly new. There are no individual departments; rather, you'll find a mix of items in every corner of this former meat-processing plant. From shoes to furniture to housewares, the styles range from urban chic to rustic. You can find paper lanterns made in the Mideast and jewelry crafted in the Midwest. This is a festive place to shop. Open daily; closed on major holidays. (812) 333-6076.

Yarns Unlimited. 129 Fountain Square Mall, Bloomington, IN 47404. This is not your grandmother's yarn shop. This shop lures textile and fiber artists as well as hobbyists with is broad selection of yarns and its wide offerings of classes and workshops. You can also buy your own spinning wheel or loom here. Open Monday through Saturday. (812) 334-2464; www.yarnsunlimited.com.

WHERE TO EAT

The dining choices in Bloomington are so abundant that it is impossible to cover anything but a sampling of options here.

Bakehouse. 125 North College Avenue, Bloomington, IN 47404. On the courthouse square, this casual dining spot bakes fabulous breads, muffins, and more and prepares delicious sandwiches and pizzas. Mouthwatering choices include grilled portabello mushrooms on foccacia and roasted turkey with cream cheese and more on whole wheat. There's a minismorgasbord of samples by the counter so that you can try the homebaked goods. Open for breakfast, lunch, and early dinner Monday through Saturday and for breakfast and lunch on Sunday; closed Thanksgiving, Christmas, and New Year's Day. $. (812) 331–6029.

The Brewpub at Lennie's & the Bloomington Brewing Co. 1795 East Tenth Street, Bloomington, IN 47408. Located in a strip center on the north side of Tenth Street just west of the bypass, Lennie's doesn't look interesting from the exterior, but it's a top choice for casual dining. Booths and tables accommodate diners munching thick roast beef sandwiches on sourdough, Lennie's Voodoo Chili, and the wild beet spinach salad. At both lunch and dinner, gourmet pizzas receive accolades. Before or after you dine, you can peek in the brewery where the many famous beers are made, including award-winning Quarrymen Pale Ale and Big Stone Stout. For the enthusiastic there's a small gift shop with mugs, T-shirts, and other logo wear. Open daily for lunch and dinner; closed major holidays. $–$$. (812) 323–2112; www.bloomington.com.

Hartzel's Jiffy Treet. 425 East Kirkwood, Bloomington, IN 47408. Well, you won't get a full meal here, but you'll fill up on scrumptious frozen treats. Ice cream flavors created on site include such standbys as mocha almond fudge and rainbow sherbet; seasonal treats like pumpkin ice cream and gingerspees (a gingerbread and cinnamon concoction); and such exotic flavors as mango yum-yum and green-tea ice cream. Dieters can order Carbolite—a low-carbohydrate, fat-free, sugar-free, eight-calories-per-ounce frozen dessert. Open daily; closed mid-December through early January. $. (812) 332–3502.

Michael's Uptown Cafe. 102 East Kirkwood, Bloomington, IN 47408. The Uptown is new American cuisine, where the focus is on seasonal and regional items, although many preparations have Cajun flavors. Everything from soups to breads to desserts is made from scratch. The atmosphere is casual. Open for breakfast, lunch, and dinner Monday through Saturday and for brunch on Sunday; closed Thanksgiving and Christmas. $$. (812) 339–0900.

Samira Restaurant. 100 West Sixth Street, Bloomington, IN 47408. Perhaps the only restaurant in the state to feature Afghanistan cuisine, Samira blends flavors from India, the Mideast, and nouvelle American. The menu includes diverse offerings, such as grilled salmon salad, lamb kabobs, and dumplings stuffed with seasoned leeks. The restaurant is quiet, which draws those who actually want to converse during their meal. Open for lunch Wednesday through Friday and for dinner Monday through Saturday. $$. (812) 331-3761.

Scholar's Inn Gourmet Cafe & Wine Bar. 717 North College Avenue, Bloomington, IN 47404. This home, more than 150 years old, now houses one of Bloomington's most elegant eateries. Beautifully restored and refurbished rooms have cozy tables for intimate dining. The dinner menu, much of which changes about three times a year, includes salmon filet and lemon-thyme chicken. Luncheon choices include crab cakes and pita pizzas, while brunch has spicy sausage scramble, French toast, and more. Desserts, including crème brûlée and chocolate pâté, are superb! Open for lunch Tuesday through Friday, for brunch on Sunday, and for dinner Tuesday through Sunday; closed major holidays. (800) 765-3466 or (812) 323-1531; www.scholarsinn.com.

WHERE TO STAY

Grant Street Inn. 310 North Grant Street, Bloomington, IN 47408. The inn is a few blocks east and north of the courthouse square. Divided among three buildings, twenty-four rooms offer some of Indiana's most elegant inn accommodations. The lobby is cheerful and polished, and all the rooms are individually and fashionably furnished using both antiques and newer items. Bathrooms are gleaming and modern. The gourmet breakfast buffet is served in a sunny dining room. Rates are higher during the fall and on special events weekends. The inn accepts neither children under twelve nor pets. $$-$$$. (800) 328-4350 or (812) 334-2353; www.grantsinn.com.

Scholar's Inn. 801 North College Avenue, Bloomington, IN 47404. Although there are only five rooms, every one is a winner in this charming old home. The Caleb Mills Room, a garden suite on the first floor, has its own fountain and Jacuzzi. Each room has its own bathroom. $$$. (800) 765-3466 or (812) 332-1892; www.scholarsinn.com.

WHERE TO STAY AND EAT

Fourwinds Resort and Marina. 9301 Fairfax Road, Bloomington, IN 47401. Although the address is Bloomington, this resort is on Lake Monroe, a good fifteen minutes south of downtown. Take College Avenue South, curving as it merges with Walnut. Continue past the mall, past other shops and a car dealership to Fairfax Road, where you will turn left. Fairfax wends through the countryside and deposits you at the resort. Here the wind really does whisper through the trees and the water does lap the shore as boats bob on the lake. With hiking, miniature golf, an indoor/outdoor pool, and large rooms, this is an ideal family getaway. There is a PGA golf course nearby, and you can rent canoes and pontoon boats. Ask for a room with a view. The dining room, the Tradewinds Restaurant, is attractively decorated and provides a great view of the lake. The chef has created a popular menu, including bourbon strip steak and a pan-seared pork chop served with cheese grits. $$. (800) 538–1187 or (812) 824–9904; www.fourwindsresort.com.

HELTONVILLE

Heltonville is southeast of Bloomington and northeast of Bedford, and there is no shortcut to get there. Take State Road 446 south of Bloomington, across the Lake Monroe causeway, and through the Hoosier National Forest until you get to the caution light, which is in Heltonville.

WHERE TO GO

Turner Doll Factory. Rural Route 1, Heltonville, IN 47436. From the caution light turn right, which is State Road 58; follow it to the Heltonville School. The highway takes a sharp left around the school, but go straight. A sign points to the Turner outlet store. At the ball diamond turn left; the factory is about ¼ mile down that road. Road signs are few and far between! Tour the small factory, where you'll discover how dolls are fashioned from head (including popping in the eyes) to toe. You can see artists painting precious faces and seamstresses sewing outfits. There are boxes of wigs, shelves of heads, and racks of dresses. Following the short tour, visit the factory shop where the dolls are sold, some at a discount. Few Turner Dolls retail for less than $100, and many cost much more. The shop contains a variety of other toys and dolls. Open for tours Monday through Friday year-round; closed on major holidays. The doll shop is open Monday through Saturday; closed on major holidays. Free. (800) 887–6372 or (812) 834–6692; www.turnerdolls.com.

STINESVILLE

To get to Stinesville take State Road 46 west from Bloomington. Beyond Ellettsville you'll see a small sign pointing northward to Stinesville. Follow this winding road for a couple of miles into town. There are really just two commercial buildings in Stinesville (although there is a facade that the Historic Landmarks Foundation is trying to save). One houses the local mercantile, with its old-time post office; the other houses the Quarry Diner.

WHERE TO EAT

The Quarry Diner. 8248 Main Street, Stinesville, IN 47464. Definitely worth the trip, this quirky little diner serves gourmet food with fresh ingredients and imaginative combinations, such as pork chops with salsa. A big plus: The portions are not gargantuan. You won't feel guilty eating the whole meal, and you'll have room for the superb desserts. The menu changes regularly and there are a variety of specials, which are invariably good. Try the diner's very own Quarry Diner Crunch ice cream for dessert, homemade scones, soup of the day, and fries. The restaurant is small (make reservations), casual, and spotless, with works of area artists on display. Open for breakfast and lunch Tuesday through Friday, dinner Friday and Saturday, and brunch on Sunday. $-$$. (812) 876-8039; www.quarrydiner.com.

SPENCER

Although the address for McCormick's Creek is Spencer, the town itself is actually farther west on State Road 46. Spencer was long known for its wood products; notably, the common clothespin.

WHERE TO GO

McCormick's Creek State Park. Route 5, Box 282, Spencer, IN 47460. Heading west out of Bloomington on State Road 46 past Ellettsville, you'll see the entrance to McCormick's Creek on the north side of the road, just west of the junction of State Roads 46 and 43. Opened on July 4, 1916, McCormick's Creek was Indiana's first state park. Once hunting grounds for Miami Indians, the parkland was claimed by John McCormick in 1816. In 1888 the land was purchased as the backdrop for a sanitarium for the wealthy, today's Canyon Inn. Hiking trails lace through the nearly 2,000 acres of forest, dramatically sculpted by canyons, cliffs, the creek, and waterfalls. There's a recreation center on the grounds as well. You'll pay a fee to enter during the summer, but it's free the rest of the year. (812) 829-2235.

WHERE TO STAY AND EAT

Canyon Inn. McCormick's Creek State Park, P.O. Box 71, Spencer, IN 47460. Although the building has been around since sanitarium days, it has been updated regularly, providing modern if modest rooms. $. On the main floor there's a large dining room with plenty of windows overlooking the park. Specials change daily and might include fried chicken or beef tips on noodles. There is always a buffet on Sunday. Open daily for breakfast, lunch, and dinner. $-$$. (877) 922-6966 or (812) 829-4881.

FOR MORE INFORMATION

Monroe County Convention & Visitors Bureau. 2855 North Walnut Street, Bloomington, IN 47404. There is a gift shop, as well as brochures. (800) 800-0037 or (812) 334-8900; www.visit bloomington.com.

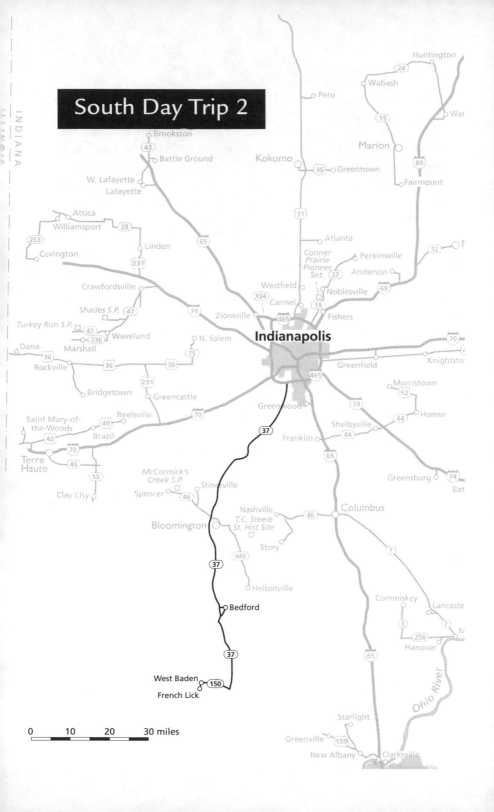

South Day Trip 2

Driving down through Bedford and Paoli (with its pleasant court-house square) to French Lick and West Baden really does consume almost every minute of two hours, taking State Road 37 south to Paoli, where you go west on U.S. Highway 150 then south on State Road 56. West Baden and French Lick are just a skip down the road. These two small towns are side by side; you won't even recognize when you have left one and entered the other.

Your drive to these resort towns will take you farther and farther from city centers, making it hard to imagine that at the turn of the twentieth century, more than a dozen trains a day chugged in and out of the town's train stations, disgorging vacationers and others who came to take the healing waters of the mineral springs. In season these were bustling towns, rich in romance and excitement. Today French Lick remains a resort, while West Baden is open only for tours.

If you have at least an extra half hour, take the long route on your drive home. At the junction of State Road 56 and Highway 150, just north of French Lick, head west instead of east. This route diverts you through a large swathe of the Hoosier National Forest and wends its way through several sweet little hamlets, including Natchez and Lacy. When you reach Shoals you can turn right to take U.S. Highway 50 northeast to Bedford, or you can follow the road left and then right on State Road 450, which also leads into Bedford but by an even more circuitous route. The vistas are grand, whichever route you choose. Other outstanding natural attractions in the area include Spring Mill State Park in Mitchell and Patoka Lake, south of French Lick.

BEDFORD

Bedford is the capital city of Indiana's world-renowned limestone business, a business that put the facings on many buildings in Washington, D.C, as well as on the Empire State Building. An exhibit chronicling the history of the quarries is on display at Oakland City University, just north of the courthouse square downtown. To get to downtown Bedford, take U.S. 31 South, exiting east on U.S. 50, which is also Sixteenth Street.

WHERE TO GO

Antique Auto & Race Car Museum. Stone City Mall, 3348 Sixteenth Street, Bedford, IN 47421. Once you get onto U.S. 50 heading east, the mall is the first turn to the left. For those who enjoy simply staring at race cars, this museum has plenty to see, ranging from midgets and sprint cars to Nascar and Indy cars. There are some classics, such as a 1931 Rolls Royce, as well as an odd selection of old items, including stoves, washing machines, and sewing machines. Open Monday through Saturday, April 1 through December 31. Fee. (812) 275-0556; www.autoracemuseum.com.

Bluespring Caverns Park. Bluespring Caverns Road, Bedford, IN 47421. Heading on State Road 37 south of Bedford, signs point the way west on U.S. 50, then north on a short side road to the caverns. Before recorded time, the White River cut deep caverns and passages through this area, creating a complex system for underground exploration. Quiet electric tour boats propel visitors through the limestone formations. The trip takes about an hour and includes some walking. There's a gift shop. Open daily Memorial Day through October 31; open Saturday and Sunday April 1 through Memorial Day. Tours may be canceled due to heavy rain. Fee. (812) 279-9471.

Green Hill Cemetery. 1202 Eighteenth Street, Bedford, IN 47421. From Sixteenth Street take M Street south to Eighteenth Street, where you turn left, or east. The entryway will be on your right. The limestone carvers in Bedford wanted to be remembered through the ages in style, so grave markers here are exceptional. You'll see logs, benches, angels, and a golfer. One monument is topped with tools of the limestone trade, also carved in limestone. A child's grave has the little girl's hat and high-button shoes sitting amidst ivy, lilies, and roses. The tourism bureau (see below) has two walking-tour brochures of the cemetery, one featuring a variety of monuments and the other featuring solely carvings of trees, of which there are many. (812) 275-5110.

WEST BADEN

In the beginning of the twentieth century, this town was known nationally for its pleasure palace, with its casino, opera house, and covered two-story bicycle and pony track.

WHERE TO GO

West Baden Springs Hotel. 8538 West Baden Avenue, West Baden, IN 47469. Imagine: One of the most beautiful buildings in the state is tucked away in this tiny little town, barely a blip in the state's population bubble. If it weren't for Historic Landmarks Foundation and the Cook family of Bloomington, who jointly rescued the building in the late 1990s, there wouldn't be anything to see. When it was built, this hotel, with its immense suspended dome, was considered one of the architectural wonders of the modern world. The dome remained the largest of its kind until the Astrodome was built in 1967, but the glory of this once-grand hotel had long since faded. Today parts are restored so that you can see statuary, beautiful tile work, intricate carvings, gardens, and more. You and twenty-seven friends can fit into the fireplace in the atrium to have your photo taken; when used, it burned 14-foot logs. The large gift shop has a wide selection of Indiana memorabilia as well as things of architectural interest. Open daily for tours April 1 through October 31 and Wednesday through Sunday November 1 through March 31. Call for tour times. Fee. Historic Landmarks Foundation, (317) 262-8080, (800) 450-4534, or (812) 936-4034; www.historic landmarks.org.

FRENCH LICK

Named after an eighteenth-century French trading post and the area's substantial salt lick, French Lick enjoyed its heyday in the late nineteenth and early twentieth centuries, when resort hotels near mineral springs flourished. Today it is also know as the hometown of basketball great Larry Bird.

WHERE TO GO

French Lick Winery. 8498 West State Road 56, French Lick, IN 47432. The winery is located in the Beechwood Mansion, which you will spot on the main road. The winery offers tastings of more than twenty wines, and you can walk through the cellar, viewing production work during the weekend. The tasting room doubles as the gift shop, mainly selling wines, wine-related items, and snacks. Open Tuesday through Sunday April through December, and Friday through Sunday January through March. Free. (812) 936–2293 or (888) 494–6380.

Indiana Railway Museum. 1 Monon Street, French Lick, IN 47432. Train aficionados will recognize the signs of a former rail hub: many sets of tracks leading into the station. Today old trains of many sorts sit on those tracks, making up part of the museum, and visitors can clamber on and around them. Inside the waiting room there are more exhibits. The highlight of this visit should be the moving portion: the train ride aboard the French Lick, West Baden & Southern Railway, which creaks and sways from French Lick to tiny Cuzco and back—a 20-mile, two-hour journey, including the stop. You'll see a couple of caves, Larry Bird's house, a lake, forests and, if you look carefully, deer; plus you'll travel through a dark, dark tunnel. On special weekends the train is apt to be robbed by riders who come galloping up on horseback and then get chased off by the sheriff and his men. It's great fun, especially for youngsters. Call ahead to find out when the robberies are scheduled. Open Saturday and Sunday April through November and Tuesday June through October. Fee. (800) 748–7246 or (812) 936–2405.

WHERE TO STAY AND EAT

Beechwood Country Inn. State Road 56, French Lick, IN 47432. Situated on a hill overlooking the Boulevard (State Road 56), the Beechwood Country Inn is easy to spot, with its impressive brick facade and stately white pillars. Built in 1915 the mansion was home to the owner of West Baden Springs Hotel and many other enterprises; today it retains its richly designed decorative touches, such as beautiful paneling and decorative crown molding. There are six bedrooms, all nonsmoking, and each furnished elegantly and with private baths. The Ballard Room contains the family's original bedroom suite, a marble fireplace, and a modernized bath with Jacuzzi; the bathroom in the Blue Room has pewter fixtures; and the Club Room has carved cherubs flying above the headboard. Because there are only six rooms and conventions are often held in the town, reservations should be made in advance. The Web site pictures some of the rooms. Breakfast is included in the price of the room. $$-$$$. Downstairs at the Beechwood, stylishly decorated with many Ballard family antiques, is dedicated to dining and relaxation. The chef changes the menu regularly; however, you might find Veal Oscar or duck a l'orange. Open for lunch and dinner Tuesday through Saturday. Reservations recommended. $$-$$$. (812) 936-9012; www.beechwood-inn.com.

French Lick Springs Resort. 8670 West State Road 56, French Lick, IN 47432. This massive hotel dominates downtown French Lick with its yellow brick facade. A long, broad staircase leads to the grand old lobby, usually bustling, although the hotel has seen busier and grander days. The wide range of activities available provide happy diversions for many tastes: archery, tennis, golf (with two courses), swimming (indoors under a dome and outdoors), bicycling, horseback riding, bingo, croquet, and more. Or perhaps you just want to rock in a chair on the spacious front porch. There's also a spa on site, which takes advantage of the mineral springs. The guest rooms are a bit tired, but the resort, with its cheerful staff and aura of pleasant well-being, more than makes up for the rooms. With all the resort has to offer, it's easy to see why it is popular with conventioneers and families alike. Ask about special packages; they have them for golfing, the spa, and more. The resort serves breakfast, lunch, and dinner at its three restaurants; plus there's an ice cream shop for snacks. Prices vary. $$. (800) 457-4042 or (812) 936 9300; www.frenchlick.com.

FOR MORE INFORMATION

Lawrence County Tourism. 1116 Sixteenth Street, Bedford, IN 47421; (800) 798-0769 or (812) 275-7637; www.limestonecounty.com.

Orange County Tourism Commission and French Lick–West Baden Chamber of Commerce. 1 Monon Street, French Lick, IN, 47432; (877) 422-9925 or (812) 936-2405; www.orangecountyin.com; www.frenchlick-westbadencc.org.

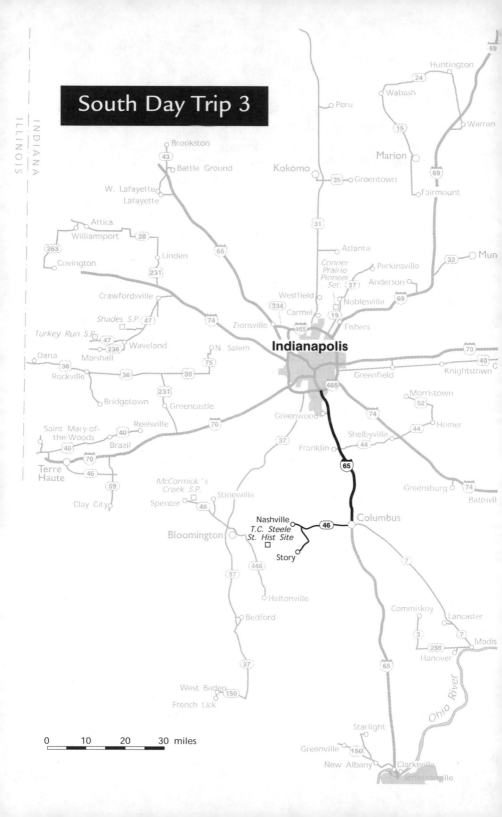

Indiana's original artists' retreat, Brown County trumpets its natural beauty and famed purple haze, prominent in paintings of the county. In addition to its natural charms, the county is rife with artists' studios, a legacy of the Hoosier Group—a contingent of five artists who painted here in the early twentieth century and brought other artists as well as worldwide attention to the county. There are outdoor recreation options here, including skiing in the winter, and Brown County is home to those quaintly named towns of Gnaw Bone, Bean Blossom, and Needmore.

NASHVILLE

The swiftest route to Nashville is I–65 south to State Road 46 West. Nashville has more than a hundred shops, appealing restaurants, and a wide variety of entertainment options, including the Little Nashville Opry, the Pine Box Musical Theatre, and the Melchior Marionette Theatre. The town's galleries display works by many Indiana artists.

WHERE TO GO

Brown County Art Gallery. One Artist Drive, Nashville, IN 47448. Located east of the courthouse, the gallery has the works of Indiana artists, including both permanent and rotating exhibits. A central room shows works of current gallery members. Make sure to note the two portraits of Bill Pittman, painted on a door. Pittman was an innkeeper and friend to local artists in the late 1800s and early 1900s. One portrait is of Pittman from behind; the other from the front—each painted by seven artists, including notables T. C. Steele and Adolph Schulz. Open daily from March through December; open Friday though Sunday during January and February. Free. (812) 988–4609.

Brown County Art Guild. 48 South Van Buren Street, Nashville, IN 47448. This gallery displays works by current Indiana artists but is particularly notable because it always includes a selection of works by the Brown County School or Hoosier Group, including Steele, Marie Goth, and Gustave Baumann. Open daily March through December; open weekends during January and February; closed major holidays. (812) 988–6185; www.browncounty.org and follow the links.

Brown County Historical Museum. Old School Lane, Nashville, IN 47448. Here you will learn about early Brown County life, through a variety of displays spread across several buildings: a log cabin, blacksmith's shop, doctor's office, jail, and loom room. There are a number of curiosities, including a rocker for two children, an old-fashioned apple peeler, and a logbook detailing what goods the doctor accepted for his services. The jail demonstrates how grim prison must have been more than a hundred years ago. Open weekends and holidays May through October. Fee. (812) 988–4153.

Brown County State Park. State Road 135–46, Nashville, IN 47448. Enter the park west of Nashville by crossing a covered bridge spanning Salt Creek. The largest Indiana State Park, Brown County sprawls across more than 16,000 acres of hilly, wooded terrain. There are walking trails, horseback trails, nature trails, and a self-guided auto tour; many trails follow old Indian footpaths. Camping, fishing, and picnicking round out the mix of activities; the pool is open Labor Day through Memorial Day. When fall paints the trees, cars snake through the park. Fee. (812) 988–6406.

T. C. Steele State Historic Site. 4220 T. C. Steele Road, Nashville, IN 47448. Although the address is in Nashville, this home is actually west of town near Belmont. Follow Indiana State Road 46 west through Belmont. You'll see signs, which will direct you to turn south to the site. You can tour the home, which is substantially as it was in Steele's day (he and his wife moved here in 1907), as evidenced by a painting he did; the studio, where a selection of Steele's art hangs; and the gardens, which meander through the property.

During spring daffodils coat the hillsides, a tribute to Steele's wife, a dedicated gardener. Annually scores of artists gather to paint the vistas. Open Tuesday through Saturday; closed holidays; closed mid-December to mid-March. Free. (812) 988–2785; www.state.in.us/ism.

Yellowwood State Forest. 772 Yellowwood Lake Road, Nashville, IN 47448. About 6 miles west of Nashville on State Road 46, you'll see a convenience store. Just past it, turn north into Yellowwood. About 2½ miles down that road you'll find the office, which is where you can pick up a map, register to camp, get a hunting and fishing license, and obtain a permit to pan for gold. You can rent rowboats here, as well. Visitors love Yellowwood because it is not an overly groomed state forest. Although there are picnic and camping areas, the forest seems pristine. The forest is open year-round, but the office is open Tuesday through Saturday from Easter until Thanksgiving and Monday through Friday from Thanksgiving until Easter. Free. (812) 988–7945; www.ai.org/dnr/forestry.

WHERE TO SHOP

Colonial Craft Gift Shop. Franklin at Van Buren Street, Nashville, IN 47448. Located in the Artist's Colony Inn, the shop is inviting and packed with an unusual assortment of intriguing merchandise. One of the best-sellers is Brown County basket jewelry: charms and earrings woven to resemble little baskets or teapots and made in Nashville. Other items include pottery, hand-painted paper boxes, hooked rugs, original folk-art dolls and Santas, papier-mâché creations, and mohair bears. Open daily year-round; closed major holidays. (812) 988–8813.

Lawrence Family Glass Blowers and Quintessence Gallery. 37 East Franklin Street, corner of Franklin and Van Buren Streets, Nashville, IN 47448. These side-by-side shops are owned by the Lawrence family, glass artists. Both shops carry glass figurines, sculptures, and ornaments—although those in Quintessence tend to be the larger and more expensive pieces—as well as stained glass by a local artist. Lawrence Family Glass Blowers has a small production facility where you can see artisans at work. Open daily February through December. (812) 988–2600.

Lexington House. 46 West Main Street, Nashville, IN 47448. This shop can dress any home or room in cabin style. The best-seller is

Old Hickory furniture. Bob Timberlake—a line of lamps, mirrors, rugs, men's apparel, and top-end cherry furniture licensed by the North Carolina artist of the same name—also sells well. Outfit your home with a lamp made out of snowshoes, a towel holder with a moose on it, a carved wooden bear, and antler accessories—including silverware and chandeliers. Featured pottery heralds from Monroe Saltworks, known for its patterns of mooses, bears, and ducks. Open daily; closed Thanksgiving and Christmas. (812) 988-6610; www.browncountycabinware.com.

JAR's Pet Palace. 44 West Gould Street, Nashville, IN 47448. For pet lovers, this shop delights. There are pet fashions, such as rain-coats, hats, bandanas, and boots; doggie doorbells; grooming aids, including breath sprays; ID tags; and treats. Open daily March through December and on weekends only during January and February. (812) 988-8950; jarspetpalace.com.

Totem Post. 78 South Van Buren Street, Nashville, IN 47448. For former Gnaw Bone campers and other old-time regulars in Nashville, no visit is complete without a stop at the Totem Post, which sells Indian jewelry, carvings, moccasins, and other souvenirs. Kids like rabbits' feet, toy Indian drums, and small beaded bags. Open year-round; closed major holidays. (812) 988-2511.

Touch of Silver, Gold and Old. Old State Bank Building, 66 East Main Street, Nashville, IN 47448. The jeweler's forte is custom work, made to order based on your specifications or created from stones you already have. The shop also carries a selection of jewelry from artists around the world, costume jewelry, and estate jewelry. Prices range from about $5.00 to $15,000.00 and sometimes more. Open daily; closed holidays. (812) 988-6990.

Trilogy Gallery. 120 East Main Street, Nashville, IN 47448. Pottery, lamps, tables, and glassware are just some of the items carried in this large gallery. The specialty is handcrafted furnishings, and there are accessories, home-decor items, and works by American artisans. Open daily; closed major holidays. (800) 922-3460 or (812) 988-4030; www.triologygallery.com.

WHERE TO EAT

Nashville House. 15 South Van Buren Street, Nashville, IN 47448. At the corner of Main and Van Buren Streets, this Indiana original has rustic charm. Built as a hotel in 1859, the Nashville House was rebuilt after a fire in 1947. It has been serving fried chicken, ham, and turkey dinners for decades. The famous fried biscuits with apple butter melt in your mouth. Pecan pie is dreamy. In the gift shop kids can buy rock candy and parents can stock up on apple butter. Open Wednesday through Monday for lunch and dinner; during October the restaurant is open daily. $$. (812) 988-4554.

The Ordinary. 61 South Van Buren Street, Nashville, IN 47448. A longtime Brown County favorite, the Ordinary is a Colonial-style tavern with a hearty menu. Roasted turkey, wild game, steaks, ribs, and a selection of vegetarian items are among the regular selections. An unusual and popular luncheon selection is the turkey and pheasant sandwich. A meat and cheese plate appetizer lets diners sample the restaurant's offerings. Open for lunch and dinner Tuesday through Sunday. $$. (812) 988-6166.

Overlook at Salt Creek Golf Club. 2359 State Road 46 East, Nashville, IN 47448. From Nashville head east on State Road 46; in about a mile you will see the sign for Salt Creek on your right. This dining room overlooks the golf course and seats about a hundred, with white tablecloths for dinner, although it is a casual spot. The chef enjoys creating specials, so each month is apt to be themed. For example, during lobster month there would be a variety of dishes created around lobster, as well as the regular steaks, seafood, and pastas. Weekends bring a special menu and additional new entrees. Open for lunch Wednesday through Sunday and for dinner Thursday through Saturday; closed in winter. $-$$$. (812) 988-7888; www.theoverlookrestaurant.com.

Soup to Nuts. 76 East Main Street, Nashville, IN 47448. Although it is tucked away behind Old State Bank Building, diners flock to this small place, popular for its fresh ingredients, good prices, and wide range of dishes. Menu items change daily and seasonally; for instance, sirloin chili is always on the winter menu. Soup and sandwich specials are offered daily, and there is always a vegetarian soup or quiche. Daily specials might include grilled salmon fillet and rice pilaf. Open for lunch Wednesday through Monday and for dinner Thursday through Saturday year-round. $-$$. (812) 988-4411.

WHERE TO STAY AND EAT

Artists Colony Inn and Restaurant. Franklin at Van Buren Street, Nashville, IN 47448. This charming inn is a one-stop-shop for all that Brown County is known for, except the forests. The rooms, each named after a Brown County artist, are tailored and warm, with interesting and sometimes antique furnishings, and quilts or coverlets. Eight of the rooms have balconies and there are three suites. The dining room walls display works of area artists, and diners sit in Windsor chairs. A large stone fireplace is the centerpiece of the room. Stir-fry, potpies, and cheeseburgers are among the items served. Open year-round; closed Christmas Day. $$-$$$. (800) 737-0255 or (812) 988-0600; www.artistscolonyinn.com.

WHERE TO STAY

Abe Martin Lodge. Brown County State Park, State Road 46, Nashville, IN 47448. This rustic facility is set in the forest, so you can stroll out the door and into woods, where early in the morning you may see deer gamboling. There are two lobby areas, one with a fireplace set up for reading or chatting and the other with a large-screen TV and a popcorn maker, used every night. In addition to modern and comfortable lodge rooms, there are family cabins and smaller, primitive cabins. The dining room serves three meals a day. Open year-round. $. (877) 265-6343; www.abemartinlodge.com.

   Hilltop Cabin & Suites. 304 Whippoorwill Lane, Nashville, IN 47448. These country-style suites all have fireplaces; some have decks; and all are roomy with great views of Brown County. Each has a private entrance, and some have kitchenettes. For those looking for views and plenty of space, this is a good choice. Open year-round. No children allowed. $$$. (812) 988-0984; www.hickoryshades.com.

STORY

The Story Inn is the story in Story, which you reach by taking State Road 46 east of Nashville, turning south on State Road 135, and driving for 11½ miles.

WHERE TO STAY AND EAT

Story Inn. 6404 South State Road 135, Story, IN 47448. The Story Inn, a collection of structures, is the reason to come to Story. An old general store, complete with broad-planked floors and a tin ceiling, houses a gourmet dining room. Mouthwatering entrees include strip steak with blackberry barbecue sauce. For breakfast the signature dish is banana-walnut pancakes, while lunch items include home-made soups and such treats as a grilled artichoke sandwich and turkey Waldorf. The more casual Old Mill Bar and Grill offers soups, sandwiches, and salads. The lodging provides charming guest rooms in several different buildings. (The rooms above the old general store are widely believed to be haunted by a spirit called the Blue Lady.) Generally rooms have wooden floors and country-farmhouse decor. You might get a porch with a swing, a deck, or a hot tub, but you won't find a television or telephone. The Bonham Barn, also on site, puts on musical entertainment periodically, and Story hosts a number of festivals. Open year-round, but the dining room is by reservation only. Dining room and lodgings, $$-$$$. (800) 881-1183 or (812) 988-2273; www.storyinn.com.

FOR MORE INFORMATION

Brown County Visitors Bureau. 10 North Van Buren Street, Nashville, IN 47448; (800) 753-3255 or (812) 988-7303; www. browncounty.com.

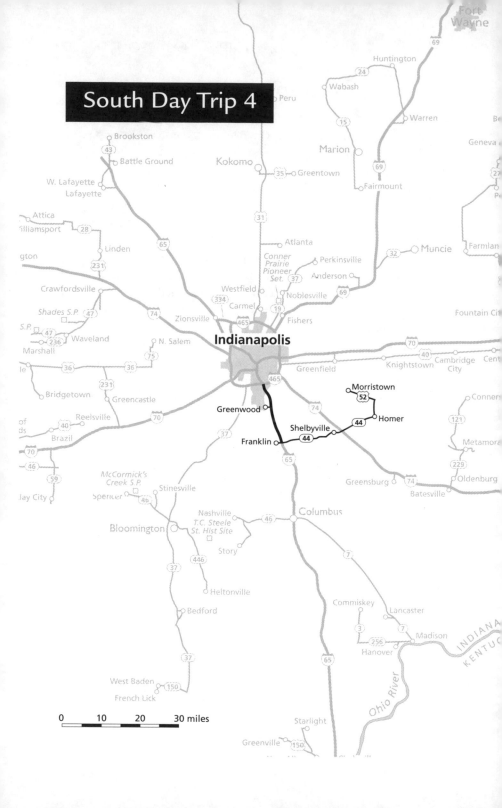

This route encompasses typical Hoosier towns, with antiques shops and a variety of places to eat. Shelbyville has an exceptional county history museum. Head south on I–65 to Greenwood and from there to Franklin. Pick up State Road 44 East to Shelbyville. From Shelbyville you can head back on I–74 or continue east on 44 to Homer for furniture, through Rushville, and back via U.S. 52 and the Kopper Kettle.

GREENWOOD

Like Carmel, Greenwood still has its old downtown, complete with small shops and restaurants, making it a pleasant place to while away time. The heart of what is called Olde Towne Greenwood is at the intersection of Madison Avenue and Main Street. Drive south a startlingly few blocks and you'll find yourself back in sprawl.

WHERE TO EAT

The Bay Window. 202 West Main Street, Greenwood, IN 46142. The Bay Window has the feel of a tearoom, with small bouquets of flowers on each flowered tablecloth and plenty of landscapes of floral still-life paintings on the walls. Homemade soups, quiche, scrumptious chicken salad, and desserts all bring customers back again and again. Many of the items decorating the restaurant are for sale. Open for lunch Monday through Saturday. $. (317) 882–1330.

Colonnade Room. 250 West Main Street, Greenwood, IN 46142. Greenwood's best white-linen dining spot is the Colonnade Room, where diners are pampered, fed a multicourse meal, and encouraged to linger. The menu, which can include such items as stuffed veal loin, chateaubriand, and duck confit, changes every quarter but always centers on seasonal, local ingredients. Each dinner includes soup, salad, and a palate-cleansing scoop of sherbet. Crown your dinner with the restaurant's award-winning, signature dessert, white chocolate crème brûlé. Open for dinner Tuesday through Saturday; closed on some holidays. Reservations recommended. $$$. (317) 887-6980; www.columnsballroom.com.

WHERE TO SHOP

Accents. 170 North Madison Avenue, Greenwood, IN 46142. Right in Olde Towne Greenwood, Accents occupies an old home where each room—upstairs and down—holds little treasures. You'll find candles, stuffed animals, gourmet foods, lace, china, baskets, and many other decorative and gift items. There are even a few pieces of painted furniture available. (317) 889-4863.

FRANKLIN

Franklin is an attractive small town with a lovely courthouse and courthouse square and is home to Franklin College. Beyond the tree-lined streets and a small railroad depot museum (also home to the chamber of commerce), the draw here is the antiques shopping.

WHERE TO SHOP

Jeri's Antiques and Interiors. 56 East Jefferson, Franklin, IN 46131. Located on the northeast corner of the courthouse square, this old building is well stocked but not cluttered or jammed with items. There are one-of-a-kind antiques in a variety of styles and from many eras, as well as new home accessories. A variety of buyers contribute to the array of merchandise, giving the store broad appeal. Merchandise is enticingly displayed, giving any shopper an idea of how he or she might use an item at home. Open daily; closed major holidays. (317) 738-3848.

Lighthouse Antiques. 62 West Jefferson Street, Franklin, IN 46131. This is a fine antiques shop, with items well organized and spaces easy to explore. Fine furniture is on the second floor, items in need of repair are in the basement, and the main floor houses everything else—from Coke machines to armoires, glassware, and more. The owners have a particular interest in old clocks and cameras. There is a bookshelf of reference materials, including price guides, so that you can check to make sure that you are getting a fair deal as well as learn other facts about the items that interest you. Open daily; closed major holidays. (317) 738-3344.

Thanks for the Thyme. 396 East Jefferson Street, Franklin, IN 46131. Next door to the railroad depot, which is also home to the chamber of commerce, this old Victorian home now houses the antiques, art/craft items, and new things, all chosen by the various individuals who have items displayed here. There is one room devoted to primitives of all sorts. Open Tuesday through Sunday. (317) 736-9866.

WHERE TO EAT

The Willard. 99 North Main Street, Franklin, IN 46131. The original building on this site, a home, was built in the 1860s, and the hotel was built around it in the 1920s. Interesting tiled floors, high ceiling, old fireplaces, and brickwork all combine to create a pleasing atmosphere, which draws a good local crowd. The specialties of the house are breaded tenderloins and pizza, both of which are created by hand on site. An awning-covered patio creates a nice spot for outdoor dining. The owners of the Willard also own the Art Craft Theater next door, which features live music and vintage films on weekends. Open for lunch and dinner daily; closed major holidays. $-$$. (317) 738-9668.

SHELBYVILLE

The town square has a statue depicting a scene from *The Bears of Blue River,* an adventure story written in the late 1800s by local author Charles Major and still in print.

WHERE TO GO

Grover Museum. 52 West Broadway, Shelbyville, IN 46176. This small history museum stands testament to what imagination, organization, hard work, and volunteer effort can do with limited funds. Don't tarry in the front of the museum; the outstanding portion is in the back—the Streets of Old Shelby, which is the re-creation of an early-twentieth-century Indiana town. You enter the hamlet by walking through an interurban train car, designed to transport you back about a hundred years. You find yourself in a town where all the buildings are three-quarter scale. A hotel, barber shop, printer, dress shop, saloon, bank, cemetery, and even a latrine are all painstakingly detailed to help visitors picture the past. Most of the artifacts are period pieces, including an old map in the school, hats in the millinery shop, and the fixtures at the soda fountain. The entire exhibit is comprehensive, well documented, and fascinating. Open Friday through Sunday; closed January. Not wheelchair accessible. Free. (317) 392-4634.

WHERE TO EAT

Good Fellows. 20 South Harrison Street, Shelbyville, IN 46176. Just south of the square in Shelbyville, Good Fellows is small and inviting, with black-and-white tiled floor, marbleized black tables and chairs, and plenty of art on the walls. A small bar stands at the far end of the room, although it serves only beer and wine. Parmigiana—chicken, veal, or eggplant—is one of the most popular dishes on this menu of Italian edibles. If the soup of the day is Italian wedding soup, don't pass it up. For the lunchtime crowd, favorites are heroes in several varieties and crab cakes. Open daily for lunch and dinner; closed holidays. $$. (317) 392-0575.

Hamilton House. 132 West Washington Street, Shelbyville, IN 46176. Built in 1853 this grand old home has been a restaurant since 1996. Lavishly decorated, the former front parlors and dining room are now filled with tables; upstairs there is plenty of room for special parties. Evening meals are leisurely and feature such items as prime rib and shrimp scampi. The pastry chef whips up delicious desserts, which may change with the season, and include cheesecake and crème brûlé. At lunch restaurant staff pride themselves in getting diners in and out quickly, while serving a broad range of items, such as waffles, omelettes, and hand-breaded tenderloin sandwiches. Pasta is a good choice at any meal. Open for lunch and dinner Wednesday through Saturday, with an a la carte brunch served on Sunday. $$. (317) 392–1350.

HOMER

Heading east from Shelbyville on State Road 44, you'll reach Homer in about fifteen minutes.

WHERE TO SHOP

The Sampler. 7138 West 235 South, Homer, IN 46146. For hand-crafted, Hoosier-made furniture, this is an ideal place to shop. The showroom, 1 block north of State Road 44, displays a wide range of the products available: Empire armoires, Early American bedsteads, Shaker tables, and more. All the furniture is made of wild black cherry, hand-rubbed to a beautiful sheen. The craftsmen pride themselves on creating furniture and other wood pieces to customers' specifications. Open daily year-round; closed some holidays. (765) 663–2233.

MORRISTOWN

WHERE TO EAT

Kopper Kettle. U.S. Route 52, Morristown, IN 46161. Long before the interstates, the Kopper Kettle was a popular stopping point for travelers, who ate, as many do now, seated at old pianos. Travelers still come here, although today their destination is apt to be this quaint restaurant, with its famous fried chicken. Dining is family-style, where large platters of food are brought to your table. The decor is elaborate, with murals on the walls depicting the Gay Nineties and brightly colored goblets on the tables. Parking is in the lot to the west of the restaurant. (765) 763–6767.

FOR YOUR INFORMATION

Franklin Chamber of Commerce. 370 East Jefferson Street, Franklin, IN 46131; (317) 736-6334.

Greenwood Chamber of Commerce. 550 U.S. 31 South, Greenwood, IN 46142; (317) 888-4856; www.greenwood-chamber.com.

Rush County Chamber of Commerce. 315 North Main Street, Rushville, IN 46173; (765) 932-2880.

COLUMBUS

For the most dramatic entrance into Columbus, take exit 68 off I–65 and head east on State Road 46. If you are a shopper, you'll probably be lured off I–65 at the first Columbus exit, home to Prime Outlets (one of the state's dandiest outlet malls). If so, you can follow U.S. 31 south and east until you see the sign pointing to downtown Columbus, where you turn right. Columbus, Indiana, is the type of town where we dream, or dreamt, of raising our children: safe, clean, and community-minded, with a low crime rate and a healthy economy. And beyond the tree-lined streets and sturdy Midwestern buildings, Columbus is rife with architectural masterpieces. Edward Larrabee Barnes, who designed the IBM headquarters in New York City, did Richards Elementary School in Columbus. Cesar Pelli, who designed the World Financial Center in New York, did the Commons (an indoor park/mall) in Columbus. Hardy Holzman Pfeiffer Associates, of the Cooper-Hewitt Museum in New York City, created Mount Healthy Elementary. Harry Weese, who crafted the Time and Life Building in Chicago, created the clubhouse for Otter Creek, a public golf course. I. M. Pei, who created the glass-pyramid addition to the Louvre in Paris, designed the public library. Robert A. M. Stern, who designed the Disney Animation building in Burbank, California, designed the hospital. Eero Saarinen, who did the St. Louis Arch and Dulles Airport, did Irwin Union Bank. More than fifty internationally known architects and artists have left their mark

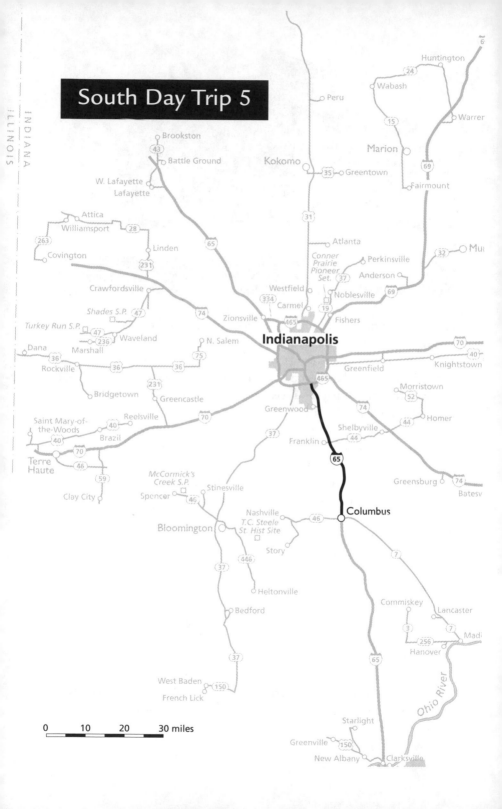

South Day Trip 5

on this Indiana town—many with more than one structure. During the course of the year there are many, many festivals, including the Chautauqua of the Arts and the Scottish Festival.

WHERE TO GO

Architectural Tour. Columbus Area Visitor Center, 506 Fifth Street, Columbus, IN 47201. The city's premier attraction is its world-renowned architecture, and the visitor center has made viewing the grandeur as easy and convenient as anyone could wish. You can take a self-guided tour; maps are available at the visitor center, a wonderful piece of architecture itself, blending old and new and crowned with a fabulous yellow chandelier by Dale Chihuly, famous glassmaker. Or you can take the minivan shuttle through town, a bargain at twice the price. You'll see Eliel Saarinen's 1942 First Christian Church, just across from the visitor center, and then see the North Christian Church, built by his son, Eero, in 1964. The post office, the library, the bank, schools, fire stations, and even the jail are all designed by world-renowned modern architects. The advantage of the guided tour is the store of lore the guides impart on the way. However, if you choose to drive yourself, you'll find the route well marked and easy to follow. Fee for guided tour. (800) 468–6564 or (812) 378–2622; www.columbus.in.us.

　Indianapolis Museum of Art–Columbus Gallery. 390 The Commons Mall, Columbus, IN 47201. This satellite museum shows changing exhibits, as diverse as the selection in the IMA: paintings, sculpture, photography, prints, furniture, and decorative arts representing all corners and cultures of the globe. It is the only regional branch of the IMA in Columbus. Open Tuesday through Sunday; closed major holidays. (812) 376–2597.

　Irwin Home and Gardens. Fifth Street, Columbus, IN 47201. This majestic mansion was built in 1864, but the formal gardens weren't completed until 1911. From then until 1996, when the last member of the Irwin family to occupy the home died, the family opened the garden up every weekend to the public. It continues to be open. You enter through gates on Fifth Street and roam through the gardens, enjoying the fountains, pools, terraces, Japanese teahouse, and beautiful flowers and greenery. Take a book and perch yourself on a step or bench for real tranquility. Open Saturday and Sunday spring, summer, and fall. Free.

Kidscommons. 325 The Commons Mall, Columbus, IN 47201. Part museum, part activity center, this nook in the mall is an ideal space for kids to play and learn. There is a different theme each month, and kids can work on a craft or science activity tied into that theme. For instance, during a month focusing on astronomy, children might make glowing moon rocks. There are plenty of other things as well, including experimenting with magnets or pulleys, role-playing in the kid's café, or scrambling through the toddler tunnels. Open Thursday through Sunday; closed major holidays. Fee. (812) 378–3046; www.kidscommons.org.

Mill Race Park. Fifth and Lindsey Streets, Columbus, IN 47201. The park, which has received national attention for its good use of land, sits on the western edge of downtown on property that once held the city's slums. Today these eighty-three acres contain picnicking and play areas, a covered bridge, an outdoor amphitheater, and courts for basketball and horseshoes. In warm weather you can take the elevator to the top of a tower for a panoramic view. Open daily year-round. (812) 376–2680; www.columbus.in.us.

WHERE TO SHOP

Baker's Fine Gifts and Accessories. 433 Washington Street, Columbus, IN 47201. The owner here stocks items that strike his fancy, and his selection has struck a chord with shoppers since 1984. Looks are sophisticated (don't expect country cuties here) and range in style from traditional to contemporary, encompassing gifts, tabletop wares, and decorative accessories. There's a wonderful line of door knockers and the largest collection of European-glass Christmas ornaments in the state, according to the owner. Open Monday through Saturday year-round and on Sunday during the holiday season; closed holidays. (812) 372–9635.

Cooks and Company. 534 Washington Street, Columbus, IN 47201. Like a grab bag of goodies, Cooks and Company is full of treats. You can stop for a latte or chai at the cappuccino and espresso bar; pick up packaged gourmet foods and decadent San Francisco chocolates; take a cooking class or attend a wine tasting; and shop, shop, shop. The retail store features high-end gourmet cookware and accessories, such as knives, aprons, and gadgets. Finally, you can order take-out lunches ($) through the week; potato chowder, walnut-chicken salad, and smoked turkey on homebaked French bread are just some of the menu selections. Open Monday through Saturday; closed holidays. (812) 379–2240.

Dell Brothers. 416 Washington Street, Columbus, IN 47201. This haberdashery opened its doors in 1916 and is still going strong, selling menswear and accessories. From sportswear to suits, the lines carried here are classic and handsome. There are some gift items as well. Open Monday through Saturday; closed holidays. (812) 372–4486.

Stone House Antiques. 748 Franklin Street, Columbus, IN 47201. North of downtown on the corner of Franklin and Eighth, this English-style home has a slate roof, steeply pitched gables, and a tidy yard, beckoning shoppers. Most of the items sold here are previously owned: gently used, newer items as well as antiques. There are many new accessories, including an extensive lamp selection. A bonus: This shops offers weaving of cane and rush chairs. Open Tuesday through Saturday from the middle of April through the middle of December; open by chance or appointment the remainder of the year. Call ahead for handicapped accessibility. (812) 376–0249.

Viewpoint Books. 358 The Commons Mall, Columbus, IN 47201. This large, general bookstore prides itself on service and selection and competes with larger stores in offering discounts. Staffed by people who cherish the printed word, the bookstore hosts its own book club each month. Open daily; closed holidays. (812) 376–0778 or (812) 378–9677; www.viewpointbooks.com.

WHERE TO EAT

The Daily Ritual. 1120 Washington Street, Suite A, Columbus, IN 47201. North of downtown, this slip of a restaurant is a reliable stop for good sandwiches, omelettes, salads, and soups. There are good choices for the health conscious, including a fruit platter and a salad with couscous and vegetables. Open for breakfast and lunch Monday through Saturday and dinner Friday and Saturday, when there is live entertainment. $. (812) 379–9287.

Divino. 425 Washington Street, Columbus, IN 47201. In an old downtown storefront, tables and booths are cozily situated beneath framed Italian posters. Soups are made from scratch and vary day to day. Signature dishes include the lasagna di casa, veal marsala, and encrusted chicken (in walnuts and sun-dried tomatoes). Tiramisu and *pana cotca*, a crème served with different sauces, are popular desserts. Open for lunch Tuesday through Friday and for dinner Monday through Saturday. $$. (812) 373-9644.

Peter's Bay. 310 Commons Mall, Columbus, IN 47201. Located in the mall right by the Fourth and Jackson Streets entrance, Peter's Bay is a dining landmark. Upscale and casual, the restaurant has an extensive menu, with an emphasis on fish dishes, such as Atlantic salmon and Indiana catfish. Open for lunch Monday through Friday and for dinner Monday through Saturday. $$. (812) 372-2270.

Smith's Row. 418 Fourth Street, Columbus, IN 47201. Once blacksmiths crowded around this area; now diners flock to this beautifully refurbished building to relax and enjoy an elegant evening. The menu changes seasonally, but some items, such as the medallions of steak Diane, rack of lamb, and baked French onion soup, are always available. The wine list may be the best in town. In nice weather you can dine on the upstairs balcony, with its view of downtown. Open for lunch and dinner Monday through Friday; open for dinner on Saturday. $$-$$$. (812) 373-9382.

Zaharako's Confectionery. 329 Washington Street, Columbus, IN 47201. There is nothing fancy about the food here, but there is a spectacular soda fountain, brought in from the 1904 World's Fair in St. Louis. Where else can you still find a Green River or a genuine ice cream soda? The most popular ice cream treat is the hot fudge sundae, with hot fudge from scratch. Sandwiches, fries, and salads are also available. The confectionery celebrated its one-hundredth anniversary, all under the ownership of one family. Open for lunch and snacks Monday through Saturday; open longer hours during the Christmas season; closed major holidays. $. (812) 379-9329.

WHERE TO STAY

The Columbus Inn. 445 Fifth Street, Columbus, IN 47201. The Romanesque old city hall, built in 1895, has been transformed into a luxurious inn. A floor was added, creating windows at floor level on the top floor. Rooms are large, elegant, and decorated in the Empire style. There is an exceptional two-floor suite, larger than most homes. Ask for a room with a view of the Dale Chihuly chandelier in the visitor center catty-corner. There's a breakfast buffet in the large, cheery dining room. A truly British tea is served there each afternoon Monday through Saturday. $$$. (812) 378-4289.

Ruddick-Nugent House Bed & Breakfast. 1210 Sixteenth Street, Columbus, IN 47201. This B&B is north of downtown and east of Washington Street. Laced in by a wrought-iron fence, this home and its grounds fill a city block. The house began life in 1884 as a Queen Anne home to the Ruddick family. In 1924 the Ruddicks' daughter, Martha, who had inherited the home, and her husband turned it into a Colonial Revival, using pillars salvaged from the St. Louis Exposition in 1904. (Elizabeth Ruddick Nugent moved into the house when she was ten and died there eighty-seven years later.) There are four rooms, one named after each of the Ruddicks. All are handsomely furnished with private baths. A family-style breakfast is served in the morning and refreshments are offered each evening. $. (800) 814-7478 or (812) 379-1354; www.ruddick-nugent-house.com.

FOR MORE INFORMATION

Columbus Area Visitors Center. 506 Fifth Street, Columbus, IN 47201; (800) 468-6564; www.columbus.in.us.

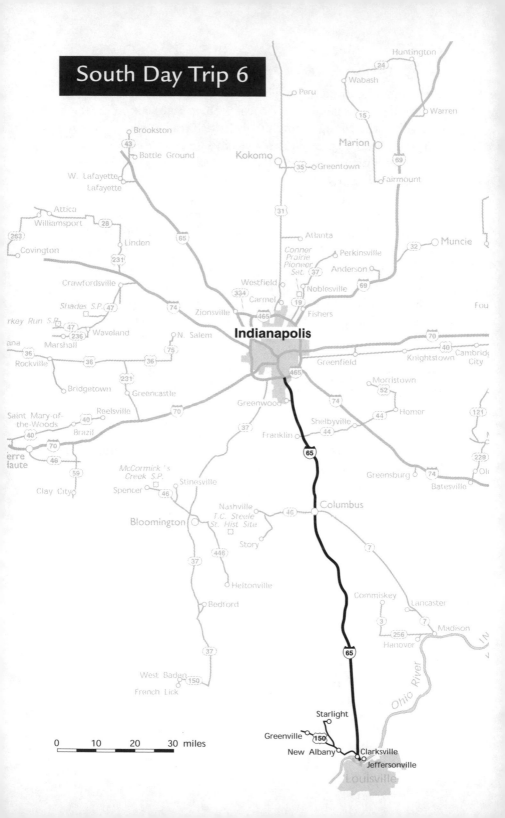

Jeffersonville · Clarksville
New Albany · Greenville · Starlight

Rather than attempting to compete with their more famous neighbor to the south, Louisville, these Indiana suburbs have latched onto Kentucky and refer to their area collectively as the Sunny Side of Louisville. However, the sites deserve a trip of their own because there are many interesting and diverse attractions. The Forest Discovery Center and the Falls of Ohio State Park are popular stops for schoolchildren because information is presented in such an engaging manner. These sites are easily accessible from I–65 and I–64.

JEFFERSONVILLE

To reach downtown Jeffersonville, get off I–65 at exit 0 and head east on Court Avenue to Spring Street. At this intersection you'll spot hallmarks of many small Indiana towns: a Carnegie Library and Masonic Temple, both with new uses. There are several other interesting buildings, and farther south on Spring there is a pretty little park. The town was originally platted using a concept suggested to Territorial Governor William Henry Harrison by President Thomas Jefferson, giving the town its name.

WHERE TO GO

Howard Steamboat Museum. 1101 East Market Street, Jeffersonville, IN 47131. Don't be deceived by the name: This is not a museum of steamboats, although there is some of that. This is a

93

magnificent twenty-two-room Victorian mansion, which happened to belong to America's premier builders of steamboats. There are plenty of steamboat artifacts and rooms on the third floor devoted to steamboat life and lore. The home itself is a masterpiece of workmanship, with intricately carved woodwork, created by the boatbuilders during the winter months when they would have otherwise been laid off. There are beautiful chandeliers, stained glass, and elegant furnishings. Open Tuesday through Sunday year-round; closed major holidays. Fee. (812) 283–3728.

WHERE TO EAT

Inn on Spring. 415 Spring Street, Jeffersonville, IN 47130. Located in the city's chunk of restored buildings, this restaurant has an old-world aura. For lunch you might choose a reuben sandwich, home-made soup, or sesame shrimp salad. For dinner you could get venison, rabbit, quail, or duck. There are vegetarian choices as well on this menu, which changes seasonally. The chef is a favorite among Louisvillians, who cross the river to eat here. Open for lunch Tuesday through Friday and for dinner Thursday through Saturday. $$. (812) 284–5545.

Schimpff's Confectionery. 347 Spring Street, Jeffersonville, IN 47130. Gustav Schimpff began cranking out candies here back in 1891, and the family is still at it. There are old-fashioned horehound drops, cinnamon red hots, and turtles, along with many other varieties of sweets. Nestled in a brick building built just after the Civil War, Schimpff's has an old-fashioned soda fountain, where the staff dishes out sundaes, sodas, and other treats. You can also pick up soup and sandwiches. If the sweets don't tempt you, stop by to look simply because the building is a superior restoration. Open for lunch Monday through Saturday. $. (812) 283–8367.

CLARKSVILLE

Clarksville, which lies just west of Jeffersonville, is named for General George Rogers Clark, who lived here in the eighteenth and early nineteenth century.

WHERE TO GO

The Falls of the Ohio. 201 West Riverside Drive, Clarksville, IN 47129. To reach the park take exit 0 off I–65 and follow the signs. Wear your walking shoes and prepare to be amazed by this Indiana treasure, one of the largest Devonian fossil beds in the world and a huge hunk of limestone spanning the Ohio River, creating rapids that impeded early river travel. Today the falls are avoided by the McAlpine Locks and Dam. Begin your tour in the interpretive center, with its life-size mastodon skeleton and must-see movie about the history of this area, going back 375 million years. Then tour through the various hands-on exhibits, which show this region from its tropical days through Native-American culture and into the present. (Don't neglect the dandy gift shop.) Once you have toured inside, head for the outdoors; there are hiking trails across the limestone and through the prettily landscaped park, picnic areas, and fishing, for those inclined. At the northwestern edge of the park is Clark's Point; General George Rogers Clark had a small cabin from which his younger brother, William, and Merriwether Lewis gathered with their full party for the first time and set off to explore the west. Open daily; closed Thanksgiving and Christmas. Fee. (812) 280–9970; www.fallsoftheohio.org.

NEW ALBANY

From Clarksville follow Spring Street west into New Albany. A pre–Civil War shipbuilding center, New Albany became famous for its wood products, such as plywood and veneer, in the twentieth century. In the late nineteenth century the town's wealthy built mansions along Main and Market Streets, which came to be known as Mansion Row, now on the National Register of Historic Places.

WHERE TO GO

Culbertson Mansion State Historic Site. 914 East Main Street, New Albany, IN 47150. The only mansion on Mansion Row open for touring is the most elegant one built. Considered the wealthiest man in Indiana in his day, William Culbertson began the twenty-five room French Second Empire home in 1867, which was completed in

1869. Marble fireplaces, fabric-covered walls, and frescoed ceiling are some of the spectacular features of this Victorian jewel. Open Tuesday through Sunday mid-March until the end of December. Free. (812) 944-9600.

GREENVILLE

To get to Greenville, head west on I-64 to exit 119, which is State Road 150.

WHERE TO STAY

Stone's Rest Inn. 8757 Rufing Road, Greenville, IN 47124. From State Road 150 head north through Galena to the Borden/Greenville Road. Turn right, or east, about 1½ miles to Rufing Road. Turn left, or north, and you'll see the Stone Rest Inn on your left in about 2 blocks. A rustic-style modern inn, the Stone Rest is set amidst 150 acres of woods, including a fishing lake and hiking trails. Rooms are individually decorated in a country style, and all have bathrooms with Jacuzzis. A full farm breakfast is served each morning. It is a lovely respite, quite close to Louisville. $$. (812) 923-8242; www.bbonline.com/in/stonerest.

STARLIGHT

To reach Starlight from Greenville, take U.S. 150 south to Navilleton Road, where you turn north, or left, and follow the signs to Starlight and the Forest Discovery Center. If you are coming from I-64, take U.S. 150 north to Navilleton (the third stoplight) and continue on.

WHERE TO GO

Forest Discovery Center. 533 Louis Smith Road, Starlight, IN 47106. Southern Indiana has long been a source of lumber, and this center is designed to help visitors understand forest management—when it's okay to chop a tree and when it's not. A pathway leads you through a lifelike indoor forest, across a bridge, which overlooks the process of taking a tree from log to finished wood product. In addition to the conservation lesson, you'll see craftspeople at work. There is a gift shop with handcrafted wood items, as well as other items. Open Tuesday through Saturday year-round; closed holidays. Fee. (812) 923–1590; www.forestcenter.com.

WHERE TO GO, SHOP, AND EAT

The Hubers are related, and these popular tourist attractions are a lot alike, including the lake in the front of the property. One, however, has a winery and the other has a sit-down restaurant. Either can be a leisurely day unto itself.

Huber Orchard & Winery. 19816 Huber Road, Starlight, IN 47106. You can see the vineyards, tour the cellars, and taste the wines produced here. There is also a cheese factory; a farm market, with fresh baked breads in addition to produce; a picnic area; a petting zoo for the youngsters; and a large gift shop. The last sells a large variety of items, including Beanie Babies, antiques, and gifts. There is a grill where you can purchase sandwiches, salads, and drinks. Winery open daily May through December; closed major holidays and on Mondays January through April. Call for the days of operation for the zoo and market. Fee, for the zoo. (800) 345–9463 or (812) 923–9463; www.huberwinery.com.

Joe Huber Family Farm Orchard and Restaurant. 2421 Scottsville Road, Starlight, IN 47106. Pick your own fruits, buy vegetables at the farm market, take a tractor-pulled wagon ride, or dawdle in the gift shop. Kids will enjoy the minifarm. Come in the fall for the annual fall festival. One of the key attractions here is the restaurant, with its family-style meals featuring such Hoosier favorites as fried chicken, fried biscuits with apple butter, and fruit cobbler. Smaller portions are available for some of the most popular entrees. Open daily year-round, closed December 24 through January 1. The restaurant is open for lunch and dinner Monday through Saturday and for lunch and early dinner on Sunday. $$. (812) 923–5255; www.joehubers.com.

FOR MORE INFORMATION

Clark–Floyd Counties Convention and Tourism Bureau. Louisville Municipal Bridge Building, 315 Southern Indiana Avenue,

Jeffersonville, IN 47130. You can't miss this sunny, yellow building; (800) 552-3842 or (812) 282-6654; www.sunnysideoflouisville.org.

Louisville, Kentucky

LOUISVILLE, KENTUCKY

With its river-city heritage, Louisville, Kentucky, like Cincinnati, Ohio, bubbles with activities, sites, and shopping—far more than one could cover in a single day trip. Highlights include the $60-million-plus waterfront development, which features fountains, picnic areas, a playground, and trails. Main Street downtown has visually appealing iron-facade buildings, the second-largest collection in the country following that of New York City's Soho District. To the southeast is Bardstown Road, home to a potpourri of shops and restaurants; to the southwest is Old Louisville, site of St. James Court, with its elegant homes.

The city is home to the internationally renowned Kentucky Derby, a two-minute race encased by a couple weeks' worth of parties, parades, and one of the largest annual fireworks displays in the nation. In addition to the attractions detailed here, interesting sites include the American Printing House for the Blind, Cathedral of the Assumption, the Louisville Palace theater, Riverside (an interpretive center for nineteenth-century farm life along the Ohio River), the Thomas Edison House, and a number of house museums.

Louisville is a direct route on I–65 South.

WHERE TO GO

Farmington Historic House Museum. 3033 Bardstown Road, Louisville, KY 40205. Heading southeast on Bardstown Road, you'll

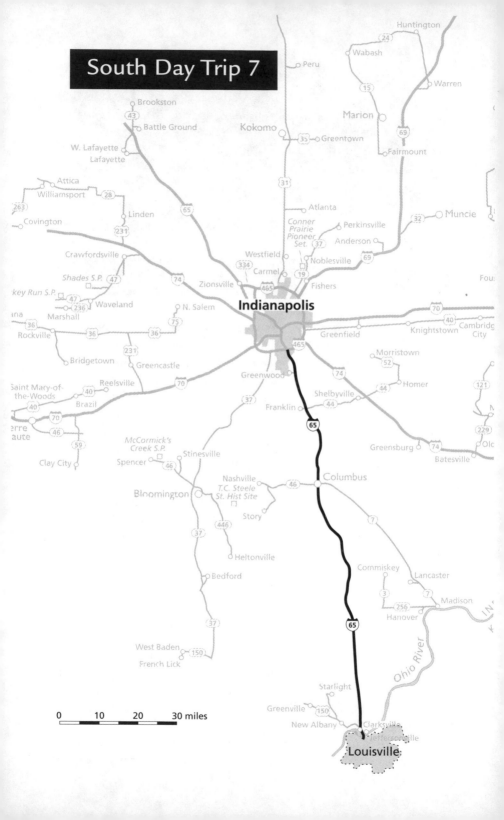

South Day Trip 7

see signs for this home off to the left, just before the entrance to I-264. A graceful Federal-style home built in 1810, Farmington figures into Lincoln lore as the place Abraham Lincoln sought refuge when Mary Todd initially spurned him; a copy of his thank-you note to homeowners John and Lucy Speed is on display. There are many beautiful period furnishings on display, as well as manicured gardens. The gift shop carries a number of Kentucky-made items. Open Tuesday through Sunday year-round. Fee. (502) 452–9920.

Kentucky Derby Museum. 604 Central Avenue, Louisville, KY 40208. For horse-racing enthusiasts and those simply curious to discover what all the fuss is about, this museum is a treasure trove of information. Equine experts can watch film clips of races dating to 1918; novices can learn the art of betting. Be sure to see the movie *The Greatest Race,* filmed for the 2000 reopening of the museum, following a multimillion-dollar renovation. You can learn about horses, jockeys, and history, too. Grounds tours, which vary by the time of year, are also available. Open daily; closed Derby Day, Breeder's Cup Day, Thanksgiving, and Christmas. Fee. (502) 637–1111; www.derbymuseum.org.

Locust Grove. 561 Blankenbaker Lane, Louisville, KY 40207. To reach Locust Grove take the River Road east from downtown, past the water tower, to Blankenbaker Road, where you turn south. The home will be on your left. Noted as the home where George Rogers Clark died, Locust Grove was actually the family home of Clark's sister, Lucy, and her husband, Major William Croghan. Clark, a Revolutionary War general and brother of William Clark of Lewis and Clark fame, moved in with his sister when his health began to fail and he could no longer cope on his own. The home, probably designed by Croghan himself based on drawings in books, was a bastion of gentility when Kentucky was still the wilderness. A ballroom and a separate room for travelers are interesting features, as are the many family portraits throughout the home. Original furnishings are rare, but the home is nicely filled with period pieces. There are various outbuildings and gardens to examine, plus a dandy visitor center with movie, artifacts, and a well-stocked gift shop. The visitor center and first floor of the house are wheelchair-accessible. Closed major holidays, including Derby Day. Fee. (502) 897–9845; www.locustgrove.org.

Louisville Science Center. 727 West Main Street, Louisville, KY 40202. Street parking is scarce downtown, so turn right just past the museum and go north 1½ blocks to a big garage; a pedestrian bridge connects it to the museum. A magnet for youngsters, this museum has scores of interactive exhibits, all designed to help a child visualize the wonderful world of science. For example, children can play in a small space shuttle or see the effects of gravity on an endless chain of balls as they move up on conveyor belts and fall through chutes. KidZone is strictly for the age-seven-and-under crowd. The area's only Imax theater is housed here, and there's a gallery for a parade of temporary exhibits. There's also a snack bar and a dandy gift shop. Closed Thanksgiving, Christmas Eve, and Christmas Day. Fee. (800) 591-2203 or (502) 561-6100; www.LouisvilleScience.org.

Louisville Slugger Museum. 800 West Main Street, Louisville, KY 40202. Less than a block from the Science Center, this new museum is easy to spot, with the world's largest bat—all 120 feet of it—standing outside the building. Inside, visitors are treated to a movie and a tour showing how bats are made. You'll learn about wood versus aluminum and how to customize a bat for its batter. At the end of the tour sluggers are unleashed in the gift shop, where they can buy all manner of baseball paraphernalia. Each tour comes with a free minibat. Open Monday through Saturday; closed major holidays. There is no bat production on Saturday December through March. Fee. (502) 588-7228; www.slugger.com/museum.

Speed Art Museum. 2035 South Third Street, Louisville, KY 40208. Part of the University of Louisville campus, the Speed, with its large galleries, good parking, and accessibility, has the right combination for hosting successful exhibitions. Brought in from museums around the world, these traveling shows attract wide attention. The permanent collection, too, is good, with a broad selection ranging from the ancient world to Native American and modern art. There is a nice gift shop, and a small cafe is open for lunch Tuesday through Saturday. Museum open Tuesday through Sunday. Free for permanent collection; fee for some special exhibitions and fee for nonmembers to enter the children's Art Learning Center. (502) 634-2700; www.speedmuseum.org.

WHERE TO SHOP

Hadley Pottery Company. 1570 Story Avenue, Louisville, KY 40206. Take I-65 South to I-64 East, and get off at the first exit (7), Story Avenue. At the bottom of the exit ramp, the factory is about a block to your left, but because Story Avenue is one-way, you must turn right and take the next four left turns, getting yourself around the block. Pigs, chicken, children, flowers, birds, and barns are just some of the familiar designs on Mary Alice Hadley's famous blue-and-gray pottery. Each piece is painted by hand, meaning there are slight variations among them. Here at the headquarters there is a seconds shop, as well as a section where you'll find cracked pieces and personalized overruns. Although the shop isn't large, Hadley lovers will depart well supplied. Open Monday through Saturday; closed major holidays. (502) 584-2171; www.hadleypottery.com.

Joe Ley Antiques. 615 East Market Street, Louisville, KY 40202. You can't miss this building, on the north side of Market, just east of downtown, with its behemoth toy soldiers flanking the entry. Inside there are four floors of antiques, ranging from trinkets to regal treasures. Whether you are in the mood to buy or browse, strolling through here is a marvelous pastime. Open Tuesday through Saturday year-round. Small entrance fee is credited against a purchase. (502) 583-4014; www.joeley.com.

Kentucky Art and Craft Gallery. 609 West Main Street, Louisville, KY 40202. As much for viewing as for buying, the gallery presents the works of Kentucky arts and craftspeople in changing exhibits on two floors. A large shop in the rear of the gallery sells a range of items, including Churchill Weavers throws and body butter. Open Monday through Saturday. (502) 589-0102; www.kentuckycrafts.org.

Louisville Stoneware. 731 Brent Street, Louisville, KY 40204. The factory and store are just off Broadway, near Barrett, west of downtown. An enjoyable part of shopping here is being able to watch craftspeople as they make the pottery. In addition to classic dinnerware, the factory shop sells quaint figurines, birdhouses, mugs, platters, and more in an array of designs, using the company's trademark color palette of browns, blues, greens, and white. Open daily year-round; closed major holidays. (800) 626-1800 or (502) 582-1900; www.louisvillestonewarecompany.com.

WHERE TO EAT

In addition to these restaurants, you can find coffee shops, cafes, and Irish, Korean, Mongolian, and Mayan restaurants sprinkled about the city.

English Grill. Camberley Brown Hotel, 335 West Broadway, Louisville, KY 40202. The English Grill celebrates the city's Thoroughbred pedigree, with portraits of Kentucky Derby winners and other famous horses hanging on the walls. The service may seem a bit slow, but this is fine dining, where one is supposed to savor both the food and the atmosphere. The menu changes seasonally; popular items from season to season include lamb, fillet of beef, and salmon. For a special treat, ask about the chef's table, served by the chef in the kitchen Tuesday through Saturday; reservations required well in advance. Reservations recommended. Open for dinner Monday through Saturday. $$$. (502) 583–1234.

Lilly's. 1147 Bardstown Road, Louisville, KY 40204. Out on Bardstown Road, which might be called Restaurant Row, Lilly's is another one of Louisville's many elegant dining spots. Let's go to the heart of the matter: The smoked pork, however it comes prepared, is top notch. There are many other good items on the menu, which changes regularly, as well as mashed potatoes, soups, halibut, and the bread. The atmosphere is cozy but sophisticated, with dark green walls with a large mural painted on one, and white-tablecloth service. Open for lunch and dinner Tuesday through Saturday; closed holidays. $$$. (502) 451–0447.

Lynn's Paradise Cafe. 984 Barret Avenue, Louisville, KY 40204. Take Broadway east to Barret (just past the train trestle) and turn right. The restaurant is a few blocks down on your right; look for the giant coffeepot and cups. As much of a sight-seeing attraction as a restaurant, this camp eatery has received national media attention and is a must-stop on your visit to Louisville. Lawn art and a corncob mural decorate the exterior; remarkably hideous lamps and kitsch adorn the tables. You'll find yourself gawking at the decor, when you are not chowing down on generous portions of delicious food, such as the breakfast burrito, walnut-crusted chicken, homemade mashed potatoes, and cheese grits. The waitstaff seems uniformly upbeat and knowledgeable. Open for breakfast, lunch, and dinner Tuesday through Sunday. Reservations recommended. $$. (502) 583–3447; www.lynnsparadisecafe.com.

Vincenzo's. 150 South Fifth Street, Louisville, KY 40202. You'll find this restaurant in an old bank building, just south of the river on the corner of Fifth and Market Streets. Founded in 1986, the elegant restaurant has a most soothing atmosphere, with richly

colored walls, large oil paintings, white tablecloths, and crisply effi-
cient service. As the name implies, the menu bent is Italian, but the
dishes have broad appeal and always include specialties such as
swordfish or poached salmon, plus a large selection of heart-healthy
items. The mixed green salad with raspberry vinaigrette is tasty.
Open for lunch Monday through Friday; dinner, Monday through
Saturday. Reservations recommended. $$$. (502) 580-1350.

WHERE TO STAY

Camberley Brown Hotel. 335 West Broadway, Louisville, KY 40202.
In Louisville's theater district, with a trolley stop just outside the
door, the Camberley Brown makes a good spot for a getaway. The
hotel's elegant lobby has marble, antiques, and elaborate moldings.
Rooms are comfortable and nicely appointed with furnishing in
keeping with the lobby decor. Inquire about special packages. $$$.
(800) 555-8000 or (502) 583-1234; www.thebrownhotel.com.

    Seelbach Hilton Hotel. 500 South Fourth Avenue, Louisville, KY
40202. Just by the enclosed downtown Galleria and near the waterfront, the Seelbach has been a social gathering point in Louisville
since it was built in 1905. The lobby is elegant and ornate; on the
lower level is a function room, the Rathskellar, decorated in Ohio's
famous Rookwood tile. The hotel's main restaurant, the Oak Room, is
the only AAA five-diamond restaurant in Kentucky. Because the hotel
is older, the rooms are different sizes; furnishings are eighteenth-
century reproductions, including four-poster beds. $$$. (800)
333-3399 or (502) 585-3200; www.theseelbachlouisville.hilton.com.

FOR YOUR INFORMATION

Historic Homes Foundation. 3110 Lexington Road, Louisville, KY
40206. This foundation operates four historic homes; (502)
899-5079; www.historichomes.org.

    **Louisville and Jefferson County Convention and Visitors
Bureau.** Third and Market Streets inside the Kentucky International
Convention Center, Louisville, KY 40202; (800) 792-5595 or (502)
582-3732; www.gotolouisville.com.

    Main Street Association. 641 West Main Street, Louisville, KY
40202. This organization has information on the historic downtown
Main Street district and offers walking tours; (502) 561-3493.

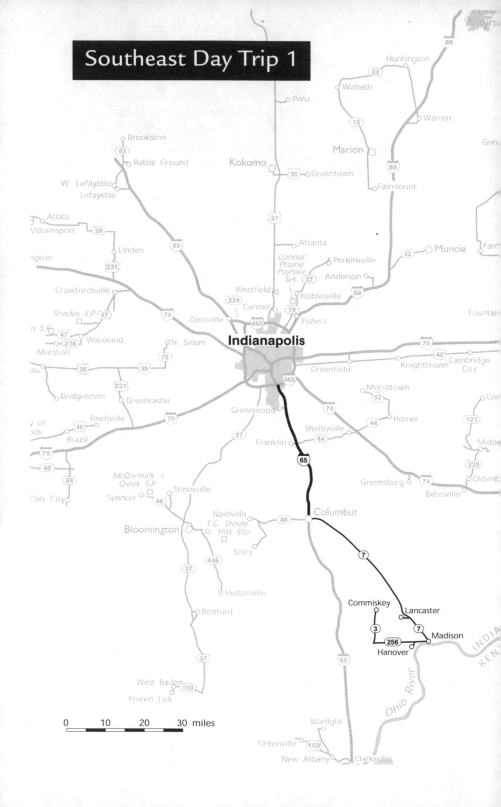

Lancaster · Madison
Hanover · Commiskey

The most pleasant route down to Madison is on State Road 7, through North Vernon and Vernon, two towns blessed in that they were passed over by bulldoze-and-build developers, leaving both with a bevy of nineteenth- and early-twentieth-century structures—albeit some are sagging. This route curves on south through hilly country until it drops down to historic Madison, one of the most picturesque towns along the Ohio River; turn left when you hit Main Street, where SR 7 abruptly ends. If you have extra time, take the scenic river route east to Vevay (pronounced *Vee-vee*), a small community with an imposing and elegant B&B, the Schenck Mansion (812–427–2787), and an interesting county museum.

LANCASTER

Beyond the hamlet of Dupont, look for State Road 250 heading west; you can only turn right. Eleutherian College is about 2 miles down this twisting road.

WHERE TO GO

Eleutherian College. 6927 West State Route 250, Lancaster, IN 47250. Lancaster has only one site, the college. You'll see it perched on a hill as you approach town, but wait to turn in at the visitor center, just west of the driveway to the school. The school's drive is treacherously invisible to highway traffic. Founded in 1848 by an abolitionist preacher from Ohio, this college welcomed African

Americans and whites. As a college, its star shone briefly, and it was dissolved after the Civil War. Call to make an appointment for tours of the interior. Free; donations appreciated. (812) 273–9434.

MADISON

The belle of Indiana's small towns, Madison sits on the Ohio River, where settlers heading west stopped off and stayed. As a port and a railroad hub, Madison prospered from the beginning of the nineteenth century until the Civil War, when main transportation routes circumnavigated the town, leading to a decline not reversed for a hundred years, when tourism revived the burg. The architecture is older than in other parts of the state, and its wealth represents an earlier era as well. You'll find references to the flood of 1937, when the Ohio overflowed its banks and crept into town. Madison has an unusually rich selection of festivals and special events throughout the year. Begin your visit at the tourism office, where you can pick up a good brochure with a map of town, a brief history, and local highlights.

WHERE TO GO

Clifty Falls State Park. 1501 Green Road, Madison, IN 47250. The park entrance is 1 mile west of Madison on State Road 56–62. Water spilling down from melting Ice Age glaciers helped carve this park of canyons and cliffs. There are miles of hiking trails of varying difficulty, as well as a renovated inn with an indoor pool, tennis courts, and a dining room ($–$$). (812) 273–8885 or (812) 265–1331; www.state.in.us/dnr.

Dr. William Hutchings's Office. 120 West Third Street, Madison, IN 47250. Although this Classic Revival building was built in the 1840s, it didn't become a doctor's office until 1882, when Dr. Hutchings purchased it. He practiced here until 1903, and a descendent presented the museum with many of the original pieces of equipment he used, along with some of his furniture. These, along with a book about his life, provide insight into late-nineteenth-century medicine. Open daily mid-April through October. Fee. (812) 265–2967.

Francis Costigan House. 408 West Third Street, Madison, IN 47250. Built by the architect of the Shrewsbury-Windle and Lanier homes and many other notable area structures, this skinny house is designed to create a sense of interior spaciousness, with a 30-foot-long parlor and other features. Woodwork, moldings, and ceilings are intricate and elegant. Open mid-April through October. Fee. (812) 265-2967.

Jefferson County Historical Society and Rail Station. 615 West First Street, Madison, IN 47250. This is the spot that reveals Madison history, including the great role the river, floods and all, has played in the town's development. Exhibits change, but there are always displays on the Civil War, steamboating, and Victorian life. Open daily late April through the end of October; open Monday through Friday November through late April. Fee. (812) 265-2335; www.seidata.com/~jchs.

Jeremiah Sullivan House. 304 West Second Street, Madison, IN 47250. Between 1811 and 1818, when this house was built, Madison grew from a village of only a dozen families to about 800 citizens, with its path seemingly paved to prosperity. Jeremiah Sullivan was an attorney, a leading citizen, and one of the founders of nearby Hanover College. When built, the Federal-style home was a mansion in the frontier. Open daily from April through October. Fee. (812) 265-2967.

Lanier Mansion State Historic Site. 511 West First Street, Madison, IN 47250. The crown jewel of Madison's historic homes, this Greek Revival–style mansion has a three-story cantilevered spiral staircase and a panoramic view of the river. Begun in 1840 by wealthy industrialist James Franklin Doughty Lanier, the 13,500-square-foot home wasn't completed until 1844. Family pieces on display include a 1793 Parisian harp and portraits. In the late nineties the home was restored to its 1840s glory, and the gardens have been restored to what historians believe is their 1850's visage, including antique roses, dwarf fruit trees, and patterned cinder paths. Open Tuesday through Sunday. Free. (812) 265-3526; www.state.in.us/ism.

Shrewsbury-Windle House. 301 West First Street, Madison, IN 47250. This home, an example of Regency architecture, was built by noted architect Francis Costigan. Ceilings soar to 13 feet, with 12-foot doors. The drawing room, with its Corinthian columns and twin fireplaces, and the free-hanging spiral staircase are outstanding features. Open April through October; appointment advisable. Fee. (812) 265-4481.

Walking Tours. The visitor bureau has mapped out two separate tours of town. The West Tour features homes and churches primarily, including several structures listed above, and Madison's signature fountain at Broadway and Main. The East Tour includes more commercial structures, such as the courthouse (a Classic Revival building constructed in 1854-55), the 1841 fire house, the Masonic Temple, and Dr. Hutchings's medical office. For those who prefer, there's a guided trolley tour on weekends, leaving from the visitor center (812-873-7868); fee. For those who bring their own wheels, the visitor bureau has mapped four separate bicycle routes of the county, ranging from moderate to difficult and covering a variety of terrain, with flat farmland, hills, and river views.

WHERE TO SHOP

Americana Interiors. 510 West Main Street, Madison, IN 47250. Americana art and home decor fill this shop. Interesting items include papier-mâché figures by artist Debee Thibeault—some seemingly inspired by early-twentieth-century illustrators, some seasonal, and all charming. Open daily year-round; closed major holidays. (812) 265-1999.

The Birdhouse. 108 East Main Street, Madison, IN 47250. Bird lovers will linger over bird-watching guides, bird feeders, wind chimes, and all manner of accessories to create your own bird sanctuary. There's bird feed in bulk as well as other items of interest to naturalists. Open daily May through December; open Monday through Saturday January through April. (800) 279-1193 or (812) 273-1193.

Lanham House. 709 West Main Street, Madison, IN 47250. Owned by the B&B of the same name, this shop carries a sophisticated mix of classic American accessories, such as elegant candle holders and vases, antiques, paper goods, silk flowers, china, and books, mostly on home decor. The small shop brims with merchandise. Open daily year-round; closed holidays. (812) 273-3200.

Trolley Barn. 719 West Main Street, Madison, IN 47250. A historic building on the west end of Main Street, the Trolley Barn is now home to about a half dozen specialty stores. Home decor, clothing, cigars, and gourmet foods are among the mix you will find here. Wakefield's Gift Gallery, one of the shops, is owned by the Trolley Barn owner. Open Tuesday through Sunday year-round; additional closing during January. Wakefield's, (812) 273-0566.

WHERE TO SHOP AND EAT

The Attic. 631 West Main Street, Madison, IN 47250. Half gourmet-food and gift emporium, half coffee shop, the Attic exudes warmth and coziness. Order a grilled sandwich, the house specialty, or soup or salad, and peruse the gourmet-food display while you wait for your lunch to be prepared. There are also gifts, home decor items, prints—which you can have framed right there—and pottery. The pastries, cinnamon rolls, and coffees are delicious. $. (888) 295-0707 or (812) 265-5781; www.atticmadison.com.

   Lanthier Winery & Restaurant. 123 Mill Street, Madison, IN 47250. Lanthier produces a variety of wines, about fifteen of which are available daily during free tastings. Visitors can also view wine production and shop in the gift shop, which sells wine-related items, gourmet food, home decor, and accessories, including silk flowers and garden statuary. The oldest part of the winery, where the tasting room is, dates to 1775; the newest portion was built in the 1940s. A restaurant, in a loft overlooking the tasting area, serves gourmet wraps, sandwiches, soups, salads, and a variety of heartier dishes. The buildings sit amidst a French country garden with fish ponds, fountains, and a menagerie, including three pet groundhogs. The restaurant serves lunch on Saturday and Sunday; the winery and shop are open Wednesday through Sunday year-round. $-$$. (800) 419-4637 or (812) 273-2409.

WHERE TO EAT

Key West Shrimp House. 117 Ferry Street, Madison, IN 47250. The restaurant is housed in an old button factory along the river, just east of the bridge that crosses over to Kentucky. Long gone in Indianapolis, the Key West Shrimp House is still going strong in

Madison. Catfish, shrimp, whitefish, and lobster are among regular treats. There are daily specials for lunch and dinner, as well as some nonseafood items. Smaller portions of many dinner entrees are available, and the children's menu offers more than half a dozen choices. Open for lunch and dinner Tuesday through Sunday. $$. (812) 265-2831; www.keywestshrimphouse.com.

Mundt's/JWI Confectionery. 207 West Main Street, Madison, IN 47250. This historic building was already more than eighty years old when Mundt's Candies moved here in 1917. Although the original candy company is gone, this restaurant satisfies any sweet craving with Kentuckiana pie (chocolate chips, walnuts, and rum), homemade ice cream (made in a vintage 1948 machine) with hot fudge, carrot cakes, and more. Luncheon specials include quiche, meatloaf, salads, and sandwiches. Lemonade is freshly squeezed. Open for lunch Tuesday through Saturday, February through December, and on Sunday and Monday during festival weekends. $. (812) 265-6171.

Ovo Cafe. 209 West Main Street, Madison, IN 47250. Pastas are the strong point at this cozy restaurant, where you might choose mustard chicken capellini or shrimp penne primavera. The home-made soup-and-salad combination (you can pick one of several salads) is a tasty luncheon option. Open for lunch Tuesday through Saturday and for dinner Monday through Saturday; open Sunday only on festival weekends. $$. (812) 273-8808.

Pronto Pizza & Pasta. 104 East Main Street, Madison, IN 47250. In a historic building, once a theater and later a confectionery, Pronto serves gourmet pizza and pasta for both lunch and dinner. Most offerings are simple, such as five-cheese pizza and linguine with clam sauce, but preparations are well done and tasty. There are also calzones and submarine sandwiches. Open for dinner Monday through Saturday. $–$$. (812) 273-9339.

The Red Pepper. 902 West Main Street, Madison, IN 47250. At the corner of Main Street and State Road 7, the bright-yellow converted gas station is easy to spot. Strictly casual, the Red Pepper is a deli and cafe, with a robust carryout business. Inside diners eat sandwiches, such as chicken salad or honey ham and melted Swiss cheese, served on thick slices of bread and delivered in red plastic baskets. Soups and salads are homemade daily. The dinner menu, seasonal and limited, features items you can easily take home and heat up, such as chicken, pork, and pastas. Open for lunch and dinner Monday through Saturday. $-$$. (812) 265-3354.

WHERE TO STAY

Lanham House. 703 West Main Street, Madison, IN 47250. Period furnishings, fireplaces, television, and goose-down duvets are some of the amenities in these well-appointed rooms. Breakfast is served in the warm library, while tea is served in the cheery front parlor. $$. (812) 273-3198; www.lanhamhouse.com.

Schussler House. 514 Jefferson Street, Madison, IN 47250. Just north of Main Street, the Schussler House has three well-appointed guest rooms, each individually decorated and including plenty of room to stretch out and relax. Breakfast is served in the sunny dining room, where the ceiling soars 12 feet high. $$. (800) 392-1931 or (812) 273-2068; www.schusslerhouse.com.

HANOVER

The town itself lies about 2 miles west of Madison on State Road 56-62, but the entrance to the college, Hanover's attraction, lies east of Hanover at the intersection of that highway and Scenic Drive, aptly named.

WHERE TO GO

Hanover College. 359 Lagrange Road, Hanover, IN 47243. As you enter this college, you may think you've turned into a state park. A long, winding road leads through beautiful forest, past cataracts, cliffs, and gorges, making hairpin turns until the road opens up at the top of a bluff dotted with Georgian-style buildings. Follow the main drive straight to the administration building, then follow it to the left on a river-view drive, with several overlooks with spectacular views of the Ohio River. The oldest private college in Indiana, Hanover was founded in 1827 and today has a student body of more than 1,100. (800) 213-2178 or (812) 866-7000; www.hanover.edu.

COMMISKEY

From Hanover, follow State Road 256 west to State Road 3 north, which leads to Commiskey, a dot on the road marked by a general store.

WHERE TO GO AND EAT

Stream Cliff Herb Farm. 8225 South County Road 90 West, Commiskey, IN 47227. Traveling on State Road 3, turn east at the Commiskey Corner Store; the farm is about ½ mile down this winding road. Cluttered and charming, this nest in the country sells plants, garden art and tools, books, cards, decor, and more, spread across three buildings. A fourth building is dedicated to classes, teaching garden design, plant care, cooking with herbs, and the like. The polished tearoom, Twigs and Sprigs, serves traditional tea with scones, Devonshire cream, and little sandwiches. The luncheon menu leans heavily toward homemade soups, which may come in a bread bowl, and sandwiches. All items use herbs from the garden, and plates are garnished with edible flowers. You can scoot down here from Columbus, but the site ties in more closely with the thematic attractions of Madison: history. After lunch meander through gardens planted in traditional quilt designs. Open for lunch Thursday through Sunday and for tea each day that the farm is open. Farm is open Thursday through Sunday early April through the end of October and Saturday and Sunday November 1 through the second week of December. Free; $ for tearoom. (812) 346–5859; www.streamclifffarm.com.

FOR MORE INFORMATION

Historic Madison, Inc. 500 West Street, Madison, IN 47250; (812) 265–2967.

   Madison Area Convention & Visitors Bureau. 301 East Main Street, Madison, IN 47250. The CVB anticipates moving to 601 West First Street, near the Lanier Mansion, by the end of 2001 or the following year; (800) 559–2956 or (812) 265–2956; www. visitmadison.org.

Greensburg · Batesville
Oldenburg · Metamora · Connersville

There are two ways to get down to this part of the state. The simplest is to take I-74 southeast, which leads to the progression of towns laid out here. If you are feeling leisurely, take U.S. 52 back, through Rushville and Morristown, covered in their own day trip.

GREENSBURG

There are two Greensburg exits. Get off at the northern one of the two and meander south on State Road 421 for the best vantage point of the famous courthouse. There are a number of attractive buildings and homes in town, many of which are marked on a walking tour brochure, available from the local Chamber of Commerce, which is also Decatur County Tourism.

WHERE TO GO

Decatur County Courthouse. 150 Courthouse Square, Greensburg, IN 47240. Around 1870, an aspen began growing in the tower of the courthouse. After a while, it sprouted out of the tower, visible to those in the square and attracting attention. The original aspen eventually died and was put in the local history museum, but it had already been joined by other trees—up to five—two of which remain today. Residents have grown fond of the trees, which are regularly trimmed and cared for. Beyond looking up at the trees, you can go into the courthouse, where the second floor affords a nice vista of town. (812) 663-8223 (County Clerk's office).

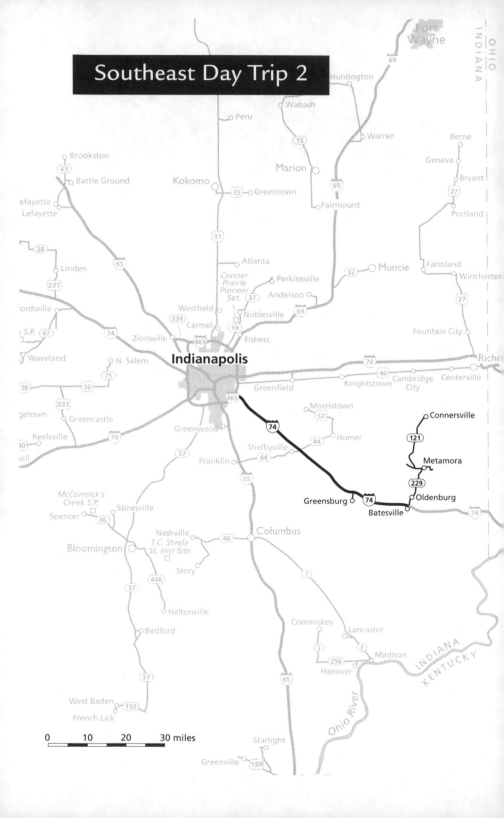

Skydive Greensburg. Greensburg Municipal Airport, 215 South Road 200 West, Greensburg, IN 47240. To reach the airport take Main Street west to the entrance of the Greensburg Municipal Park and turn south. Daredevils take note: It takes about twenty minutes for a plane to take off and climb to 14,000 feet, but it takes only three minutes to get back down via parachute. Here novices, experts, and those in between can thrill to the experience while being coached, instructed, and monitored by skydiving experts. (Novices will want to begin with a tandem jump, where the student is attached to a certified instructor and the two fall together.) Although weekdays are less crowded, up to one hundred people flock here daily on weekends. Reservations are essential. Open Wednesday through Sunday, March 1 through December 1. Fee. (800) 990-5509 or (812) 663-3483; www.skydivegreensburg. com.

WHERE TO SHOP

The Wooden Bench. 132 North Franklin Street, Greensburg, IN 47240. This furniture and gift store occupies two floors and two storefronts on the town square. There's a large selection of clocks, afghans, and gift items, including collectibles such as Boyd's Bears. Upstairs you'll find Victorian and wicker furniture. Open Monday through Saturday; closed holidays. (812) 663-6572.

WHERE TO EAT

Heritage Acres. 5084 West Old Highway 46, Greensburg, IN 47240. Jean Reed created this family-style restaurant in an 1880 farmhouse, which once belonged to her great-great-grandparents. Reed chats with guests and tells stories as servers bring out bowls of coleslaw, baked beans, and noodles; platters of fried chicken; and baskets of homemade yeast rolls—all served family style. Arrive before the designated meal time so that you can stroll through the gardens or play a bit of croquet or volleyball. The restaurant has gained national publicity for its combination of entertainment, homestyle cooking, and recreation. Open for breakfast, lunch, and dinner most days. Reservations absolutely essential. $-$$. (888) 663-1088 or (812) 663-1088; www.heritageacres.com.

BATESVILLE

Although it is best known for its casket company, Batesville has a history of fine woodworking. In the early and mid-1800s, area hardwood forests attracted woodworkers and cabinetmakers, many of them German immigrants, who have given this area many of its German traditions. Once home to Shawnee Indians, Batesville was first peopled by white settlers in 1835. The town was named after its surveyor, Joshua Bates.

WHERE TO SHOP

Weberding's Carving Shop Inc. 1230 State Road 46 East, Batesville, IN 47006. Coming east on State Road 46, go through the intersection of State Roads 46 and 229 and drive another mile. You'll see the shop on your left. This custom woodworking shop specializes in religious artifacts, such as nativity scenes, and furniture, such as baptismal fonts. But the shop creates many other custom items, including chairs, fireplace mantles, and entertainment centers. Open Monday through Saturday; closed holidays. (812) 934-3710.

WHERE TO EAT AND STAY

Sherman House. 35 South Main Street, Batesville, IN 47006. Opened in 1852, this spot has always been an inn and restaurant. The building is distinctive for its timber-frame architecture, and the restaurant interior has that Old World feel as well. The restaurant serves a broad selection of dishes, but the German and veal entrees are the most popular. The bakery is rightfully famous for German chocolate cake, praline pie, cheesecake, and apple strudel—all fresh daily. Open daily for breakfast, lunch, and dinner; closed Christmas Day and New Year's Day. $$.

Above the restaurant are a number of charmingly decorated rooms and suites, a selection of which are shown on the Web site. All have comfortable chairs and a cozy atmosphere. $. (800) 445-4939 or (812) 934-2407; www.sherman-house.com.

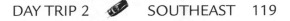

OLDENBURG

In this Village of Spires, you'll see the pinnacles as you drive north on State Road 229. Turn east on Main Street and drive uphill to see the many quaint buildings in this town, listed in its entirety on the National Register of Historic Places. The influences here are German (streets are labeled as *Strasse*) and Catholic, with a bevy of religious structures dating back to the mid-1800s, when the village was founded by Franciscans. The village is so small that you will quickly notice its whimsy: Fire hydrants are all little bits of art, painted to look like monks, firemen, or other characters. The addresses here may seem puzzling, but there are really only three principle streets in town, so you won't get lost. The small Franciscan visitor center has a brochure showing a walking tour of town.

WHERE TO GO

Michaela Farm. State Road 229, Oldenburg, IN 47036. Take State Road 229 East through town. Just after the road turns sharply north, you'll see the farm on your right. For organic produce and a tour of a working organic farm, stop here on a Sunday afternoon. You can tour the barn and hike the nature trails at this bucolic spot, operated by the Sisters of St. Francis since 1854. Open May through October. Free. (812) 933-0661.

WHERE TO SHOP

Oldenburg Flower Shoppe. 22163 Main Street, Oldenburg, IN 47036. Although the shop's main stock is in flowers, both fresh and silk, it also carries a charming selection of birdhouses, handmade by an area craftsman. There's an eye-catching selection of them, sure to please your favorite cardinal or robin, as well as some other gift items. Open Monday through Saturday; closed major holidays. (877) 312-1333 or (812) 934-6223.

WHERE TO EAT

The Brau Haus. Wasserstrasse, Oldenburg, IN 47036. Despite the German name and many good German specialties, this restaurant is best known for its fried chicken. The atmosphere is rustic, with booths, captain's chairs scrunched around tables, and beer signs and basketball memorabilia sharing wall space. Open daily; closed Thanksgiving, Christmas, and Easter. $–$$. (812) 934-4840.

METAMORA

To reach Metamora, continue along State Road 229, which T's into U.S. Highway 52. Turn right, then travel less than a mile until you see the sign on your right pointing toward the village. When the canals failed, Metamora, a thriving nineteenth-century burg, fell into a long, slow decline. Happily, no one had the interest or the money to rip down the Greek Revival, Federal, and solid commercial businesses and homes, so they stood into the twentieth century, even as the town's inhabitants died or drifted away. By the mid-twentieth century the population had dwindled to about 200, when Milford Anness, a boy raised in town, decided to save his hometown. Determined, he brought in investors, persuaded shop owners to gamble on the town, got buildings restored, and turned state attention and, eventually, funds toward this remnant of Indiana's canal system, now restored. Tourism drives business hours, so only a handful of shops are open from January through the beginning of March; more are open between then and late April. The village springs to life in late April and continues at a lively pace through Canal Days in October and the special Christmas Walk festivities, four weekends in late November through the weekend before Christmas. Merchants fly a flag (American, holiday, Metamora—any kind) when their shop is open. There are more than one hundred shops and eateries, but there's not an adequate sewage system, so the only rest rooms are at the western end of the village.

WHERE TO GO

Whitewater Canal State Historic Site. 19083 Main Street, Metamora, IN 47030. This historic site comprises a 14-mile stretch of the old canal, built in the early 1800s, and a gristmill. The gristmill, which is the place to begin your tour, was originally built in 1845 and rebuilt in 1900 after a fire. A waterwheel on the canal powers the mill even today, and you can see wheat and corn milled (and buy the flour and cornmeal in the gift shop). You can walk along the canal to see its most distinctive feature: a covered aqueduct, believed to be the only one of its kind in the country. (For a pittance you can cruise the canal aboard the *Ben Franklin III*, a horse-drawn canal boat, which runs May 1 through October 31.) Gristmill open Tuesday through Sunday mid-March through mid-December; closed some holidays. Free. (765) 647-6512; www.state.in.us/ism.

Salt Creek Ranch. 21040 U.S. 52, Metamora, IN 47030. To reach Salt Creek Ranch, return to U.S. 52 and travel west a little more than a mile. Saddle up and roam 600 acres of woodland laced with trails. You go with a guide for rides that can range between forty-five minutes and four hours. There are trails of varying degrees of difficulty, from easy to rough. If you are inclined, you can even buy a horse at this ranch. Open daily year-round. Fee. (765) 698-2044.

WHERE TO SHOP

Anne's. Mill Street at Bridge, Metamora, IN 47030. Once a drugstore, the shop is now a melange of candles, gift items, stuffed animals, and dolls. Open Tuesday through Sunday year-round, except January if the weather is bad. (765) 647-2606.

The Fudge Shoppe. Duck Creek Crossing, Metamora, IN 47030. Thick slabs of fudge in more than a dozen flavors are made here. You can buy the fudge by the slab or in decorative gift packs. There are other candies as well, including taffy, peanut brittle, chocolate-covered pretzels, and an extensive line of sugar-free candies. Open Tuesday through Sunday early April through the fourth weekend after Thanksgiving. (765) 647-5003.

The Lace Place. 19041 Lover's Lane, Metamora, IN 47030. Aptly named, this shop carries a broad selection of lace items—old and new—including clothes, dresser scarves, framed lace, and the largest selection of lace curtains in the Midwest. There are also a number of gift items, such as teapots and cozies, with a Victorian-era flavor. Open Tuesday through Saturday April until Christmas and on weekends January through March, weather permitting. (765) 647-3883.

Meeting House Antiques. 19025 Lover's Lane, Metamora, IN 47030. One of the nicest antiques shops in town is located in an old church. There is a wide selection of furniture, quilts, and coverlets, as well as some art and home furnishings; they try to stick to pre–Civil War items. They carry nothing mass-produced and no collectibles. There are new handsome lamps and lampshades. Open Tuesday through Sunday May through December. Shop and Gingerbread House, (765) 647–5518.

Misty Mountain and **Quiet Eagle.** Duck Creek Village, Metamora, IN 47030. One of the largest stores in Metamora houses two shops. The Quiet Eagle purveys primarily Southwestern and Native American arts and crafts. You'll find sand paintings, Kachina dolls, drums, jewelry, pottery, and more. Misty Mountain sells floral-designed accessories, pottery, and other home accessories. Open Tuesday through Sunday May through the fourth weekend after Thanksgiving. (765) 647–5293.

The Sampler. 19033 Lover's Lane, Metamora, IN 47030. Craftsmen create each piece of this cherry furniture by hand in Homer, Indiana (See Greenwood and East Day Trip1). Outside the factory showroom, this is the only spot where you can order and buy these satin-finished items—dining room tables, Windsor chairs, armoires, tea carts, and more. Open Tuesday though Sunday April through December. (765) 647–2597.

Sweet Annie's Farm. 19053 North Main Street, Metamora, IN 47030. This sweet shop was once a bank, but today the vault might hold dried flower arrangements or picture frames. The focus of the store is on home accents, with an eye toward the whimsical and fun. You might take home, for example, a fountain shaped like an old bucket or a watering can. In the spring there are fresh herbs; in the summer, roses; and in the fall and winter, bulbs for forcing. Open Tuesday through Sunday March through December and on weekends in January and February. (765) 647–6697.

WHERE TO EAT

Cappuccino's. Main Street, Metamora, IN 47030. The aroma is wonderful in this little coffee bar with big variety. In addition to a wide variety of beans, there are forty-five different flavors that you can add to your drink, whether you order coffee, espresso, or hot chocolate. The food items are all made from scratch: muffins, turnovers, croissant sandwiches (the chicken salad is tops), cookies, soups, and more. The cheesy cream of potato soup has become so popular that it is now available frozen in bulk. You can also buy coffee beans in bulk; there are thirty varieties, each available in both decaf and regular. Open Tuesday through Sunday May through December and on weekends during March; closed January and February. $. (765) 647-3072.

Hearthstone. 18149 U.S. 52, Metamora, IN 47030. To reach the Hearthstone, go back to U.S. 52 and head east about ¼ mile, where you'll see the restaurant on the left. Relaxed and welcoming, the Hearthstone offers family-style dining of several entrees, including skillet-fried chicken and country-cured ham. You go to the salad bar and the waitperson brings large bowls of potatoes and vegetables to your table, along with your entree. If you prefer, you can order from the regular menu, which includes catfish, ribs, and steak for a hearty meal and breaded tenderloins, burgers, and ham sandwiches for lighter fare. There is a seafood buffet on Friday night and a buffet on Saturday and all day Sunday. Open Tuesday through Sunday year-round for lunch and dinner; winter hours may vary. $$. (765) 647-5204.

WHERE TO STAY

Gingerbread House Bed & Breakfast. 19072 Clayborn Street, Metamora, IN 47030. Constructed by a Metamora carpenter in the 1870s, this quaint house is a riot of gingerbread styles and trims, including a cupola, and has always been painted pink. Filled with Victorian furniture, the house is rented as a single unit to accommodate up to four people in the eight rooms. Breakfast is brought in: apple dumplings and sausage or quiche and fresh fruit. $$. (765) 647-5518.

CONNERSVILLE

From Metamora take U.S. 52 West to State Road 121 North. From Indianapolis, however, the swiftest way to reach Connersville is to take I-70 East, exiting on State Road 1 and heading south.

WHERE TO GO

Whitewater Valley Railroad. 450 Market Street, Connersville, IN 47331. If you love trains, you can take a scenic train ride along the old canal path from Connersville down to Metamora, where you'll have a two-hour layover. This trip makes a pleasant day's excursion all by itself. You get the scenic ride, plus the visit to quaint Metamora. There are some dinner trains and special holiday excursions. Trains depart at 12:01 Saturday, Sunday, and most holidays. Fee. (765) 825-2054; www.whitewatervalleyrr.org.

FOR MORE INFORMATION

Decatur County Tourism. 325 West Main Street, Suite 2, Greensburg, IN 47240; (800) 210-2832; www.treecity.com.

Franciscan Visitor Center. P.O. Box 100, Main Street, Oldenburg, IN 47036. Here you can pick up a walking tour brochure and learn more about the Sisters of St. Francis. To tour the convent, you must make reservations. (812) 934-2475; sonak.marian.edu/oldenburg.

Metamora Welcome Line. (765) 647-2109; www.metamora.com.

Cincinnati, Ohio
Newport and Covington, Kentucky
Fairfield, Ohio

While traveling to three states in a day might seem a stretch, Cincinnati is really less than two hours away, and these interesting portions of Kentucky are just across the Ohio River, a trip on a bridge that will take less than a minute in clear traffic.

CINCINNATI

To reach downtown Cincinnati from Indianapolis, take I-74 southeast to I-75 South and get off at Fifth Street, which exits off the left lane of I-75. Cincinnati's grid of one-way streets can make it difficult for the novice to get around. Fortunately, streets are well marked, with numbered streets running east/west and the lowest numbers being closest to the river. Many north/south streets in the heart of downtown have arboreal names, such as Sycamore and Elm. Fountain Square, at Fifth and Vine, is the symbolic center of town.

Cincinnati seems like a stretch for a day trip because it is in another state, but it is really less than two hours away. Situated on the Ohio River, the city, founded in 1788, was the first capital of the Northwest Territory and a key stop for settlers on the way west. It became an important shipping city for both pioneers and farmers. Its craftspeople busily created the refinements of life that newly prosperous citizens in the frontier desired: furniture, clothing, china. Having furnishings from Cincinnati was on a par with New Orleans and New York. This shopping legacy lives on and Cincinnati

125

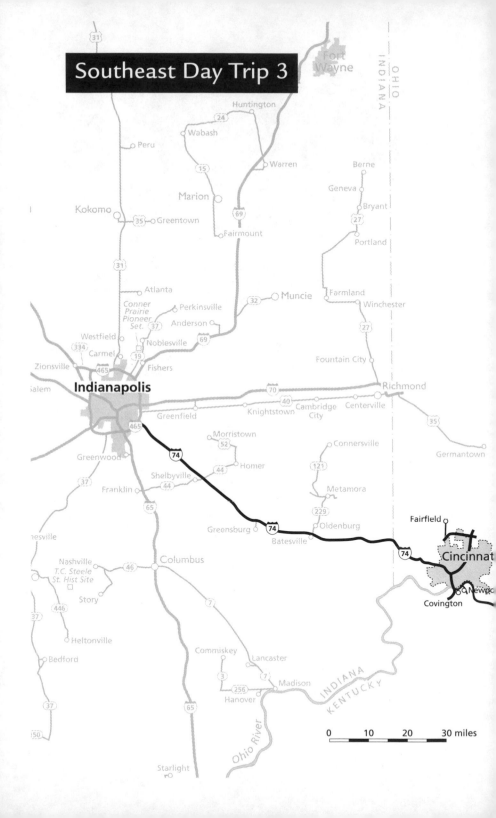

Southeast Day Trip 3

is still considered a center for upscale shopping, with major department stores, such as Saks Fifth Avenue, as well as Tiffany's, Brooks Brothers, and many other nationally known chains.

The city has many notable landmarks, including the Roebling Suspension Bridge, opened in 1867, which connects the city to Covington and Newport, Kentucky, both up-and-coming cities. Carew Tower, an Art Deco gem built in 1930, is still the tallest building in town and has an observation deck on top for panoramic views of the Queen City.

Cincinnati is also a sports town, with the Cincinnati Reds, Bengals, and Cyclones, a professional hockey team. Plus there are biking trails, public parks, and boating opportunities.

There must be something about Cincinnati that likes museums, because there are an unusually large number of them—from the big guys, such as the Museum Center, to smaller, quirkier ones, such as the Cincinnati Medical Heritage Museum and the Gray History of Wireless Museum, to house museums, such as the John Hauck House.

WHERE TO GO

Cincinnati Art Museum. 953 Eden Park Drive, Cincinnati, OH 45202. To get to Eden Park from downtown, take Seventh Street north—staying in the middle two lanes—which turns into Gilbert. Turn right on Eden Park Drive, which wends its way up to the museum and to Mount Adams. A classical building in a park setting, the Cincinnati Art Museum has an internationally renowned collection, ranging from ancient Egyptian to modern folk art. European paintings, American paintings, decorative arts, and Rookwood pottery are some of the specialties. The museum regularly hosts special events. Open Tuesday through Saturday. Fee. (513) 721-ARTS; www.cincinnatiartmuseum.org.

Cincinnati Zoo & Botanical Garden. 3400 Vine Street, Cincinnati, OH 45220. From I-74 go east to I-75 North to the Mitchell Avenue exit, exit 6. Turn right on Mitchell Avenue, right on Vine Street, left on Forest Avenue, then right on Dury to the auto entrance. Beautifully landscaped and easy to navigate, this zoo is thoughtfully designed. For example, the Children's Zoo is located near the main entrance, so parents with little ones in tow don't have to walk so far. Kids go buggy over Insect World and the vampire bats in Nocturnal House. Rare bonobo chimpanzees, lordly white Bengal tigers, cuddly red pandas, and majestic bald eagles are among the many inhabitants here. The variety of plant and animal life packed into sixty-five acres makes this a particularly worthwhile excursion to one of the country's finest zoos. Open daily year-round. Fee. (800) 944–4776; www.cincyzoo.org.

Cincinnati Museum Center Union Terminal. 1301 Western Avenue, Cincinnati, OH 45203. Creative thinking turned the town's grand old train station into museum central, home to the Cincinnati Historical Society Library, Cincinnati History Museum, Cinergy Children's Museum, Museum of Natural History & Science, and the Robert D. Lindner Family OMNIMAX Theater. A large information desk with maps and a schedule of events and activities helps you sort through the options as soon as you enter.

The **Cincinnati History Museum** has a grand diorama of the city, with lots of buttons to push and sites to light up, along with an exhibit on Cincinnati during World War II. The **Cinergy Children's Museum** has a warren of play areas, such as a pint-size soda fountain, vet's office, gas station, grocery store, and kitchen, particularly appealing to three- to nine-year-olds; The Woods, an awesome woods-themed climbing area; and Energy Zone, where youngsters are busy pulling levers, tossing balls, and ringing bells. The **Museum of Natural History & Science** draws visitors through three levels, including a look at the Ice Age and a tour of a cavern, with two paths—one for the adventuresome and another for the more timid.

Do not leave Museum Center without stopping at the ice cream parlor, run by United Dairy Farmers. The ice cream is good, and the setting is divine. The parlor, an original station feature, is created of Rookwood tile. If you are unfamiliar with Ohio's renowned tile, you'll leave the ice cream parlor a devotee. Open daily except Thanksgiving and Christmas. Fee. (800) 733–2077; www.cincymuseum.org, with links to the individual sites.

Krohn Conservatory. 1501 Eden Park Drive, Cincinnati, OH 45202. Eden Park itself is a public park on a grand scale, with many diversions and amusements, including this enormous conservatory, where you'll find thousands of plants thriving year-round. The Tropical Rainforest room, with its waterfall and fish, is the most popular area. For a little more than a month each year, there is a butterfly show, when thousands of butterflies flutter throughout the conservatory; there is a charge during this period. The gift shop has limited hours. Open daily. Free; donation requested. (513) 421–4086.

Taft Museum. 316 Pike Street, Cincinnati, OH 45202. Once the home of Charles Taft (an elder half-brother of President Howard Taft) and his wife, Anna, this elegant Federal-style mansion is decorated with paintings, including works by Rembrandt, Franz Hals, Whistler, and Gainsborough; decorative arts, such as Limoges enamels; and other treasures, such as a nineteenth-century watch collection. Built in 1820, the home went through a number of appearance-altering changes, until it was donated to the city in 1930 and the restoration process began. Carefully restored interiors give visitors an idea of a gilded lifestyle. The gift shop is small but well stocked. Open daily; call for holiday hours. Fee. (513) 241–0343; www.taftmuseum.org.

WHERE TO SHOP

Batsakes Brothers Hat Shop. 605 Walnut Street, Cincinnati, OH 45202. Hat shops are so rare in the states that this one will catch your eye the moment you see it. Whether you want a Stetson, a tam, or a custom-made hat, you'll find it here, where Presidents Ronald Reagan and George Bush had their hats made. Open Monday through Saturday. (513) 721–9345.

The Gilded Age. 1120 St. Gregory Street, Cincinnati, OH 45202. On the main drag of Mount Adams, an upscale, artsy neighborhood just east of downtown, The Gilded Age carries jewelry, antiques, and decorative items, such as feather-trimmed pillows made by a local artist and art glass chandeliers. For lovers of distinctive silver jewelry, there's much to delight the eye. Closed Monday in warm weather and additional days in the dead of winter. (513) 421–6122.

Library Friends' Shop. 800 Vine Street, Cincinnati, OH 45202. On the mezzanine level of the main library downtown, there's a large gift shop, adjacent to a coffee bar. The display isn't enticing, but the gift selection is—with items such as Shakespearean note cards, hand-carved checkerboard games, and, of course, books. The library itself is airy, warm, and inviting. A stop to shop could turn into an afternoon of delights. Open daily, except holidays. (513) 369–6920; plch.lib.oh.us.

Michael's Ludlow Village. 329 Ludlow Avenue, Cincinnati, OH 45220. From downtown take Vine to Jefferson. Turn left on Jefferson, cross Clifton Avenue and go to Telford, where you'll see the shop. A must-see for lovers of Pooh, Piglet, Eeyore, and the gang, this shop claims to have the largest collection of Winnie the Pooh items in the world. You'll also find games, puzzles, Madeline merchandise, and other sundry things, including coffee beans and loose teas. Open Tuesday through Sunday. (513) 221–8030.

WHERE TO EAT

Cincinnati has an exceptional number of good restaurants, and this list is by no means comprehensive. Here we've tried to present a variety of prices, cuisines, and experiences, all of which are sure to please.

Cafe Cin/Cin. 25 West Sixth Street, Cincinnati, OH 45202. (In the Crowne Plaza but with a street entrance.) Pronounced Cafe *chin-chin*, the self-proclaimed new-world bistro has a tantalizing array of delicious offerings, all in generous portions. Vegetarian Napoleon is an architectural feat; garlic mashed potatoes are wonderful, even on pizza; the dinner salad is filling, with caramelized walnuts and Gorgonzola-pear dressing. The atmosphere is warm but sleek, and staff is first rate. You can see the kitchen and, often, owner Henry in there preparing food. Open daily for lunch and dinner. $$. (513) 621–1973.

The Celestial. 1071 Celestial Street, Cincinnati, OH 45202. There's complimentary valet parking, luckily, considering the jam you can run into on Mount Adams. Once you've dined here, you'll not be sure which is more uplifting: the French cuisine or the view. Perched on a promontory of Mount Adams, the restaurant has a glorious view of the city and the river beyond and is considered an ideal spot for romantic moments. Open for lunch Tuesday through Friday and for dinner Tuesday through Saturday; during cooler months the restaurant may be open on Mondays as well. $$$. (513) 241–4455.

Cherrington's Restaurant. 950 Pavilion Street, Cincinnati, OH 45202. First you drop off your party at the door; then you go searching the narrow streets of Mount Adams for a place to squeeze in your car. There is a public garage a few blocks away on St. Gregory

Street. At this small, casual restaurant you'll find a sophisticated menu of exceptionally fresh ingredients. Dishes change daily, depending on what owner Dixie Cherrington finds at the market, and items are posted on the chalkboard. The hundred-year-old building is warm and cozy but seats only forty; in warm weather another thirty can be seated in the courtyard. Open for lunch and dinner Tuesday through Saturday and for brunch on Sunday. Weekend dinner reservations essential. Not easily wheelchair accessible. $$. (513) 579–0131.

First Watch. 700 Walnut Street, Cincinnati, OH 45202. Despite the address, the restaurant is actually on Seventh Street between Walnut and Main. A local chain, with three other restaurants in Cincinnati, First Watch is friendly, spotless, fast, and inexpensive. Plus the food is tasty, and you can get a bottomless cup of coffee. It's an ideal choice for weekend brunch (egg dishes are the specialty) or a fast lunch. Arrive early on Sunday to avoid waiting. No smoking allowed. Open for breakfast and lunch daily. $. (513) 721–4744.

Graeter's. 2704 Erie Avenue, Cincinnati, OH 45208. Dessert heaven best describes this local favorite, which was founded in 1870. While there are a number of Graeter's around the city, the one here, in picturesque Hyde Park, one of Cincinnati's grand old residential neighborhoods, gets the star for most charming. They are best known for the various flavors of chocolate chip, including black raspberry chip, the most requested flavor. Open Monday through Saturday. $ (513) 381–0653.

Izzy's. 800 Elm Street, Cincinnati, OH 45202. For sandwiches (corned beef and potato pancakes are famous), homemade soups, and other deli delights, this is one of the best stops in the city. There are two others, in addition to this location. Open for breakfast, lunch, and dinner Monday through Saturday. $. (513) 721–4241.

Nicholson's Tavern & Pub. 625 Walnut Street, Cincinnati, OH 45202. At this slice of Scotland, the bartender may be wearing a kilt and the piped in music is sure to actually be pipes, bagpipes, or hornpipes. The menu, too, has a British Isles bent, with bangers and mash (sausages and whipped potatoes); shepherd's pie, and fish-and-chips. The bar has an exceptional selection of ales and scotch. Open for lunch and dinner Monday through Saturday and for dinner on Sunday. $$. (513) 564–9111; www.nicholsonspub.com.

The Palace Restaurant. 601 Vine Street, Cincinnati, OH 45202. Located in the Cincinnatian Hotel, this posh restaurant serves delicious food, beautifully presented. Soups are served steaming; lettuce is crisp; meats are precisely cooked; and desserts taste just as good as they look, which is darned good. Service is with a flourish. If a band is playing in the bar, the restaurant can be too noisy. Broadly, though, you'll leave smiling, even after paying the tab. If you sit in the bar area, the Cricket Lounge, you can order off a limited menu, which is prepared in the Palace kitchen. Open daily for breakfast, lunch, and dinner. $$$. (800) 942-9000 or (513) 381-6006; www. cincinnatianhotel.com.

Skyline Chili. 254 East Fourth Street, Cincinnati, OH 45302. Downtown at the corner of Fourth and Sycamore, this Skyline Chili outlet is classic in its decor and offerings, although you will find similar decor and tasty chili at all the shops in Cincinnati and elsewhere. Admittedly, we are trying to avoid chains in this guidebook, but Cincinnati is the home of this one and dining where it all began is fun. Skyline was actually created back in the 1940s by a Greek immigrant, whose family continues to keep the recipe for the famous chili a secret. Completely different from other kinds of chili, Skyline chili is really layers including spaghetti, meat sauce, cheese, and often onions. The name comes from the view the owner had at his original location. Open for lunch and dinner Monday through Friday, lunch on Saturday, and on Sunday when the Cincinnati Reds play a game at home. $. (513) 241-4848; www. skylinechili.com.

WHERE TO STAY

Cincinnatian Hotel. 601 Vine Street, Cincinnati, OH 45202. On the corner of Sixth and Vine, this charming hotel is the Cincinnati equivalent of Indianapolis's own Canterbury. Elegant rooms have all sorts of amenities, including plush bathrobes and turndown service with a sweet treat. Built in 1882 as the Palace Hotel, the eight-story hotel has a broad marble staircase with a walnut bannister, the centerpiece of the atrium, which is capped with a vast skylight. There's a small health club and a posh restaurant, called the Palace, in honor of the original hotel. $$$. (800) 942-9000 or (513) 381-3000; www.cincinnatianhotel.com.

NEWPORT, KENTUCKY

WHERE TO GO

Newport Aquarium. One Aquarium Way, Newport, KY 41071. To reach the aquarium from Cincinnati, take I–471 South across the Ohio River, exiting immediately at the Newport/Route 8 exit, which leads directly into the parking garage. Acrylic tunnels that allow visitors to walk through the water tanks, where sharks can swim on all sides of you, are only one of the ooh-ahh features of this spanking new aquarium, just south of Cincinnati. There are more than sixty exhibits, including a movie with a surprise ending in the Pirate Theater, a jellyfish gallery, and opportunities to touch some sea creatures. The gift shop, too, is a winner, with sharks of every sort, as well as cuddly penguins, games, books, pencils, jewelry, and more. Allow two full hours for your visit; there's a restaurant on site. Open daily. Strollers aren't allowed, but you can borrow a backpack to tuck your toddler in. Fee; free for children age two and under. (800) 406–FISH or (859) 491–FINS; www.newportaquarium.com.

COVINGTON, KENTUCKY

WHERE TO GO

Cathedral Basilica of the Assumption, 1140 Madison at Twelfth Street, Covington, KY 41011. To reach the cathedral from Cincinnati, take I–471 South across the Ohio River, exiting immediately at the Newport/Route 8 exit. Turn left on Fifth Street, taking it to Scott Boulevard, where you turn right. Go south on Scott to Eleventh; turn right and go 1 block, where you'll see the parking lot on the left. This Gothic cathedral boasts one of the world's largest stained-glass windows, as well as flying buttresses and gargoyles. The exterior is modeled after Paris's Notre Dame and the interior is modeled after that city's St. Denis. You can take one of the scheduled tours for $2.00 or guide yourself through for free. There's a museum shop as well. Open daily year-round. (859) 431–2060.

MainStrasse Village. To reach MainStrasse Village from I–75/71, head south across the Ohio River, take exit 192, the Covington/Fifth Street exit, and follow the signs to the area roughly bounded by Philadelphia, Fifth, Main, and Ninth Streets. A little slice of Germany, this village has a variety of shops and restaurants, many of them in restored homes, once part of a thriving nineteenth-century German community. You will find plenty of places to dawdle and browse, looking at antiques, vintage clothes, hand-blown glass, German nutcrackers, and more. Strudel Haus and Wertheim's Gasthaus Zur Linde serve traditional German items; other restaurants, including Chez Nora Kitchen and Bar, the Dee Felice Cafe (cajun food and jazz bands), and the Cock and Bull English Pub, offer a variety of cuisines. There are special events year-round, the two biggest being Maifest and Oktoberfest. (859) 491–0458.

WHERE TO SHOP

Donna Salyers' Fabulous Furs. 20 West Pike Street, Covington, KY 41011. From downtown Cincinnati, follow I–75 South across the Ohio River and take exit 192, the Covington/Fifth Street exit. Go east on Fifth Street, turn right on Madison Avenue, and go 2 blocks. Turn right on Pike Street, where you'll see the showroom. When you are watching stars strut across the silver screen in luscious lynx, they may in fact be wearing Donna Salyers' fabulous fakes. With a world-wide Internet and catalog business, this company is actually head-quartered in Covington, where you can wrap yourself in luxury and take home a fake; samples are discounted. Open Monday through Friday; call for Saturday hours. (859) 291–3300; www.fabulousfurs. com.

WHERE TO STAY

Amos Shinkle Town House Bed and Breakfast. 215 Garrard Street, Covington, KY 41011. Amos Shinkle, one of the area's leading citizens in the mid-nineteenth century and the fellow who commissioned John Roebling to build the suspension bridge, built this beautiful home, now a B&B. Beautiful cornices and woodwork and Victorian opulence are hallmarks of the main house, which contains three of the bedrooms. Four smaller rooms are in the carriage house. This B&B has a long-standing reputation for fine food, lodgings, and service. $$. (800) 972–7012 or (859) 431–2118; www.amosshinkle.net.

FAIRFIELD, OHIO

To get to Fairfield, take exit 41 (Hamilton/Fairfield, Route 4) off I-275. Turn right (north) at the end of the exit ramp and go a little less than 4 miles.

WHERE TO SHOP

Jungle Jim's International Farmers Market. 5440 Dixie Highway, Fairfield, OH 45014. You will spot Jungle Jim's on the right, with the large animal figures in the parking lot. Inside, the amusements continue, the Honey Nut Cheerios mechanical band playing near the cereal aisle, a gyrating Elvis, and a gum ball/pinball machine that releases your gum ball when you lose the pinball game. You will also find an outstanding selection of international foods, beers from around the world, and exotic fruits. Open daily. (513) 829–1919; www.junglejims.com.

FOR MORE INFORMATION

Greater Cincinnati Convention and Visitors Bureau. 300 West Sixth Street, Cincinnati, OH 45202; (513) 621–2142; www. cincyusa.com.

  Northern Kentucky Convention & Visitors Bureau. 605 Philadelphia Street, Covington, KY 41011; (800) 447–8489; www. nkycvb.com.

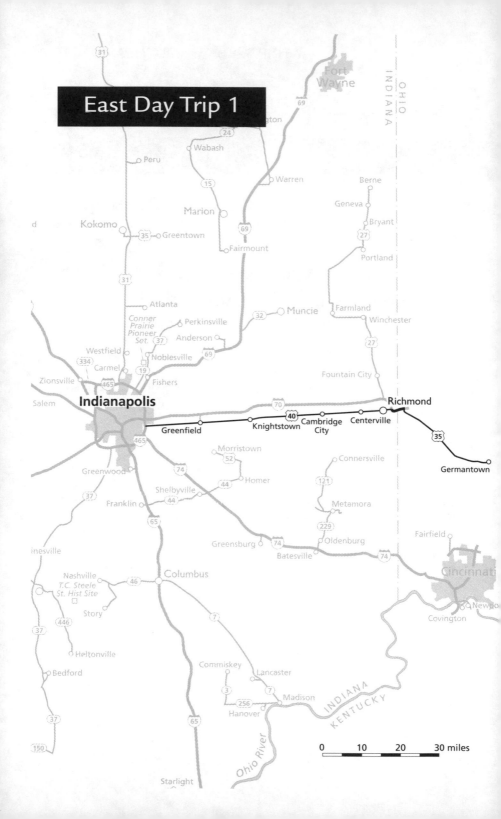

Greenfield · Knightstown
Cambridge City · Centerville · Richmond
Germantown, Ohio

Once you have traveled the Old National Road east of Indianapolis, you may swear off I-70. You'll find this road uncrowded, well maintained, and dotted with interesting small towns. However, it is easier to exit Indianapolis on I-70 and head east to the Greenfield exit, where you travel south to the National Road, U.S. 40, and avoid that road's congested section on the east side of Indianapolis.

GREENFIELD

Although Indianapolis likes to lay claim to James Whitcomb Riley, the bard actually spent much time in this little town, which he called "the best town outside of heaven." In early October, the town celebrates his birthday with a festival, which has grown to be one of the largest in the state.

WHERE TO GO

James Whitcomb Riley Home & Museum. 250 West Main Street, Greenfield, IN 46140. If you get off I-70 at the Greenfield exit, you'll need to turn west on Main Street to reach the Riley boyhood home. James Whitcomb Riley, the Hoosier bard, was born in Greenfield and lived here off and on his entire life. Begin your tour in the museum, which is the building just to the east of the Riley home. Here learn about Riley and his times, and see artifacts that belonged to him and his family. There's a small gift shop with postcards, Riley's books, some cookbooks, and period books. Next you tour the Riley home, guided by one of the volunteers. You'll see the Victorian-style home, with its formal parlor containing an old hammered dulcimer and some original Riley items. Upstairs you'll see the alcove Riley shared with at least three others. Local garden clubs tend the lovely back-yard, which has a gazebo, site of many local weddings. Open Tuesday through Sunday from April 1 through November 12; closed holi-days. Fee. (317) 462–8539; www.heen.org.

WHERE TO EAT

Carnegie's. 100 West North Street, Greenfield, IN 46140. A red awning on the west side of the old library is the entrance to Carnegie's, which has an Italian bent in look and menu. Although the menu changes regularly, you will always find pastas and red bell pepper soup at both lunch and dinner. The luncheon menu will also include sandwiches and salads, while the dinner menu generally offers salmon, Indiana duck breast, and beef tenderloin medallions. Open for lunch Tuesday through Friday and for dinner Tuesday through Saturday. Not wheelchair accessible. $$. (317) 462–8480; www.carnegiesonline.com.

KNIGHTSTOWN

Appropriately, Knightstown is named for one of the engineers of the National Road, Jonathan Knight. For its charming architecture (the town is rife with brick Italianate buildings), the entire town is listed on the National Register of Historic Places. The Hoosier Gym, 335 North Washington Street, was used in the consummate Indiana basketball movie, *Hoosiers*.

WHERE TO GO

Carthage, Knightstown, and Shirley Railroad. 112 West Carey Street, Knightstown, IN 46148. The depot is at the intersection of Carey, which is 3 blocks north of the National Road, and Harrison Streets. Indiana never seems to get its fill of excursion train rides.

This station doesn't hold much promise, but the bright-orange train cars have character. You have a choice of sitting outside, uncovered, covered, or in an enclosed car. Interior seats are lumpy; exterior is mostly bench seating. The train chugs south across the National Road and the Big Blue River about 5 miles to Carthage, and then back in about an hour. The depot is open and the train runs Friday, Saturday, and Sunday, May through October. Call for departure times. Fee. (800) 345-2704 or (765) 345-5561; www. homestead.com/cksrailroad.

Trump's Texaco Museum. 39 North Washington Street, Knightstown, IN 46148. Just behind Michael Bonne's store, this gas station is a blast from the past, modeled to remind the owner of his father's 1950s-era Texaco station, with its old-time pumps showing Sky Chief gasoline at 35.9 cents a gallon. Spotless and beautifully restored, the old station contains antique cars and a formidable collection of Texaco memorabilia, including signs, uniforms, cigarette lighters, and toys. (Owner Bruce Trump is a nationally recognized expert on Texaco items.) Old cars sit in the service bays. Donations welcome. Open by appointment and chance. (765) 345-7135.

WHERE TO SHOP

Hats Off. 102 East Main Street, Knightstown, IN 46148. This Victorian gift shop carries old hats, handkerchiefs, and occasionally old linens, but most of the items are new: cards, plush animals, glassware, teapots, angels, and plenty of seasonal items. Open daily; closed major holidays. (765) 345-7788.

Michael Bonne Coppersmith. 224 East Main Street, Knightstown, IN 46148. Oversized cookie cutters, bowls, candle holders, greeting cards, plates, mailboxes, and more are all individually hammered here in the factory. Noted nationally, Michael Bonne creates the copper for Martha Stewart and Williams Sonoma and started the business when a severe head injury prevented him from pursuing his construction business. The back room is the Indiana Prospecting Company, also Bonne's, and one of very few places where you can buy gold-prospecting equipment. Open Monday through Saturday; closed major holidays. (765) 345-7831; www. michaelbonne.com.

CAMBRIDGE CITY

Cambridge City was home to the six Overbeck sisters, who created art pottery, much sought after in the first half of the twentieth century. Samples of the prized pottery can be seen at the public library, 33 West Main Street. There are a number of lovely old homes in town, as well.

WHERE TO GO

Huddleston Farmhouse Inn Museum. 838 National Road, Cambridge City, IN 47327. You can't miss this spot, an imposing white three-story home, right on the southern edge of the Old National Road; it's actually in Mount Auburn but the mailing address is Cambridge City. Built by a prosperous Quaker family, the farmhouse was a wayside inn during an era when more than one hundred wagons trundled past the house daily on their way to settle the west. Travelers didn't actually stay in the farmhouse but were given a resting place and cooking privileges in the kitchen. The home contains a variety of interesting pieces, including the cradle that rocked the twelve Huddleston children and curious kitchen utensils. In addition to the home, there are several restored outbuildings. During the year, a number of dinners are held using antebellum recipes and cooking methods; participants help churn butter, make soup, and more. Open Tuesday through Saturday February through December and Sunday afternoons as well May through August; closed major holidays. Partially wheelchair accessible. Free; donation requested. (765) 478–3172.

CENTERVILLE

Centerville feels farther east. Houses are scooted up closer to the road, there's more Federal-style architecture, and more brick than you find in little towns as you head west. You can pick up a brochure pointing out some of Centerville's 137 historic structures at the City

Building, on the corner of First and East Main Streets, and at various antiques shops in town.

WHERE TO GO

Salisbury Courthouse. 214 East Main Street, Centerville, IN 47330. You may have to drive around the block twice to find this tiny little log courthouse, located on the north side of U.S. 40, between First and Second Streets. It sat in Richmond for more than a century and was moved here in the 1950s. Although you can step inside during local festivals and by appointment, it's worth stopping by to walk around the exterior and marvel at the size of the logs used to create this structure, the last-known extant log courthouse in the Northwest Territory. You can peek in the windows and see the big fireplaces; the building isn't furnished. The original cost to build the two-story structure? $229.99! Inezetta Stiver, Historic Centerville, Inc., (765) 855–5387.

WHERE TO STAY

Historic Lantz House Inn. 214 West Main Street, Centerville, IN 47330. On the National Register of Historic Places, this Federal-style home was built in 1823 for Daniel Lantz, a wagon maker, and his family. In the heart of downtown, this wonderful inn has an air of hospitality, topped with exclusivity. In addition to the lovely common rooms and five guest rooms, there is a garden. The inn has been featured in several national magazines. Breakfast, an afternoon snack, and evening tea are included with the room rate. No smoking allowed. $$. (800) 495–2689 or (765) 855–2936; www.inns.com.

WHERE TO EAT

Essenhaus. 100 Main Street, Centerville, IN 47330. A rarity, this restaurant is actually run by the Amish, who get around their dictum to avoid outsiders with a buffet. Serve yourself and pay at the door on your way out. Although you will see the Amish clearing tables and restocking the buffet, no one will take a drink order or come up to your table to chat cheerily. Summer and fall are great times to eat there because all the produce is fresh from Indiana gardens. Open Thursday, Friday, and Saturday for lunch and dinner. $. (765) 855–1026.

Jag's Cafe. 129 East Main Street, Centerville, IN 47330. Two 1840s row houses serve as Jag's today, filled with antiques and artifacts, including a bar from the 1893 Chicago World's Fair. All the menu items are made from scratch, and the restaurant is famous for its tenderloins and cheesecake. Fish-and-chips and steaks are also popular. Open Friday through Sunday for lunch and Tuesday through Sunday for dinner. $$. (765) 855–2282.

WHERE TO SHOP

Tin Pig Antiques. 130 West Main Street, Centerville, IN 47330. This quaint shop carries country furniture, lamps, accessories, and other home decor items. Open daily. (765) 855–5313.

Webb's Antique Mall. 200 West Union Street, Centerville, IN 47330. Union Street is north of U.S. 40, and the mall is just west of Morton Street, the town's main north-south street. This immense mall, the largest antiques mall in Indiana, draws visitors from all over the country and could be a day trip all by itself. There are aisles packed with furniture; others lined with cases of jewelry and curios; bin upon bin of old magazines and records; shelf after shelf of glassware and china and racks of vintage clothing. Essentially, if it is old you are apt to find it here, including antique gasoline pumps. Wear comfortable walking shoes, get a map, and be grateful that there is a restaurant inside where you can revive yourself with coffee and a sandwich or just rest your feet. Open daily; closed Thanksgiving and Christmas. (765) 855–5551.

RICHMOND

Quakers and Germans were this city's earliest settlers, imbuing it with a work ethic and a level of craftsmanship that is still reflected in local culture and sites. In the early and mid-twentieth century, Richmond was world-renowned for its rose hothouses, now commemorated by the city's three rose gardens, which flourish June through September. A warning for drivers: Richmond has lettered streets, but there are two of most of them; i.e., North A and South A, North B and South B. Make sure you are on the right one!

WHERE TO GO

Gaar House and Farm Museum. 2593 Pleasant View Road, Richmond, IN 47374. East of downtown Richmond, take Hayes Arboretum Road north to State Road 121; travel west until you reach Gaar Road and turn north. You'll see the mansion on your right. One of the most remarkable things about the Gaar Mansion is the detailed record that remains of the home and the five generations of Gaars who lived there. For example, there's an 1877 bill of sale for furniture purchased in Cincinnati; there are architects' drawings of the home and photos of the various changes over the years. The home is a Victorian belle, with magnificent trims and moldings and elegant furnishings. Restored in the seventies by the original owner's great-granddaughter, the home is on the National Register of Historic Places. Open on the first and third Sundays of each month March through December and by appointment. (It's worth the effort of calling for an appointment!) Fee. (765) 966-7184 or (765) 962-5295; www.waynet.org.

    Glen Miller Park. 2500 National Road East, Richmond, IN 47374. Although Hoagy Carmichael did record "Star Dust" in Richmond, Glen Miller did not hold forth here. Created in the nineteenth century, the park was named Glen for the rolling glens and Miller for the citizen who sold the parkland to the city. The park is most famous for its rose gardens, where more than 2,000 roses bloom, a lustrous reminder that Richmond was once the rose capital of North America. Picturesque, the park has rolling hills, a stream, flowers, and wrought-iron bridges. If you exit through its eastern entrance, you'll be across from the entrance to the Hayes Arboretum. Open daily until sunset. Richmond Parks and Recreation. Free. (765) 983-7275.

    Hayes Regional Arboretum. 801 Elks Road, Richmond, IN 47374. Begin your tour in the Nature Center (an old dairy barn), where there are many displays on the flora and fauna of the region. There's a bird-watching room with comfy chairs, a glass wall, and speakers that bring the tweeting and twittering inside. Walls are lined with drawings of birds and information about them. There's also a working beehive. Outside, you can visit the butterfly house, take a hike, or enjoy an auto nature drive through the 355-acre preserve. The Leafy Loft gift shop sells wind chimes, jewelry, candles, sidewalk chalk shaped like butterflies, and other nature-themed items. Open Tuesday through Sunday; closed on Sunday from Christmas to Easter and on major holidays. Free; fee for the auto nature drive. (765) 962–3745; www.infocom.com/hayes.

Richmond Art Museum. 350 Hub Etchinson Parkway, Richmond, IN 47375. Hub Etchinson Parkway intersects the National Road just east of the new bridge on the west side of Richmond; turn south. While the museum has a small permanent display, it has a good variety of temporary exhibitions throughout the year, including an annual fall juried exhibition of area artists. Open Tuesday through Friday; closed holidays. Free. (765) 966–0256; www.richmondartmuseum.org.

Wayne County Historical Museum and Historic Scott House. 1150 North A Street, Richmond, IN 47374. The museum is 1 block north of Main Street on Twelfth Street, which is east of downtown. Inside the museum, you'll find an early-twentieth-century general store, old automobiles made in Richmond, a 1929 airplane built in the county, an intricate Wooten Desk from 1874, and some curiosities, such as Egyptian mummies. On the grounds there is a log house, a blacksmith's shop, a printing office, and Wayne County's first schoolhouse. Although the Scott House is part of the museum, it is actually about a block away at 126 North Tenth Street; tours through this Victorian mansion are by appointment only. Museum open Tuesday through Sunday. Fee. (765) 962–5756.

Whitewater Opera Company. 211 South Fifth Street, Richmond, IN 47374. Richmond has become known for this spunky opera, which has been thriving for decades. The performers put on about three shows a year and have outreach programs. All the performances are held in the Civic Hall Performing Arts Center. Fee. (765) 962–7106; www.infocom.com/~wocop.

WHERE TO SHOP

Details in Design. 201 South Fifth Street, Richmond, IN 47374. Just catty-corner from the Olde Richmond Inn, this cheery shop has an enticing selection of home-decor items, all at remarkably reasonable prices. You might find a painting, a sofa, candles, a picture frame, or a live topiary. It's an ideal spot to shop for gifts or hatch a plan to redecorate a room. Open Tuesday through Saturday; closed holidays. (765) 962–6163.

Secret Ingredient. 720 East Main Street, Richmond, IN 47374. For women's contemporary fashions, this is the place to shop. The store itself is cheerful and cleverly decorated, and there's a broad selection of items from jewelry to purses, shoes, sweaters, coats, and more. Items are generally distinctive, but the store carries only a few of each thing, so you won't see lots of other women walking around in your "one-of-a-kind" find. Open Monday through Saturday; closed major holidays. (765) 935-0990.

Veach's. 715 East Main Street, Richmond, IN 47374. They must love children in and around Richmond, because they support a whopper of a toy store—perhaps the biggest independent in the state outside Indianapolis. The inventory isn't run of the mill; rather, there's a large stock of educational and interesting toys. Costumes, things with wheels, games, dolls, books, and more fill the aisles. There's a second-floor balcony devoted to trains. Connected next door and part of Veach's is a crafts, sewing supply, and framing shop. Open Monday through Saturday; open Sunday near the Christmas holidays; closed major holidays. (765) 962-5761.

WHERE TO EAT

5th Street Coffee & Bagels. 211 South Fifth Street, Richmond, IN 47374. For a quick bite and an inventive menu, this is a good choice. All the baked goods are made right on site, as are all of the flavors of cream cheese. In an old building, the restaurant has fashioned many nooks for enjoying your sandwich and iced tea or bagel and cappuccino. Open daily for breakfast and lunch; closed holidays. $. (765) 965-5427.

Little Sheba's. 175 Fort Wayne Avenue, Richmond, IN 47374. On the east side of the heart of downtown, turn north on Seventh Street, which intersects with Fort Wayne right by the restaurant. Burgers, deli sandwiches, hoagies, gyros, reubens, and other sandwiches dominate the menu at Little Sheba's. But there are also good soups, salads, and gigantic brownies, as well as a baked spaghetti dinner every Friday and Saturday evening. In the space once occupied by a grocery, the restaurant has made use of notable old features, such as the tin ceiling and handsome woodwork. It is a standout on a block that would benefit from preservation attention. Open for lunch and dinner Monday through Saturday; closed major holidays. $–$$. (765) 962-2999.

The Olde Richmond Inn. 138 South Fifth Street, Richmond, IN 47374. Once a residence, the Olde Richmond Inn has three fireplaces with decorative Italian tiles, stained glass, and other interesting features from the late 1800s, when the home was built. Since 1984 the home has served as a restaurant. In addition to the extensive list of items on the regular menu, there are daily specials. Pounce on the hearts of palm with mozzarella salad if it's available; the spinach salad with chicken is filling and flavorful as well. In the evening Seafood Bianca with its creamy wine sauce is a superior choice. Open for lunch and dinner daily; closed major holidays. $$. (765) 962–2247.

GERMANTOWN, OHIO

Germantown is a stretch from Richmond, but it is a charming little community and one not on the regular tourist routes. To get there take I–70 east of Richmond, exiting at the first exit in Ohio, U.S. 35 South, through Eaton and Gratis, then heading east into German-town.

WHERE TO GO

Historical Society Museum. 47 West Center Street, Germantown, OH 45327. This slip of a museum contains a number of artifacts from the town's history: a big clock dating to 1804, a spinning wheel, military artifacts donated by local veterans, and such. Three display cases are changed every few weeks to display a newly themed array of items. The building was once the city's Carnegie library. Its entrance is flanked by two concrete lions, each weighing 420 pounds, which were built by native Homer Kern and are now a symbol of the village. Open Saturday and Sunday May through December. Not handi-capped accessible. Free. (937) 855–7951.

Walking Tour. Both the Historical Society of Germantown, 47 West Center Street, and the Village offices, 75 North Walnut Street, have walking tour maps, which cover many of the same sites. You can take a driving tour in about ten minutes or walk at your own leisure. Veterans' Memorial Park, on West Warren and Walnut Streets right by the Village offices, is a good place to start. You can take Walnut south to Center and turn east, which leads by a number of interesting structures (make sure to look up, where you'll see second-floor doors), including the old opera house at 9 East Center Street, and to Germantown's covered bridge, open only to pedestrian traffic. Built in 1870 the inverted truss bowstring suspension bridge is believed to be the only one of its kind in the world. Return west to Main Street and head south. Main has many lovely old homes, clear down to Shuey Mill, 313 South Main Street, once a gristmill and now a private home. Return north via Main Street, Plum to the west, or Cherry to the east. Be sure to stroll up and down Market Street, which is the main thoroughfare. On your tour you are certain to notice the concrete lions, a hallmark of this little town. Between 1985 and 1995 resident Homer Kerns made between 300 and 400 of these statues, and many of them found homes in Germantown.

WHERE TO EAT

The Cardinal Roost. 16 West Center Street, Germantown, OH 45327. Center Street is 1 block north of the highway. A jazzy little diner with a fifties-sixties feel, the Cardinal Roost serves a bit of nostalgia with every meal. Lunch and dinner specialties include the Elvis Cheeseburger, James Dean Coney Dog, Brown Cows (root beer floats), and banana splits—all at old-fashioned prices. There are two rooms: smoking and nonsmoking. Open for lunch and dinner Tuesday through Sunday. $. (937) 855-2473.

    Florentine Hotel. 21 West Market Street, Germantown, OH 45327. Once an elegant hotel, the Florentine is now a casual yet elegant dining spot. Situated in the oldest building in town, the restaurant has pictures of its elegant hotel days on the walls. Today it serves dinners that draw crowds from all around. Prime rib, swiss steak, pork chops, homemade mashed potatoes, and desserts are popular. There are four different specials during the week. Open for dinner Wednesday through Sunday; closed major holidays. $$-$$$. (937) 855-7759.

FOR MORE INFORMATION

Richmond/Wayne County Convention and Tourism Bureau and National Road Old National Road Welcome Center. 5701 National Road East, Richmond, IN 47374. In addition to brochures on Richmond and the surrounding counties and packets of information on the National Road, this tourist center has a modest gift shop and a number of interesting displays. Open daily; closed Christmas, Easter, Thanksgiving, and New Year's Day; (800) 828–8414 or (765) 935–8687; www.visitrichmond.org.

Village of Germantown. 75 North Walnut Street; Germantown, OH 45327; (937) 855–7255; www.ci.germantown.oh.us.

WayNet.org. This community-sponsored Web site has valuable information for travelers; www.waynet.org.

This route covers a melange of sites: Route 27's history as an Underground Railroad route, the heritage of Swiss craftsmen, the home of author and naturalist Gene Stratton Porter, and more. With such diversity, you may wish to study a map to determine which path makes the most sense for your interests. The route suggested here moves north and returns via I-69. At the northern end of this trip, you'll be in Adams County, home to license plates with the "1" designation.

FOUNTAIN CITY

Just south of town lies the highest elevation in the state: Hoosier Hill. To reach it from U.S. 27, turn east on County Line Road, then south on Elliott Road. Precise directions are on the Richmond Web site.

WHERE TO GO

Levi Coffin House. U.S. 27 North, Fountain City, IN 47341. From 1827 to 1847, 2,000 escaped slaves stopped at this house on their journeys northward. Levi and Catharine Coffin, Quakers, constructed the home knowing they would be using it as an Underground Railroad stop. A second-story hiding space was built behind a bedroom wall; the well was put in the basement so that nosy neighbors couldn't guess the number of inhabitants by the volume of

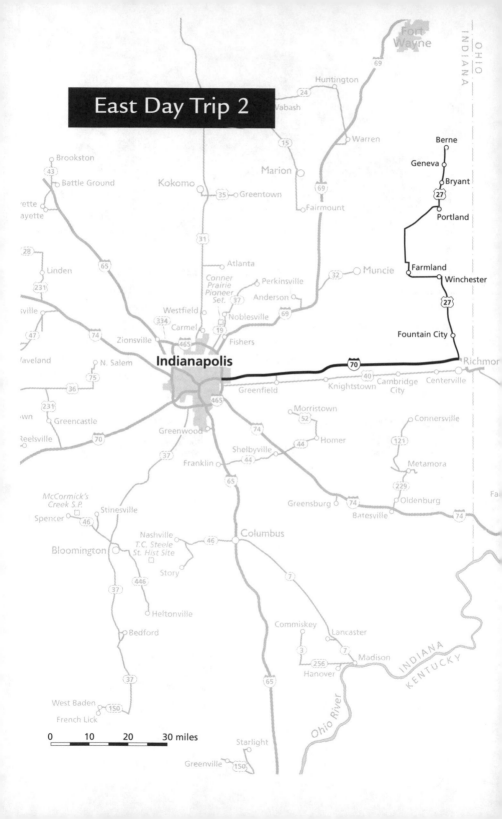

water drawn. The barn houses one of the few remaining original fugitive transport wagons. Open Tuesday through Saturday afternoons June through August; September and October on Saturday; tours given anytime by appointment. Fee. (765) 847-2432.

WINCHESTER

County seat of Randolph County, Winchester has an attractive courthouse and an imposing war memorial. The Winchester Speedway, west of town, hosts races regularly televised on ESPN and CNN. If you come into town from the south on State Road 27, veer northwest on Business 27, which is a more picturesque route into town.

WHERE TO GO

Wick's Pies, Inc. 217 Greenville Avenue, Winchester, IN 47394. Those flaky-crusted sugar-cream pies come from this factory, which is almost as famous for its pecan pies. Tours are available where you can watch pies being made. It's not the way grandma did it, but her oven couldn't hold hundreds of pies at once, and she didn't bake twelve million pies a year, like Wick's does. All the tour slots for each year fill up on January 2, so call early and don't give up if you get a busy signal. Free. (765) 584-8401; www.wickspies.com.

WHERE TO SHOP

Silver Towne. 120 East Union City Pike, Winchester, IN 47394. From the courthouse square, head east on Washington Street to Union Street. Go north, past Goodrich Park, where the road turns sharply east and becomes Union City Pike. The shop is on the left. Founded after World War II by a veteran who was fascinated by coins, this spot has gained a national reputation as a place to buy and sell coins. From new state quarters to rare nineteenth-century coins, this shop stocks thousands of coins as well as supplies, such as guidebooks and storage cases. Over the years the business has expanded to sell jewelry, sports memorabilia, and collectibles. Open Monday through Saturday and the six Sundays before Christmas. (800) 788–7481 or (765) 584–1246; www.silver towne.com.

WHERE TO EAT

Courtesy Coffee Shop. 730 West Washington Street, Winchester, IN 47394. Washington Street is State Road 32, and the coffee shop is on the western edge of town. Clean and attractive, the Courtesy, which has been around since 1947, offers a broad selection of items. The most popular items include baked steak, chicken and noodles, and breaded tenderloins. For dessert it's the town special: sugar-cream pie. In decor this spot is several steps above most other coffee shops. The lobby has a stone wall with water trickling down it into a small pond; the salad bar is in a stone well; there are murals on the wall and a stone fireplace in one room. Open for lunch and early dinner Tuesday through Saturday and for lunch on Sunday. $. (765) 584–1851.

Mrs. Wick's Pies and Restaurant. 100 Cherry Street, Winchester, IN 47394. When you walk into this simple restaurant, you'll see pie cases to your left, filled with all your favorites. You can sit down and order pie by the slice with coffee, or you can take one or a dozen pies home. Devotees shop here on Wednesday knowing that the van brings pies from the factory on Tuesday night. On Wednesday there are plenty of discounted "seconds," with imperfectly crimped crusts or other minor flaws. You can order from the regular menu, which features Hoosier home cooking, such as biscuits and gravy and beef and noodles. Open for breakfast and lunch Monday through Saturday and for early dinner Monday through Friday; closed holidays. $. (765) 584–7437; www.wickspies.com.

FARMLAND

To reach Farmland, head west from Winchester on State Road 32, which jogs north near Farmland. Farmland is an undeniably fetching little town, with an active historic preservation organization that has contributed to downtown's vitality. Train fans will want to ascend the grain silo, converted into shops and more, to view trains as they thunder in and out of town. In the fall Red Gold, Indiana's own tomato company, sponsors a chili cook-off. The first Tuesday in December there is a holiday evening, with luminarias lining Main Street, carriage rides, open houses, and refreshments.

WHERE TO SHOP

Homespun Memories. 201 North Main Street, Farmland, IN 47340. As the interest in quilts has risen, shops such as Homespun Memories have become popular. Filled with quilting fabrics, patterns, and supplies, the shop draws customers from a large area and offers quilting classes. Open Tuesday through Saturday; closed major holidays. (765) 468–7472; members.xoom.com/homespunmem.

    Little Corner Shop. 119 North Main Street, Farmland, IN 47340. Tea sets and teddy bears, books and Beanie Babies, Madeline and musical instruments fill this small shop. Merchandise is thoughtfully selected—no violent toys or videogames. There are books to read—classics, such as *Spot*, and mind-stretchers, such as the Usborne series. Open Tuesday through Saturday, with extended hours from Thanksgiving until Christmas. (765) 468–7424.

    Tanglevine Crossing. 110 North Main Street, Farmland, IN 47340. This shop draws visitors to Farmland, and you'll recognize it as you gaze down Main Street; an inviting yard and porch are dotted with creations that will lure you indoors. The store's signature items are made of wild grapevine—baskets, wreaths, free-form sculptures—and are distributed nationally through outlets including Saks Fifth Avenue and Laura Ashley. Displays brim with a range of gift and decorative items, including coasters, sweaters, stationery, the cleverest mousepads around, and pillows. Handmade candies, including cinnamon logs, divinity, and French chewing (hand-pulled taffy) are scrumptious. Open Tuesday through Saturday, with extended hours from Thanksgiving until Christmas. (765) 468–6958.

WHERE TO EAT

Chocolate Moose. 101 North Main Street, Farmland, IN 47340. A trip back in time, the Chocolate Moose has an old-fashioned soda fountain and old-fashioned atmosphere, with some booths, some

tables, and tall, tall ceilings. The specialty is that Indiana classic, the breaded tenderloin, along with shakes, Green Rivers, phosphates, and floats. Open daily for lunch and dinner. $. (765) 468–7731.

PORTLAND

To reach Portland from Farmland, head north on State Road 1 and northeast on State Road 67, which intersects with U.S. 27 in Portland.

WHERE TO SHOP

Jay Garment Antique Mall. 500 South Meridian Street, Portland, IN 47371. With 66,000 square feet of display space and items from dealers all over the country, this antiques mall draws shoppers from around the Midwest. The main thrust is merchandise from 1973 and before, although there is a post-'73 area as well as a section for craft dealers. Prices range from $2.00 to $2,000.00. An attached Victorian house carries reproduction furniture, such as curio cabinets to display your treasures. There's a coffee shop to rest after your mall foray. Open daily year-round; closed Thanksgiving, Christmas, and Easter. (219) 726–8891.

BRYANT

The attraction in Bryant is Bearcreek Farms, a huge tourist complex designed as a country resort.

WHERE TO GO, SHOP, AND EAT

Bearcreek Farms. 8339 North 400 East, Bryant, IN 47326. Discovering this enormous complex amidst farm fields surprises visitors. There's a small amusement park and train ride; the Tin Lizzie Museum; two separate shopping complexes; and a theater featuring wholesome and nostalgic musical performances. Two dining rooms—Homestead Heritage (a full-service menu) and the Marketplace

Buffet—are served by the same kitchen and feature a wide variety of items. Restaurants open Tuesday through Saturday for lunch and dinner and Sunday for lunch. Most shops, restaurants, and the theater are open early April through mid-December; some attractions are open only during warm weather. Fee for rides; other attractions are free; restaurants, $$. (800) 288-7630 or (219) 997-6822; www.bearcreekfarms.com.

GENEVA

The Amish in this part of Indiana are among the strictest in the state. Their buggies, for example, cannot have cabs, and the dress colors for women are limited to a handful of choices.

WHERE TO GO

Amishville. 844 East 900 South, Geneva, IN 46740. Signs will direct you east of U.S. 27 along a curving road to Amishville. For some it may be hard to get beyond the gift shop, the first building you come to as you turn in the drive. It contains Amish foodstuffs (such as noodles and preserves), furniture, quilts, pottery, and more. The tour of the restored Amish home is especially interesting because guides are well versed in the practices of the present day Amish living in the neighborhood. The site's restaurant is listed below, and there are campsites available. Open daily April through December. Fee for tours. (219) 589-3536.

Limberlost State Historic Site. 200 East Sixth Street, Geneva, IN 46740. Author and naturalist Gene Stratton Porter and her family lived in this spacious, refined cabin on the edge of Limberlost swamp from 1895 until 1913. Photographs and some family furnishings are on display. Of particular note is the music room with its Lincrusta wallcovering, an ornate decorative technique created by the man who invented linoleum. Separate fliers map nature tours through the property and the Limberlost area. A small gift shop carries Porter's books and other objects. Open Tuesday through Sunday from mid-March until mid-December. Not easily wheelchair accessible. Free. (219) 368-7428.

WHERE TO EAT

Essen Platz. 844 East 900 South, Geneva, IN 46740. This rustic restaurant serves buffet, family-style, and from a regular menu. Thick chicken-noodle soup, sausage and sauerkraut, and beef with noodles are some of the menu items. Thick slabs of bread come from a nearby Amish bakery. This is a tasty and inexpensive choice. $. (219) 589-3536.

BERNE

As you come into town on U.S. 27, turn right on Main Street (State Road 218), marked by the largest Mennonite church in the country. Just beyond, half-timbered plaster construction and window boxes stuffed with colorful flowers evoke the village's Swiss roots. This town is noted for its furniture production, an outgrowth of all the Swiss woodworkers who settled here.

WHERE TO GO

Swiss Heritage Village. 1200 Swiss Way, Berne, IN 46711. This pioneer village is composed of structures built by early Swiss settlers and moved here to save them from demolition. The guided tour brings each building to life. Sites include the world's largest cider press, built in the mid-1800s, and one of the original Northwest Territory schoolhouses, solid as a rock. Be sure to listen to the cheesemaker's tale! Open Monday through Saturday May 1 through October 31. Fee. (219) 589-8007.

WHERE TO SHOP

Edelweiss. 206 West Main Street, Berne, IN 46711. Although this shop bills itself as a florist, it stocks much, much more, including gifts, antiques, paper goods, silk flowers, and scads of miniature ceramic village buildings. The prices are just as pleasing as the selection of merchandise, making this a must-stop shop. Open Monday through Saturday; closed holidays. (219) 589-2125.

Et Cetera Ecke—Global Gifts. 152 West Main Street, Berne, IN 46711. One of the Ten Thousand Villages shops run by Mennonites, this store stocks goods made by Third World craftspersons. The concept is to supply these individuals with work and to pay them a fair wage for their goods. Musical instruments, clothing, toys, and jewelry are among the offerings. Open Tuesday through Saturday; closed holidays. (219) 589-2831.

Yager Furniture. 117 West Main Street, Berne, IN 46711. Locally made Berne Furniture is one of many lines carried here. The selection of furniture and accessories, spread across three floors, will amaze shoppers used to narrower offerings in small towns. There are prices for every budget. Open Monday through Saturday; closed holidays. (219) 589-3101; www.yagerfurniture.com.

WHERE TO SHOP AND EAT

The Nut Tree. 105 West Main Street, Berne, IN 46711. This rambling building serves as an antiques and crafts store cum coffee shop. Freshly baked muffins, soups, sandwiches, and casseroles complete the menu. Choices vary by the day of the week. Open Monday through Saturday; closed holidays. $. (219) 589-8466.

FOR MORE INFORMATION

Berne Chamber of Commerce. 175 West Main Street, Berne, IN 46711; (219) 589-8384; www.bernein.com.

National Road Old National Road Welcome Center. 5701 National Road East, Richmond, IN 47374. In addition to brochures on Richmond and the surrounding counties and packets of information on the National Road, this tourist center has a modest gift shop and a number of displays. Open daily; closed Christmas, Easter, Thanksgiving, and New Year's Day; (800) 828-8414 or (765) 935-8687; www.visitrichmond.org.

Hamilton County has a bevy of activities, so many that it is better to divide the county into two parts. No one could do it all in one day, or even two. The focus of this trip is the eastern portion of Hamilton County, including its best-known attraction, Conner Prairie. In general, reaching the destination on this trip involves heading north on I-69 to the 116th Street exit or taking Allisonville Road north. If you haven't traversed this latter road in a while, this trip will show you clearly just how much Hamilton County is growing and how farms are giving way to housing developments. Because it includes Noblesville and Conner Prairie, the trip offers a generous slice of Indiana history and heritage.

FISHERS

Fishers is housing divisions and shopping areas, although there is a nice visitor center in the old train station, on the north side of 116th Street, just west of the tracks.

WHERE TO EAT

Hamiltonian Dinner Train. Operated by the Indiana Transportation Museum in Noblesville, this dinner train departs from Fishers Station, which is 1 mile west of the interchange of I-69 and 116th Street at 11601 Municipal Drive, Fishers, IN 46038. Just after you cross the train tracks, turn north into the municipal center complex, where you'll see the station and Hamilton County Visitors Bureau on your right. The train provides transportation to restaurants, including the Anvil Inn

(317–984–4533), once a blacksmith shop in Cicero, and Fletchers in Atlanta (765–292–2777). Hors d'oeuvres are served on the train going north, and there's a cash bar. Generally you'll ride in stainless-steel coaches, built in 1937 for the Santa Fe Scout, but special cars are added from time to time. Prices, which cover the train trip, hors d'ouevres, and meal, are set by the participating restaurants and reservations are made through them. (317) 773-6000; www.itm.org.

Sahm's Restaurant and Bar. 11590 Allisonville Road, Fishers, IN 46038. A family-owned-and-operated restaurant, Sahm's has a warm and welcoming feel. Luncheon specials include such items as chili, clam chowder, and sandwiches on thick slices of bread made on site. At dinner mesquite-grilled items and the daily specials are popular. The tantalizing array of desserts are fresh and different each day. The Flying Horse Pub, part of the restaurant, is the spot for a predinner gathering or drinks at the end of the day. Open daily except Labor Day, Thanksgiving, and Christmas. Reservations are accepted for weekends and holidays. $$. (317) 842-1577; www.sahms.com.

WHERE TO STAY

Frederick-Talbott Inn. 13805 Allisonville Road, Fishers, IN 46038. Across the street and roughly a block north of the entrance to Conner Prairie, this inn blends happily into its historic country setting. Filled with antiques, including dining room furniture from the old L. S. Ayres tearoom and bureaus from the Atkinson Hotel, the inn is a reminder of Indiana and Indianapolis long ago and is one of the best B&Bs in the state. The ten sophisticated rooms include all the modern conveniences, including televisions and spacious private baths. The inn sprawls across two farmhouses, with plenty of charming places to relax: porches, parlors, and garden seats. A full buffet breakfast is included. Ask about package deals with Conner Prairie. $$–$$$. (317) 578-3600 or (800) 566-2337; www.fredtal.com.

CONNER PRAIRIE

WHERE TO GO

Conner Prairie. 13400 Allisonville Road, Fishers, IN 46038-4499. The most direct route for reaching Conner Prairie is to drive north on Allisonville Road, past the strip center cluster that is part of Fishers, until you see an open stretch of green on your left. This is Conner Prairie, which was a prairie among the fields when it was established in 1934, thanks to philanthropist Eli Lilly, father of historic preservation in Indiana. Today civilization encroaches at every edge of the 1,400-acre property, although the areas well trodden by visitors are thankfully and deliberately placed away from the sounds of traffic and the sights of subdivisions.

Broadly, Conner Prairie is a trip back into Indiana's history, with four areas to visit. The newly created Lenape Indian River Camp and McKinnen's Trading Post show daily life in 1816, while Prairietown is a recreation of 1836. There are plans to bring slices of 1886 and 1936 Indiana to Conner Prairie. In 2001 an 1886 Quaker Meeting House is slated to open, followed by an 1886 working farm in 2002. A 1936 working farm will be created between 2003 and 2007. In addition to the main areas described below, there is a playground, amphitheater, where the Indianapolis Symphony Orchestra performs in the summer, and a lovely covered Commons for relaxing and picnicking.

Conner Prairie's special programs, which are ongoing on a daily basis, enhance every visitor's understanding of times gone by. For example, on one day, you might find school children scraping down a real deer hide, see plowmen from all over the state compete in an obstacle-course competition, get a chance to throw a tomahawk, and taste traditional Native American food. "Follow the North Star," a highly lauded program created in 1998, immerses participants in an interactive simulation of the Underground Railroad experience.

The admission charge for Conner Prairie includes entrance to all the sites. There is an extra charge for some of the events held, such as "Follow the North Star" and December candlelight tours. Closed Monday (except holiday Mondays), Easter, and Thanksgiving. Museum Center is open year-round; other areas are open April 1 through the last Sunday in November. (317) 776-6000 or (800) 966-1836; www.connerprairie.org.

Conner Estate. Tours of the estate depart every twenty minutes from the barn; there is limited space available, so it's wise to head here first upon your arrival at Conner Prairie. William Conner, a nineteenth-century fur trader, came to Indiana in 1801 and moved into this home with his second wife in 1823. As one of the state's leading citizens, Conner had a substantial house made of brick with elegant furnishings and paper on the walls of most of its rooms. In addition to the home and barn, there is a loom house, where you can learn about weaving and textiles, and a garden, where you'll learn about nineteenth-century planting techniques. A nature trail meanders down the hill from the Conner home and eventually comes out of the woods in Prairietown. Along this walk you'll see a flatboat, once a common means of transportation on the White River.

Museum Center. The Museum Center introduces visitors to pioneer life in Indiana, displaying artifacts and showing paintings. There is a detailed section on the eponymous William Conner, who really was an Indiana pioneer and really did live on this property. There's a small play area where you can plop down your youngsters while you take in nearby exhibits. A gallery displays traveling exhibits, and next door in the theater, a twelve-minute movie sets the scene for traveling out into the property and back in time.

McKinnen's Trading Post and Lenape Native American Camp. This newest section is beyond Prairietown, a good ten-minute walk from the Museum Center. Nestled in the woods, the Indian camp is complete with shelters unlike the tepees we imagine dotting the landscape 200 years ago. These Indians, the Lenape (pronounced *Le-NAH-pay*) were almost as new to Indiana as the settlers were. Driven there in the early 1700s, the Lenape were originally from Delaware. They were ultimately forced on to Oklahoma, taking with them William Conner's first wife and their six children.

The crude trading post was actually built using tools of the time and logs cut down on the property. Hearing the interpreter explain how it took two men a full day to strip the log of bark gives visitors an idea of how much work went into carving out even a modest niche in the frontier.

Pioneer Adventure Area. This is a nineteenth-century hands-on workshop where kids and adults alike can grind corn, dip candles, and play games, such as rolling hoops. At the schoolhouse, cabin, barn, and shed, you can compare early-nineteenth-century life with that of the early twenty-first century, with the help of knowledgeable staff.

Prairietown. Sail back in time to Prairietown, an 1836 Hoosier farming community. Here Andrew Jackson is president and Abraham Lincoln is unknown. Costumed interpreters role-play characters of the times, and you simply cannot get them to talk to you about twenty-first-century subjects. Stop by to visit the Campbells, who have one of the town's few painted homes, complete with decorative interior and exterior touches, a real luxury in 1836. Harriet Campbell can tell you about her struggles to bring a bit of culture to this outpost. Life is far more austere at the primitive home of Jeremiah Hudson, a Quaker printer and abolitionist. From house to house, you'll uncover the layers that pile on to create a pioneer settlement, rich in variety, though small in size. It is particularly fun to fall in with a school group touring these homes. The students ask wonderful, and sometimes comical, questions.

WHERE TO SHOP

Museum Shop. Museum Center at Conner Prairie, 13400 Allisonville Road, Fishers, IN 46038. This large shop is well organized and focused on offering visitors a selection of items that will help them remember their Conner Prairie experience and learn even more. There are cookbooks with nineteenth-century recipes, Indiana history books, a Conner Prairie activities book for children, notecards, Indiana-made candies, pottery, toys, games, and more. Brightly colored rock candy on a stick is a big hit with kids.

WHERE TO EAT

Persimmons. On the second floor of the Museum Center, overlooking the prairie, this restaurant is a quiet and pleasant place to dine. At noon the atmosphere is more casual, with a menu of salads and sandwiches. (The fried chicken salad is legendary.) For dinner the restaurant dresses up with double-white linen service and a menu that changes seasonally. Some favorites, such as salmon and beef, are always on the menu in one visage or another. In both the luncheon and dinner menus, you'll find echoes of Hoosier cooking with a twenty-first-century bent. The children's menu is limited. $$$. (317) 776–6008.

NOBLESVILLE

A thriving little community, Noblesville has the charm we tend to bestow in our dreams to all of Indiana's county seats. Few, though, weathered the twentieth century as well as Noblesville. An elegant

French Renaissance courthouse from the nineteenth century shares the town square with what was once the sheriff's residence and the jail and is today the County Museum of History. Enticing shops and restaurants line the square. The west side, however, where the current government building stands, is given over to duller pursuits: insurance, lawyers, and city offices. You can dawdle the day away in the town square alone, but there are sites nearby you won't want to miss, including the Indiana Transportation Museum and Bundy Decoy.

WHERE TO GO

Canterbury Arabians. 12131 East 196th Street, Noblesville, IN 46060. Sleek purebred Arabians awe visitors at this ranch, where horses are bred and trained. The owners recommend visiting in spring or summer, when foals have arrived. Families often come to pet the horses and to watch them work. Open daily year-round. Free. (317) 776-0779.

Hamilton County Museum of History. On the Noblesville Square, Noblesville, IN 46060. Built in 1875 this grand house once served as the sheriff's residence and jail. Last used as a jail in 1977, the building is now a museum with a smattering of artifacts, including photos and some costumes. Exhibits change periodically. Open Thursday through Saturday. Free. (317) 770-0775.

Indiana Transportation Museum. Forest Park, Noblesville, IN 46060. To reach the museum from downtown Noblesville, head west on either Conner or Logan Street and north on Cicero Road (State Road 19). After you go under the railroad bridge, turn left into Forest Park. The museum is 0.6 mile back. With equipment ranging from 1864 through the 1960s, this museum is dedicated to preserving Indiana railroading history. Among the notable pieces of equipment, there's industrial magnate Henry Flagler's private car and the only operating steam engine in the state, Nickel Plate #587, which was built in 1918. There's an interurban trolley to ride, and the museum operates a number of excursions—all of which depart from the Fishers train station. (To reach the station, take 116th Street west about 1 mile from I-69. Just west of the train tracks, turn north into the municipal center complex, which houses the visitors bureau and the train station.)

The Atlanta Express runs every weekend and holiday April through October, departing at 1:30 P.M. and returning around 3:30 P.M., with a thirty- to forty-minute stop in tiny Atlanta. The Fairtrain ferries State Fair goers down to the Indiana State Fairgrounds each August. The Polar Bear Express has become one of the most popular excursions, taking families on a pre-Christmas outing, including a reading and slide show of the children's story *The Polar Express* and a visit from Santa. The popular Hamiltonian Dinner Train is outlined above under Fishers, Where To Eat. Forest Park itself is also home to an old-fashioned carousel ride, aquatic center, and a golf course. Museum open Tuesday through Sunday. Fee for museum entrance. (800) 234–TRAIN or (317) 773–6000; www. itm.org.

Purgatory Golf Club. 12160 East 216th Street, Noblesville, IN 46060. This course at its longest set of tees is 7,750 yards and lays claim to being the longest regulation course east of the Mississippi. Opened to much fanfare in the summer of 2000, the course, with its 125 bunkers and challenging play, has drawn praise from many quarters. Fee. (317) 776–4653.

WHERE TO SHOP

Accent Shop. 273 South Eighth Street, Noblesville, IN 46060. Sister to Indianapolis's long-loved Accent Shop, the Noblesville branch is in an old house where each room presents new treats. The hall, for instance, has a stash of candles of every sort. Dishes, glassware, and all sorts of tabletop items are in every room. Upstairs there's a sale room. Open Monday through Saturday. (317) 773–6087.

Alley Cats. 937 Logan Street, Noblesville, IN 46060. A fairly new addition to the Noblesville shopping palette, this shop is a hit with its savvy mix of home decor items, gifts, and antiques. Open daily. (317) 774–1213.

All for the Love of Water. 925 Conner Street, Noblesville, IN 46060. Next door to the well-known Lake and Lodge Outfitters, this shop began as a catalog, without a storefront. The owner of Lake and Lodge persuaded them to move in next door, and the two shops are indeed complementary. All for the Love of Water carries everything from gracefully crafted models of schooners to patio furniture and boat-themed shower curtains. Where else in Indiana can you find a lamp finial modeled after the Cape Hatteras lighthouse? Open daily. (800) 892–8371 or (317) 776–0816; www.loveofwater.com.

Bundy Decoy Company. 16506 Strawtown Avenue, Noblesville, IN 46060. Head north out of Noblesville on State Road 37 toward Strawtown. Turn east, or right, on Strawtown Road, which is just before the bridge that crosses the White River, and travel 4½ miles east. You'll first see the tall, blue dust collector, then the big sign and buildings on the north side of the road. Bundy's makes about sixty different wood objects—decoys and birds—all by a twenty-five step operation, which begins with a chunk of cedar. These handcrafted treasures are sought after nationwide. Here you can see them being made and take home one for your own. You can also call and order a catalog. (800) 387-3831 or (765) 734-1142.

The Gentleman Soldier. 876 Logan Street, Noblesville, IN 46060. Part museum, part shop, this stop is a must-see to be appreciated; clientele fly in from around the country to pick up items here. You might find a uniform trimmed in gold lace and worn at Elizabeth II's coronation, a sword carried at the Battle of Waterloo, or a rare map or manuscript—all part of this collection of militaria. Item prices start around $300. Open Tuesday through Saturday. (317) 776-8790.

Lake & Lodge Outfitters. 917 Conner Street, Noblesville, IN 46060. Teddy Roosevelt would feel at home here, where you can buy mooseheads, fur rugs, Old Hickory furniture, and African-themed items. It's the place to go to furnish your lake cabin or your svelte tent on the African veldt. It's a grand place to go exploring. Open daily. (317) 773-4777; www.lakeandlodge.com.

Noblesville Antique Mall. 20 North Ninth Street, Noblesville, IN 46060. On three levels, a variety of vendors sell furniture, toys, textiles, books, and more. Clean, neat, and easy to get around, this is an exceptionally inviting antiques mall. Open daily. (317) 773-5095.

Noblesville Emporium. 950 Logan Street, Noblesville, IN 46060. Stretching across several old buildings, this emporium houses more than one hundred separate shops, including both antiques and new items of every sort. There's a restaurant by the entrance, giving you a place to relax and have a soda and sandwich between forays into the emporium. Open daily. (317) 773-4444.

Southwest Style. 601 Conner Street, Noblesville, IN 46060. Kachina dolls, leather sofas, cowboy deco, and all manner of Native American-style furnishings and accessories fill this gallery. It also carries Hoosier Hickory furniture, made in Indiana state prisons since the 1920s. (800) 267–0224 or (317) 773–6908; www.swstyle.com.

WHERE TO EAT

Classic Kitchen. 610 Hannibal Street, Noblesville, IN 46060. A pure delight, this restaurant offers both exceptional food and service. Restaurateur Steven Keneipp is a host extraordinnaire, solicitous, charming, and never, never intrusive. Exceptionally knowledgeable about nutrition, Keneipp's knowledge and enthusiasm for the art of cooking and the joys of eating well bring bounty out of his kitchen with every meal. Dishes vary daily, with emphasis on what is fresh and in season. Open Tuesday through Saturday for lunch and Friday and Saturday for dinner. Reservations highly recommended because the restaurant is small. $$$. (317) 773–7385.

L'Opera Ristorante. 40 North Ninth Street, Noblesville, IN 46060. The decor of L'Opera Ristorante is classical, with pillars here and there and soft colors. As the name suggests, the background music is opera, while the cuisine is Italian. Open Tuesday through Saturday for dinner. $$$. (317) 770–9828.

Noble Coffee & Tea Co. Ltd. 933 Logan Street, Noblesville, IN 46060. Because this building is L-shaped, there are actually two entrances, one on Logan Street and the other around the corner on Ninth Street. A grand gathering spot for friends, this restaurant has loads of comfy chairs and sofas for relaxing and sipping a drink from the extensive and creative drink menu, including coffee, tea, and smoothies. The food menu is limited to breakfast items; baked goods, such as muffins and scones, are made from scratch on site. Open Monday through Saturday for morning coffee through afternoon tea—the latter by reservation only. $. (317) 773–0339.

PERKINSVILLE

From Noblesville you can take State Road 37 North and jog south where it intersects with State Road 13, or from I–69 take State Road 13 North, the Lapel exit. You go to Perkinsville for one reason alone:

to dine at Bonge's (pronounced *BUN gee's*). As our waiter so merrily proclaimed, it's the only building in town that doesn't have a trailer hitch on the front.

WHERE TO EAT

Bonge's Tavern. County Road 280 North, Perkinsville, IN 46011. Once you pass the Perkinsville town limits sign, County Road 280 North is the first road to your right. The exterior isn't a promising sight. The building was once an old country store but was long ago turned into a tavern. The front porch where you wait (huddled around space heaters in winter) sags, and the structure looks a bit rickety. No matter. Inside, the atmosphere is warm and casual, with rough-hewn floors and fat Christmas bulbs looped across the ceiling. Entrees vary nightly and are posted on a blackboard above the bar. Rely on your waiter to guide you to the best choices, which might include such delicacies as lobster medallions with portabello mushrooms and truffles or filet with bernaise. The zesty house tomato soup is chunked with tomatoes. Perkinsville Pork, breaded in Parmesan and fried in butter, is a standard. For dessert, sugar-cream cake is exquisite. Dinner Tuesday through Saturday. No reservations accepted. On warm summer weekends the wait can be more than an hour. $$$. (765) 734–1625.

FOR MORE INFORMATION

Hamilton County Convention and Visitors Bureau. 11601 Municipal Drive, Fishers, IN 46038; (800) 776–TOUR or (317) 598–4444; www.visitcentralindiana.org; www.hccvb.org.

NORTHEAST DAY TRIP 2

Anderson · Muncie

Shooting north on I-69, it's easy to reach both Anderson and Muncie. Although there is more than one exit off the highway for each city, exit 26 (Scatterfield Road) is the optimum choice for Anderson because the Visitors & Convention Bureau is there. To reach Muncie, some people prefer to take I-69 to State Road 332, which is actually north of downtown, but it is a four-lane road. I prefer getting off the interstate at State Road 32 and following that northeast into downtown. If you are ambitious, you can add Pendleton, which has some historic buildings and antiques shops downtown. This part of Indiana was once settled by the Delaware Indians; before them, the Hopewell; and even earlier, the Adena. From the Mounds earthworks to the very names of the cities, pieces of that Indian heritage remain. Sites, though, are diverse; Muncie, in particular, makes an excellent destination for a family outing.

ANDERSON

When the automotive industry was in its infancy, Anderson manufactured cars, as did many other Indiana towns. But by the 1920s, automobile manufacturing gave way to automotive parts manufacturing, notably through Remy Electric—later Delco-Remy, a subsidiary of General Motors. Historic Eighth Street, west of downtown, contains many lovely old homes built during the city's heyday, some converted into businesses and at least one into a bed-and-breakfast. In this area, on Eighth between Chase and Lincoln Streets,

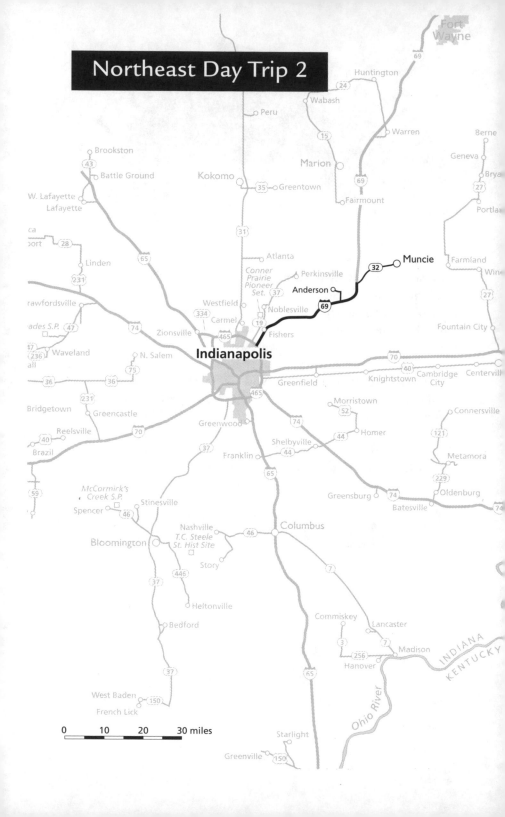

Fort Wayne

69

Huntington

24

Peru

Wabash

15

Warren

Berne

Brookston

43

Marion

Geneva

Battle Ground

Kokomo

35 Greentown

69

Brya

27

W. Lafayette

Lafayette

69

Fairmount

Portla

ca

28

31

Atlanta

Linden

65

Conner Prairie Pioneer Set.

Perkinsville

Muncie

Farmland

231

37

Anderson

32

Win

rawfordsville

Westfield

Noblesville

69

27

ades S.P. 47

334

Carmel

19

Fountain City

Zionsville

74

465

Fishers

47 236 all

Waveland

N. Salem

Indianapolis

70

40

Cambridge City

Centervill

75

465

Knightstown

36

36

Greenfield

231

Morristown

Connersville

Bridgetown

Greencastle

52

121

Reelsville

70

Greenwood

74

Homer

40

37

Shelbyville

44

Metamora

Brazil

Franklin

44

229

65

McCormick's Creek S.P.

Stinesville

Greensburg

74

Oldenburg

59

Spencer

46

Batesville

74

Nashville
T.C. Steele
St. Hist Site

46

Columbus

Bloomington

37

Story

446

Commiskey

Lancaster

Heltonville

Bedford

3

7

Madison

256

INDIANA

Hanover

37

65

KENTUCKY

West Baden

150

French Lick

Ohio River

0   10   20   30 miles

Starlight

Greenville 150

there's a sweet, well-maintained little park, Funk Park. More recently Anderson has gained fame for Hoosier Park, its horse track, and as home to the Gaither Family gospel singers. One of the city's most tranquil new additions is Indian Trails Riverwalk, downtown along the banks of the White River. Curiously, the city is actually named after an Indian, Kikthawenund, son of a trader named Anderson. An important chief, Kikthawenund lived in a village called Wapiminskink, which white settlers came to call Andersontown.

WHERE TO GO

Gruenewald Historic House. 626 Main Street, Anderson, IN 46016. The home you see from the street is a French Second Empire structure, added in 1873 onto the front of a plainer two-story brick house built in 1860. The home is beautifully restored and has many interested pieces, including a large hand-carved pianoforte. A garden and gazebo are maintained behind the house, and you can walk a few paces farther to Anderson's new Indian Trails Riverwalk, which borders the White River. Open Tuesday through Friday April through mid-December. (765) 648-6875.

Historical Military Armor Museum. 2330 Crystal Street, Anderson, IN 46012. To reach the museum from downtown Anderson, take Broadway, which is also State Road 9, north. When you cross Cross Street, go about 3 more blocks and turn right (east) onto Ames Street. Ames dead-ends into Crystal, where you turn north and immediately right into the museum's parking lot—the one containing tanks and helicopters. Inspect armored vehicles, beginning with a circa 1880 war wagon and going all the way to behemoth tanks from Desert Storm, big enough to hold their World War I counterparts. There's plenty of military paraphernalia about, as well as a real lion, the owner's pet. Open all day on Tuesday and Thursday, as well as Saturday afternoons. Fee. (765) 649-8265.

Mounds State Park. 4306 Mounds Road, Anderson, IN 46017. To reach the park entrance, follow State Road 32 east of Anderson until you reach Mounds Road. Turn south to the gates. Ten earthwork formations, built by a prehistoric Indian tribe, have been excavated and can be reached by hiking trails. They were probably used for religious ceremonies. In addition to the earthworks, there is a nature center operated in an 1840s farmhouse, open April through October. Free. (765) 642-6627.

Paramount Theatre Centre and Ballroom. 1124 Meridian Plaza, Anderson, IN 46046. One of only twelve John Eberson atmospheric theaters remaining in the nation, the Paramount sparkles like a gem, well worth a drive to Anderson. Stars twinkle in the sky, although fading sunlight glows behind the Moorish courtyard up around the balcony. The 1989 restoration of the theater was brilliant, enhanced by the 1997 salvation of its 996-pipe organ, one of only three Grande Page Organs in theaters in the country. To fully appreciate the theater, book a performance, but you can show up when the box office is open (Monday through Friday) and, for a donation, peek inside. (800) 523-4658 or (765) 642-1234; www.sparathea.org.

WHERE TO EAT

The Nile Restaurant. 723 East Eighth Street, Anderson, IN 46046. Located on the east side of downtown, near Anderson University, this restaurant stirs up Mediterranean flavors, rich in curry and other spices. Gyros are popular at every meal. Although the restaurant clearly had some previous use, nice touches of Egyptian motif give this small space character. Open for lunch and dinner Monday through Saturday. $-$$. (765) 640-9028.

MUNCIE

Like Anderson, Muncie's name has Indian origins, referring to the Munsee clan of the Delaware Indians (this is Delaware County), who once populated the banks of the White River. In 1818 the Delaware gave up the land in a treaty, and the town was platted in 1827. The town's rise to prosperity in the late nineteenth and early twentieth century was tied tightly to the Ball brothers, who created a canning-jar operation. Flourishing and branching out, Ball Corporation formed a local powerhouse lasting until the late 1990s, when it relocated to Colorado. The munificent Ball family helped endow many local charitable, cultural, and educational institutions, including Ball State University and Minnetrista Cultural Center. One of today's best-known and most generous locals is Jim Davis, creator of Garfield the Cat.

Interesting sites are scattered throughout the city. Those who admire monuments will want to take a tour of Beech Grove Cemetery, 1400 West Kilgore Avenue, which has a row of mausoleums, including those of three of the Ball brothers. The brand-new SportsPlex is drawing softball and soccer players from around the heartland. Downtown, where there seems to be a jewelry store on every corner, is a warren of one-way streets, so be prepared to go around the block to get where you are going. Ball State University, David Letterman's alma mater, is west of downtown, spreading mostly north of University Avenue; finding a place to park is a chronic problem.

WHERE TO GO

Ball State University. Campus Information Center, Pittenger Student Center, 2000 West University Avenue, Muncie, IN 47306. Endowed by the five Ball Brothers, the campus bears their legacy. The core of the school's Museum of Art, which holds works by Rembrandt, Edgar Degas, and Winslow Homer, is the private collection Frank Ball donated to the school. The Old Quadrangle, roughly bounded by University, McKinley, Riverside, and Tillotson Avenues, contains many of the school's most historic sites. Strolling through Christy Woods and visiting the Wheeler orchid collection at the northwest corner of the quadrangle makes a pleasant diversion. The Student Center has maps to the campus, the bookstore, a hotel, and the food court. Campus Information Center, (765) 285-5000; www.bsu.edu.

International Aeromodeling Center. 5151 East Memorial Drive, Muncie, IN 47302. At this complex east of the Muncie Bypass, you'll find the National Model Aviation Museum, a flying site, and the national headquarters of the Academy of Model Aeronautics. Models of all shapes and sizes hang down from the museum's ceiling, and displays chronicle the history of model aeronautics and explain the different types of flying miniature aircraft. In nice weather AMA members are often out in the field flying their creations. A gift shop has a wide selection of model aviation books and merchandise. (800) 435-9262 or (765) 287-1256; www.modelaircraft.org.

Minnetrista Cultural Center and Oakhurst Gardens. 1200 North Minnetrista Parkway, Muncie, IN 47303. Minnetrista Parkway runs between Wheeling Avenue and Walnut Street on the north side of downtown. Roughly the Sioux Indian word for "gathering place by the water," Minnetrista was a large Ball-family compound, where several family mansions stood along the banks of the White River. Today the site holds a thirty-five-acre cultural complex, given over chiefly to preserving the regions cultural heritage. Changing exhibits in the modern Cultural Center focus on history, art, and science. Oakhurst, one of the family mansions still standing on the site, tells the story of the Ball family. Oakhurst Gardens are on the western end of the property and include a charming children's garden. A gift shop in the cultural center carries pottery, toys, paper goods, and luggage and bags by Indiana designer Vera Bradley. The Orchard Shop, also within the complex, is listed separately below. Open daily year-round; closed Thanksgiving and Christmas. Fee, although most outdoor events are free. (800) 428–5887 or (765) 282–4848; www.mccoak.org.

Moore-Youse Home Museum. 120–122 East Washington Street, Muncie, IN 47305. Operated by the Delaware County Historical Alliance, this home sits next door to the Alliance headquarters, which is where you check in to get a tour. Spanning 118 years, three generations of the Moore-Youse family occupied this middle-class home, passed down through the maternal side. Remaining much as it appeared in the late 1800s and early 1900s, the house was bequeathed to the Alliance on the condition that it be maintained as an example of Victorian living. Open Wednesday through Sunday afternoon, March through November. Fee. (765) 282–1550; www.iquest.net/~dcha.

Muncie Children's Museum. 515 South High Street, Muncie, IN 47305. With cat-creator Jim Davis in residence nearby, this museum is the unofficial home of Garfield. There's a studio section where kids can learn to draw cartoons, an interactive display on bugs, a giant anthill to crawl through, an outdoor area with a treehouse, and more. The gift shop is tantalizing. Open Tuesday through Sunday; call about holiday hours. Fee. 765 286–1660; www.munciechildrensmuseum.com.

WHERE TO SHOP

House of Fogg. 418 East Main Street, Muncie, IN 47305. Muncie artist F. B. Fogg has her clever paper artworks displayed in at least 1,600 galleries across the country. Here you can see a selection of the best, as well as watch artists create collectibles, most notably paper clocks. Open Monday through Saturday. (765) 289-7464.

Indiana Glass Outlet. 1300 Batavia at Kilgore Avenue, Muncie, IN 47302. You can find plenty of bargains in this enormous warehouse, given over to candles and glass. While it isn't fine crystal, you can stock your shelves for much less than you would pay elsewhere. There are two rooms; the larger back room isn't heated. Open daily year-round; closed holidays. (765) 282-7046.

Minnetrista Orchard Shop. 311 West St. Joseph Street, Muncie, IN 47303. Fresh apples are the heart of this shop, where you can pick your favorites among the many varieties in crates near the door. Beyond apples, there is a wide selection of gourmet foods—including Indiana's own Abbott's candies, jams, soup mixes—and gift items. In season there's a farmers' market. Open daily year-round; closed Thanksgiving and Christmas. (800) 428-5887 or (765) 282-4848; www.mccoak.org.

WHERE TO EAT

Foxfires. 3300 Chadam Lane, Muncie, IN 46304. Owned by Garfield the Cat creator Jim Davis, this is one of Muncie's most popular restaurants. The cuisine is American, with French and other ethnic overtones. Dinner menus change regularly, but you might find Atlantic salmon or Indiana ostrich listed as the day's fare. The restaurant is renowned for its fine selection of wines. The restaurant has both casual and more formal dining areas. Open for dinner Monday through Saturday. $$-$$$. (765) 284-5235.

Mezza Luna. 105 East Main Street, Muncie, IN 47305. Sister to the Mezza Luna in Indianapolis, this restaurant has the same menu, complete with Italian specialties and tapas, which are lighter dishes. All the preparations are thoughtful, the food is uniformly good, and the presentation is very nice. The restaurant is situated in a renovated building right downtown, with some exposed brick walls and others plaster painted in rich golds and blues. Open for lunch

Tuesday through Friday and for dinner Tuesday through Saturday. $$-$$$. (765) 284-1921.

Vera Mae's Bistro. 219 South Walnut Street, Muncie, IN 47305. A cozy and upscale eatery, Vera Mae's is decorated in deep rose with polished wood floors. New York strip steak, pork loin, and Chicken Brie Raspberry are the popular dinner dishes and stay on the menu year-round; other items change seasonally. At lunchtime the turkey foccacia sandwich is a sure hit, as are daily specials. Open for lunch Monday through Friday and for dinner Monday through Saturday. $$-$$$. (765) 747-4941.

Vince's at the Airport. 5201 North Walnut Street, Muncie, IN 47303. North of McGalliard at the airport, Vince's overlooks the airfield and looks like it could be a passenger terminal. The broad menu contains such Hoosier classics as New York strip steak, chicken Caesar salad, and reubens, as well as some more unusual items, such as a Cajun chicken dish. Breakfast features a wide range of egg dishes as well as French toast, pancakes, and waffles. Open for breakfast on Saturday and Sunday and for lunch and dinner Tuesday through Sunday. $$. (765) 284-6364.

White River Landing. 117 West Charles Street, Muncie, IN 47305. Charles Street is one-way heading east, you'll spot the restaurant with its rustic wood exterior. Inside, the theme is nautical, with oars, old life jackets, signal flags, and fish netting. The polished wood and brick warm the atmosphere. Pizza here rates as some of the best in town, the the steak Bar-B-Q and Chicken Ranch being the two most popular combinations. There are plenty of sandwiches, salads, and full dinners. Open for lunch and dinner Monday through Saturday. $-$$. (765) 286-8133.

FOR MORE INFORMATION

Anderson-Madison County Visitors & Convention Bureau. 6335 Scatterfield Road, Anderson, IN 46013. At exit 26, turn south; you will see the bureau immediately on your right; (800) 533-6569 or (765) 643-5633; www.madtourism.com.

Muncie Visitors Bureau. 425 North High Street, Muncie, IN 47305; (800) 568-6862 or (765) 284-2700; www.muncievisitorsbureau.org.

Warren · Huntington
Wabash · Marion · Fairmount

This excursion blends early Indiana history with French traders and Indians and with more-contemporary attractions, including the Dan Quayle Museum and Fairmount's tributes to film icon James Dean. Heading farther north but out of the two-hour-trip range, you'll find the summer-place joys of Lake Wawasee; the Barbee Hotel, a thirties gangster hangout; and North Manchester, with its Italianate buildings, Thomas Marshall's birthplace (vice president under Woodrow Wilson), and Louie's Candy Kitchen, an old-time ice cream parlor and malt shop.

WARREN

Warren's Pulse Opera House, a two-story theater built in the late 1880s, is now being restored and gives performances during the summer. Take I-69 north from Indianapolis to get here.

WHERE TO SHOP

Handcrafters Marketplace. 233 Wayne Street, Warren, IN 46792. Either I-69 exit for Warren will take you right into downtown and onto Wayne Street. This small shop has handcrafted merchandise, some of which is from Indiana. Booths represent more than forty crafters, who ply pottery, rusty tin wares, custom-made sweatshirts, handwoven rugs, and a large assortment of candles. Open Tuesday through Saturday; closed January, February, and March. (219) 375-2442.

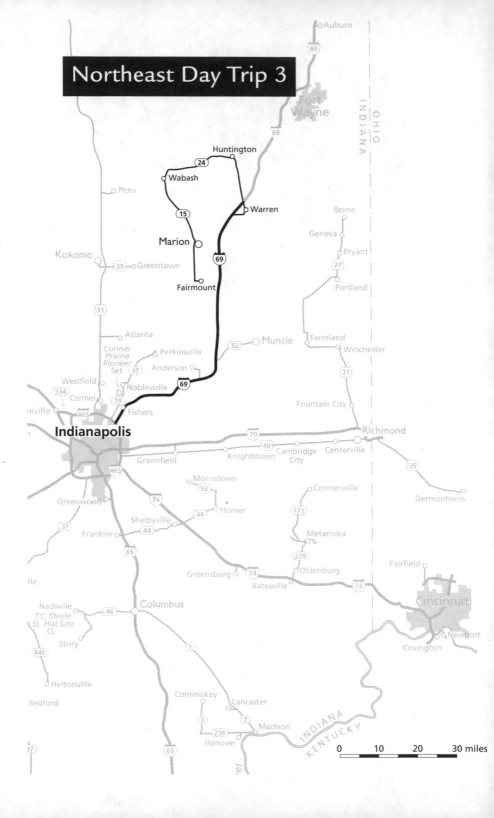

Northeast Day Trip 3

HUNTINGTON

Dan Quayle seems to have cornered Huntington's public personae, but there are some other famous local residents, including Chris Schenkel of ABC Sports and Ed Roush, who introduced our nationwide 911 system. The town's quirky claim to fame is an enormous, privately owned collection of outhouses; some are on exhibit at the Huntington County Historical Society. On your way home, stop at a grocery for Schenkel's Dairy skim milk, which is rich, not watery. From I-69 take State Road 5 north to Huntington.

WHERE TO GO

Dan Quayle Center and Museum. 815 Warren Street, Huntington, IN 46750. The Quayle Museum is at the corner of Warren and Tipton. Although you're greeted with a load of mug shots of Dan Quayle looking statesmanlike, you'll find the exhibits interesting. This has actually turned into a museum of the vice presidency, the only one in the country. Exhibits talk about the Veeps, explaining that fourteen went on to become president, five are from Indiana, and one was inaugurated in Cuba. There's a small souvenir stand with Quayle and quail memorabilia. Open Tuesday through Sunday; closed major holidays. Free. (219) 356-6356; www.quaylemuseum.org.

　　Forks of the Wabash Historic Park. 3010 West Park Drive, Huntington, IN 46750. Clearest directions to the site are on the Web page. Nomad hunters camped here as much as 10,000 years ago, followed by Miami Indians, French explorers, and European settlers. Today the site re-creates a time when the frontier was opening to settlers and the English, French, and Indians all mingled and traded here. Costumed interpreters show you through the sites, which include the home of Chiefs John B. Richardville and Francis Lafontaine, built in 1834. There's a visitor center with artifacts to gaze at and activities to try; exhibits deal with the history of the Forks of the Wabash. Open Thursday through Sunday afternoons mid-April to mid-October. Fee. (219) 356-1903; www. historicforks.org.

　　Huntington Courthouse Square National Register Historic District. In the heart of downtown, twenty-one structures are on the

National Register of Historic Places. You can pick up a brochure from the tourism office (listed below), which maps the route to see all the structures and includes line drawings, making buildings easy to spot. The courthouse warrants stepping inside. A central rotunda and a spectacular art-glass dome are treasures. On the top floor the circuit courtroom is beautifully restored, with its own art-glass ceiling. The lobby of the Hotel LaFontaine, now housing for the elderly, also rates a stop.

Wings of Freedom Museum. Huntington Municipal Airport, 1365 Warren Road, Huntington, IN 46750. This compact museum is dedicated to World War II aviation exploits. Exhibits include the P–510 North American Mustang Scat VI, a tribute to 434th Fighter Squadron pilots killed in action, and a display on the WASPS. There's a small gift shop and library. For a real treat, you can catch a ride. Open weekends and by appointment May through October. Fee.(219) 356–1945; members.aol.com/scatvii/page/index.htm.

WHERE TO SHOP

John Trook Antiques. 53 East Market Street, Huntington, IN 46750. Packed from floor to ceiling, this tiny store carries a range of antiques but has a country primitive focus. If you find the sheer mass of material daunting, ask the owner to direct you. Open Monday through Saturday. (219) 356–7072.

Korner Kupboard Kreations. 438 North Jefferson Street, Huntington, IN 46750. Purchase your souvenirs at this giftware store: a Huntington mug or wooden cutout of one of the historic buildings downtown. The shop also carries candles, decorative flags, Kennebunk afghans, cards, and locally made Bircraft giftware—wood decoratively carved and painted then encased in plastic. Open Monday through Saturday. (219) 356–1377.

WHERE TO EAT

Pizza Junction. 201 Court Street, Huntington, IN 46750. Aptly named, this restaurant occupies the former train depot, giving diners prime seats to watch trains rumble by, which they do daily. Pizzas, salads, and subs are the mainstays. Breadsticks are delicious, and service is friendly and speedy. Open for lunch and dinner daily; closed Thanksgiving and Christmas. $. (219) 356–4700.

WABASH

The town snugs up to the banks of the Wabash River, and its courthouse is perched picturesquely high above the river. The town claims to be the first in the world—1879—lit entirely with electric lights. To get here from Huntington follow U.S. 24 West and turn south on State Road 13.

WHERE TO GO AND STAY

The Honeywell House. 720 North Wabash Street, Wabash, IN 46992. Once the home of the widow of Mark Honeywell, founder of Honeywell, Inc., this mansion sits in a parklike setting and is filled with antiques, works of Indiana artists, and other treasures from Eugenia Honeywell's travels. Now property of the Indiana University Foundation, the home is a cultural center offering free concerts and exhibits and a bed-and-breakfast, where you can stay in one of the charming rooms. Open for tours by appointment year-round. Fee to tour; $$ for lodging. (219) 563-2326; www. honeywellhouse.org.

WHERE TO EAT

Market Street Grill. 90 West Market Street, Wabash, IN 46992. This restaurant is appealing for its curious decor, where you can sit in the bar in an old barber chair and watch electric trains chug around the room. House specialties are steaks and seafood, along with a piquant bacon, lettuce, and tomato soup. Open for dinner Wednesday through Sunday. No children allowed. $$. (219) 563-7779.

MARION

Once home to the Miami Indians, Marion, south of Wabash on State Road 15, claims the largest Indian cemetery in the state, located west of town at 3750 West County Road 600 North. There's an old Indiana schoolhouse there, too. North of town about 7 miles on State Road 15 is the Mississinewa Battlefield, site of the first U.S.

victory over the British during the War of 1812. Each October brings a reenactment.

WHERE TO EAT

Wilson-Vaughn Historic Hostess House. 723 West Fourth Street, Marion, IN 46952. This wonderful old home, listed on the National Register of Historic Places, was built in the beginning of the twentieth century by J. Wood Wilson for his young bride, Peggy, and furnished with items the two purchased on trips to Europe. After Wilson died Peggy married John Vaughn, and they lived in the house. After the couple died a group of enterprising women converted the house into a lunchroom and venue for social events. Soups, sandwiches, salads, and homemade desserts are the typical fare. Open for lunch Monday through Friday. $. (765) 664-3755.

FAIRMOUNT

Native son and fifties *Rebel Without a Cause* star James Dean is immortalized throughout Fairmount. You can see the motorcycle shop where he bought his first bike and the church where his funeral was held, following his death in a car accident at age twenty-four. Each September there's a festival in Dean's honor, with a fifties car show, film showings, a parade, and more. From Marion, follow State Road 9 South and turn east on State Road 26.

WHERE TO GO

James Dean Memorial Gallery. 425 North Main Street, Fairmount, IN 46928. Seven rooms are stuffed with Dean memorabilia—his signature jeans and white T-shirt, movie posters, and every conceivable collectible from gum cards to mugs. A separate room shows screen tests and other Dean film footage. Open daily; closed Thanksgiving, Christmas, and New Year's Day. Fee. (765) 948-3326; www. JamesDeanGallery.com.

    Fairmount Historical Museum. 203 East Washington Street, Fairmount, IN 46928. This museum houses Dean's motorcycles, some movie costumes, and memorabilia donated by friends and family.

Other exhibits showcase items from Garfield creator, Jim Davis, another Indiana native, and other local notables. Open daily March through November. Free. (765) 948-4555; www.jamesdeanartifpcts.com.

FOR MORE INFORMATION

Huntington County Visitor & Convention Bureau. 407 North Jefferson Street; Huntington, IN 46750; (219) 359-9754; www.visithuntington.org.

Marion/Grant County Convention & Visitors Bureau. 217 South Adams Street, Marion, IN 46952; (800) 662-9474 or (765) 668-5435; www.comteck.com/~marionin.

Wabash County Convention & Visitors Bureau. 11 South Wabash Street, Wabash, IN 46992; (800) 563-1169 or (219) 563-7171; www.wabashcountycvb.com.

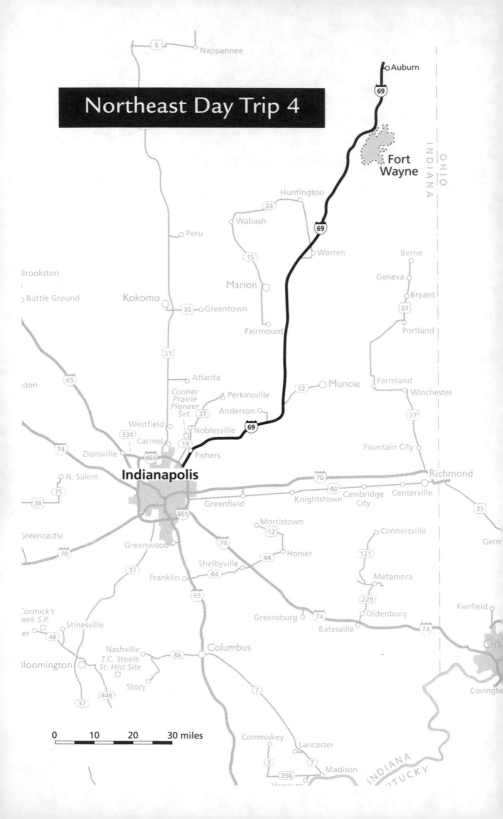

Northeast Day Trip 4

Fort Wayne · Auburn

The most expeditious route to northeastern Indiana is I-69.

FORT WAYNE

Take I-69 north to exit 102 and angle right, northeast, off the exit ramp. This street, West Jefferson, will take you directly downtown, passing Covington Plaza, a good place to shop and to grab a bite to eat, Jefferson splits as you approach downtown, becoming one-way going east, while Washington, a block to the north, is one-way heading west.

Fort Wayne, the second-largest city in Indiana and seat of Allen County, is surely one of the finest small cities in the country and one of my favorite stops. Museums, parks, more than 400 restaurants, and great shopping elevate the city beyond the ordinary. In the heart of town, the St. Marys and St. Joseph Rivers converge to form the Maumee River. Today these rivers are a focal point; their banks are gussied up to create lovely riverside drives, many of which are lined with greenways and public walks. The downtown is crowned by Headwaters Park, twenty acres of lush foliage and beautiful fountains. Beyond this park, Fort Wayne has about 2,000 acres of parklands spread across eight public parks.

The core of downtown contains enough attractions, including the Lincoln Museum, Science Central, and the Art Museum, to occupy several days. Casting your net a bit farther will take you to the fine children's zoo or twenty minutes north to Auburn, famous for antique cars.

Fort Wayne's genesis is interesting. The land near the convergence of the three rivers had long lured settlers. The Indians called the area "Glorious Gate," and both the Miami and Iroquois Nations had settlements here. A French fort went up here in the early 1700s, and that fort and its successors were fought over by the Miamis, French, British, and Americans for about a hundred years. One of those forts was built on a site selected by General "Mad" Anthony Wayne, who had routed the Indians. The fort was named in his honor, and the name stuck to the settlement. (There's a massive statue of Wayne on horseback in Freimann Square, one of the city's prettiest parks, nestled between the Performing Arts Center and the City-County Building.) A re-creation of an early fort, along with a number of rough-hewn wood buildings, lies just north of Headwaters Park off Lafayette Street and was once open to the public. Currently it is open only for special events, such as reenactments, but the city is rethinking the site's future.

Incorporated as a town in 1829, Fort Wayne got a big economic boost when the state determined that the canal would go through there. Ultimately Fort Wayne became a diverse manufacturing center, with a strong sense of civic duty resulting in many cultural and community benefits, including the symphony, art museum, and scores of restaurants. The cultural life continues to thrive. If you have extra time in the city, try to attend a performance at Embassy Theatre, a restored gem from 1928.

As you drive through Fort Wayne, look about. There are a number of lovely buildings, including the Lincoln National Bank and Trust Building, 116 East Berry Street, which looks rather like the Tribune Building in Chicago or a twenty-two-story version of the Empire State Building. The Allen County Courthouse, at 715 South Calhoun Street, is an Indiana gem, a majestic Beaux Arts building completed in 1902 and one of the largest county courthouses in the state. North of town lies the Concordia Theological Seminary, largely designed by internationally renowned architect Eero Saarinen.

WHERE TO GO

Cathedral of the Immaculate Conception. 1100 South Calhoun Street, Fort Wayne, IN 46802. The cathedral is in the heart of downtown and you can nudge into its parking lot from either Calhoun or

Lewis Street. Pick up a brochure inside for a full history, including information about the extensive renovation finished in 1999. (You'll have to come to a worship service to appreciate the full benefits, which include improved lighting and a new sound system.) A church was built on this site above a Miami Indian burial ground as early as 1834, and the cornerstone of this cathedral was laid in 1858. The Gothic interior, with its Bavarian stained-glass windows and impressive wood carving, inspires serenity. Adjacent to the Cathedral Church, located on the lower level of the MacDougal Chapel at 1139 South Calhoun Street, is the tiny Cathedral Museum, which houses religious artifacts dating back to the mid-thirteenth century. You can visit the cathedral on your own at any time, but if you want a guided tour, call in advance. Free. (219) 424–1485.

Foellinger-Freimann Botanical Conservatory. 1100 South Calhoun Street, Fort Wayne, IN 46802. Covering almost an entire city block, this conservatory includes three large greenhouses: tropical, desert, and a showcase room featuring seasonal foliage. A hunk of the funding for this venture came from the Foellinger Foundation, founded by the family that once published the *Fort Wayne News Sentinel,* and the Freimann Charitable Trust, founded by the Freimann family, whose scion headed Magnavox Corporation. When Indiana's gloomy February seems to stretch endlessly, an afternoon here is an ideal escape. A large gift shop features horticultural and gardening gifts. Open daily; closed Christmas Day. Fee. (219) 427–6440.

Fort Wayne Children's Zoo. 3411 Sherman Boulevard, Fort Wayne, IN 46808. Sprawling across forty-two landscaped acres, this small zoo has received many accolades. Look for the Sumatran tiger and vividly plumed birds in the Indonesian Rainforest; steer your own zebra-striped Jeep along a track through the African veldt; take a spin on the endangered-species carousel; gaze at exotic fish in the Great Barrier Reef aquarium; and take home something cuddly from the gift shop. Open daily from the end of April until mid-October. Fee. (219) 427–6800; www.kidszoo.com.

Fort Wayne Fire Fighters Museum. 226 West Washington Boulevard, Fort Wayne, IN 46802. Old Engine House No. 3 was initially completed in 1894, added onto twice in the early twentieth century, and remained the city's biggest fire station until 1971. Today the Romanesque structure is a museum with plenty of objects and vehicles illustrating the history of fire fighting. Kids learn fire safety through demonstrations and practice. There's a fire-safety maze for kids and a popular restaurant, Old No. 3 Firehouse Cafe. Open year-round Monday through Friday from 11:00 A.M. to 2:00 P.M. Fee. (219) 426-0051.

Fort Wayne Museum of Art. 311 East Main Street, Fort Wayne, IN 46802. As you head east on Main Street, you'll see a large red aluminum sculpture, *Crossings,* in the lawn; turn left just before it. Although the museum has a permanent collection of some 1,300 works, the gallery is not large, so only a selection of the works is displayed at any given time. The museum's own holdings are supplemented by a vigorous traveling exhibition schedule, treating locals and visitors alike to a array of art from around the world. The gift shop is well stocked with delightful objects, including jewelry, paper goods, children's toys, and ceramics. Closed Monday and major holidays. Fee, except Wednesday and the first Sunday of the month. (219) 422-6467; www.fwmoa.org.

Johnny Appleseed Memorial Park. U.S. 930 Bypass and Harry Baals Drive, Fort Wayne, IN 46805. From downtown take Lafayette north to State Boulevard. Turn right on State and then left on Parnell. Go less than a mile; just over a small bridge you'll see the entrance to the park on the right. John Chapman, known to every American schoolchild as Johnny Appleseed, spent many years spreading seed and planting trees in northern Indiana and throughout the Midwest. In 1845 he died near Fort Wayne and was buried there. The real site of his grave is uncertain, but there is a grave for him, surrounded by a wrought-iron fence, in Archer Park, which is intertwined with Johnny Appleseed Memorial Park. Signs show you the way. Beyond the grave site there's a campground, playground, and picnic areas. A Johnny Appleseed festival is held here each fall. Fort Wayne Parks and Recreation Department, (219) 427-6003.

The Lincoln Museum. 200 East Berry Street, Fort Wayne, IN 46802. Lincoln National Corporation, once based in Fort Wayne, amassed the world's largest private collection of Lincoln memorabilia, which is the font from which this museum springs. There are scores of artifacts spread through eleven galleries. Rare photographs and paintings depict Lincoln as a youth, a clean-shaven lawyer, and as the craggy, bearded president anyone who's ever seen a penny knows. You'll hear his speeches and watch videos about the era. With computer games, you can reenact a Civil War battle or redecorate the White House, facing the choices Mary Todd Lincoln had. Hands-on exhibits include nineteenth-century dress-up clothes for kids. Whatever Lincoln memorabilia you wish to own, from busts to reproductions of the White House china, you will find at the gift shop. Open Tuesday through Sunday; closed major holidays. Fee. (219) 455–3864; www.TheLincolnMuseum.org.

Old City Hall Historical Museum. 302 East Berry Street, Fort Wayne, IN 46802. As you might guess, Old City Hall Historical Museum is located in the Old City Hall Building, built in 1893. The city moved to larger quarters in 1971, and the site was taken over by the Fort Wayne Historical Society, which has an impressive collection of artifacts highlighting the history of Allen County. Holdings include Anthony Wayne's camp bed, Indian artifacts, an 1880's storefront, a nineteenth-century dollhouse, and the old city lockup located in the basement. Open Friday, Saturday, and Sunday. Fee. (219) 426–2882.

Science Central. 1950 North Clinton Street, Fort Wayne, IN 46805. Because Clinton Street is one-way south, you must jog over a block east to Lafayette, which is one-way north. Once you've crossed the river, turn left onto Elizabeth, which cuts over to Clinton just north of Science Central. You'll easily spot this old factory building topped by crayon-colored chimneys, and the cheery inside will bring a smile to every face.

Even those who claim to hate science and math will discover the fun side of numbers and physics as they enjoy a simulated moon walk, create an earthquake, bend a rainbow, and stir up some clouds. You can see your heart beat, play a tune on the stairs, and encase yourself in a giant bubble. A pedaling skeleton shows what bones you use riding a bicycle. For a thrill kids can ride a bike on a track 20 feet up in the air or sail down a three-story slide. Kids Central, with its pint-size door, is the section reserved for children ages two through seven. The gift shop features science- and math-related games and toys. There isn't a restaurant, but you can bring your own lunch to eat in a seating area on the lower level, or you can get your hand stamped so that you can go out and return later. Open Tuesday through Sunday and holiday Mondays, except Christmas and New Year's Day. Fee. (800) 442–6376 or (219) 424–2400; www.sciencecentral.org.

WHERE TO SHOP

Karen's Antique Mall. 1510 Fairfield Avenue, Fort Wayne, IN 46802. Fairfield is just west of the heart of downtown, and Karen's, which has its own parking lot, is 2 blocks south of Jefferson Boulevard. With more than sixty dealers on two floors, this mall offers a wide selection, running from early-nineteenth-century furniture to Beatles' collectibles from the sixties. There's a year-round Christmas shop and a shop featuring Boyd's Bears. Just off the lobby there's a museum room dedicated to Philo Farnsworth, who invented the TV tube. Although he wasn't born in Fort Wayne, Farnsworth experimented with the TV tube in the city, where he raised his family. The display includes one of two complete sets of *TV Guide* on display in the nation, old TVs, and memorabilia from hit shows. Open daily year-round. (219) 422–4030.

Jorgensens. 6226 Covington Road, Fort Wayne, IN 46804. Although nationally known designer Vera Bradley is headquartered in Fort Wayne, there is no outlet shop here. (There is an annual sale of discontinued lines. For the date of that sale, contact Vera Bradley at 219–482–4673; www.verabradley.com.) Jorgensens, however, carries a wide selection of the goods, including china and collectibles, as well as many other gift and home-decor items. Plus, it's just behind Covington Plaza, where you'll find some of Fort Wayne's best shopping. Open Tuesday through Saturday. (219) 432-5519.

Little Professor Book Company. Covington Plaza, 6360 West Jefferson Boulevard, Fort Wayne, IN 46804. Little Professor, a franchise of independents, is actually a cross between an independent bookstore and a chain. It has a broad selection of books, regular book talks and signings, and the kind of special service you get with an independent. There's free coffee in the cookbook section. Open daily; closed major holidays. (219) 436-7763; www.littleprofessor.com.

WHERE TO EAT

Fort Wayne has an exceptional number of very good places to dine in all price ranges. This represents only a slice of the tasty spots you might choose.

Bill's Bistro. 1802 Spy Run Avenue, Fort Wayne, IN 46805. Bill's restaurant and lounge serves a range of entrees from aged Angus beef to ostrich. You may catch a whiff of cigar in the air and hear the sounds of live music. This polished restaurant is popular with the scotch-and-soda crowd, and there is no section for the under twenty-one crowd, so leave the kids at home. The waitstaff here gets my gold star for friendliness and efficiency. Open Monday through Saturday. $$$. (219) 422-7012; www.preferredrestaurants.com.

Cafe Johnelle. 2529 South Calhoun Street, Fort Wayne, IN 46807. Since its opening in 1961, Cafe Johnelle has been touted as one of the finest restaurants in Indiana and has won national awards. A jewel in the city's dining trove, the restaurant's ambience, with soft lighting and original art, tells you that this is the sort of place where important decisions are made (mergers and marriages), where the food is cuisine, and the service is dignified. Open Tuesday through Saturday. Reservations recommended. $$$. (219) 456-1939; www. widesign.com/menus.

Catablu. 2441 Broadway, Fort Wayne, IN 46807. Located in a historical old theater on Broadway, this relatively new restaurant is casual yet quite sophisticated. Delicious breads, salads, seafood, and more are all served with an artistic flair. Portions are large, and a luncheon entree may be enough for your dinner as well, particularly if you also try one of the soups. The kitchen, open to the diners' view, is where the stage once was. The waitstaff is speedy and attentive. Open Monday through Friday. Reservations recommended. $$$. (219) 456-6563; www.preferredrestaurants@catablu.com.

Cindy's Diner. 830 South Harrison Street, Fort Wayne, IN 46808. Fort Wayne's mighty-mini, fab-fifties spot serves burgers and malts for breakfast and lunch. There are plenty of standard items on the breakfast menu, too. Kids love this stop, a slip of a diner on the edge of downtown on the corner of Wayne and Harrison. Open daily for breakfast and lunch. $. (219) 422-1957.

DeBrand Fine Chocolates. 5608 Coldwater Road, Fort Wayne, IN 46825 (219-482-4373); 6370 West Jefferson Boulevard, Fort Wayne, IN 46804 (219-432-5050). Willpower may melt in this dessert cafe, but the chocolate won't, unless it's melted over something tantalizing. Devotees of these Fort Wayne chocolates, made with all natural ingredients and without preservatives, can't get enough and believe there is no rival. Sundaes are the best-selling dessert, while raspberries n cream, caramel pecan patties, and rose carmellas are the most popular chocolates. Open daily; closed major holidays. $. www.debrand.com.

Don Hall's Tavern at Coventry. 5745 Coventry Lane, Fort Wayne, IN 46804. Coventry Plaza lies on U.S. 24, on the west side of Fort Wayne, just west of I-69. A local chain, Don Hall's has a broad menu of fare sure to please a range of palettes: homemade soups, reubens, filet mignon, fettuccine Alfredo, Italian grinders, omelettes, chicken salad, and a selection of burgers. Don Hall's is a good family choice, and there are others throughout the city. Closed major holidays. $$. (219) 459-2893; www.donhalls.com.

Munchie Emporium and Mad Anthony Brewing Company. 2002 Broadway, Fort Wayne, IN 46807. This jazzy restaurant offers home brews, entertainment (Tuesday, Thursday, Friday, and Saturday evenings), and dining. You can look behind glass to watch beers, including Big Daddy Brown, made on site. Fare features thick-crusted gourmet pizzas; the Politician, loaded with everything, is the most popular. Beyond pizza, the variety includes sandwiches, salads, and pasta. Open daily for lunch and dinner and for brunch on Sunday. $-$$. (219) 426-2537; www.madbrew.com.

Queenie's Bakery and Cafe. 2441 Broadway, Fort Wayne, IN 46807. In the lobby of the theater that houses Catablu, this tiny bakery packs powerful flavors. Lemon squares, brownies of all sorts, megacookies, and cheesecakes are all delicious. Stop in to grab some sweets for the road. Breakfast and lunch Monday through Friday. Closes at noon on Saturday. $. (219) 456-3311.

The Window Garden Restaurant. 1300 One Summit Square, Fort Wayne, IN 46802. Located on the thirteenth floor of the Bank One building on the corner of Washington Boulevard and Calhoun Street, this restaurant offers a panoramic view of Fort Wayne. To the north you can see the cheerful stacks of Science Central; a skip to the east, you'll see the graceful Cathedral of Immaculate Conception. It's cafeteria service featuring such items as Swiss steak and patty melts, but the food isn't the reason you go here. It is a handy restaurant for those visiting the Lincoln Museum. Open Monday through Friday for breakfast and lunch; open Sunday for lunch, except during July and August. $. (219) 426-4086.

WHERE TO STAY

Carole Lombard House. 704 Rockhill Street, Fort Wayne, IN 46802. The birthplace and childhood home of the unforgettable

Hollywood phenomenon is today a modest bed-and-breakfast with four guest quarters featuring period furnishings and private baths. Carole's own room, although small, is nicely furnished. $. (888) 426–9896 or (219) 426–9896.

Roebuck Inn. 5319 St. Joe Road, Fort Wayne, IN 46835. To reach the Roebuck Inn from downtown, head north on Clinton, turn east on East State Boulevard, angle northeast on Crescent, and north on St. Joe. On your left you'll see a stone wall and the entrance to Canterbury Green, where you check into the Roebuck. The main office of Canterbury Green is 2613 Abbey Drive. The inn is the B&B lodging for the Canterbury Green Country Club and apartments, and guests have the advantage of receiving a pass to use all the country club facilities, including the four pools, tennis courts, and health club. Breakfast, too, is served in the country club dining room. The inn itself has five suites, each of which will sleep three and all of which have a living area, including kitchen, and a private bath. The decor is country cozy. $$. (219) 485–9619; www.rent.net/direct/canterburygreen.

AUBURN

Auburn is more than two hours beyond Indianapolis, but it is only a 20-mile trip north of Fort Wayne. Anyone interested in automobiles and their history will make the effort to head north on I–69 and east on State Road 8 to Auburn. As seat of DeKalb County, Auburn has always had small-town bustle, but its heyday was during Indiana's automotive boom times. By 1900 Auburn already had an automotive manufacturer, and during the twenties and thirties, Auburns, Cords, and Dusenbergs were known worldwide for their innovations and sleek styling. The Depression hit the company too hard, and it closed in 1938. Today the town draws international attention for its Auburn Cord Dusenberg Festival and car auction, held early each fall.

WHERE TO GO

Auburn Cord Duesenberg Museum. 1600 South Wayne Street, Auburn, IN 46706. For vintage car lovers, this place is Mecca. More than one hundred showroom-perfect cars from horseless carriages to current sports cars fill seven galleries of a beautiful Art Deco building, once the Auburn Automobile Company showroom. The displays are well organized, well labeled, and inviting, no matter what your age. Plus, there are some other vintage items, including old radios, televisions, and an airplane dangling from one ceiling. A gift shop carries a sporty selection of car memorabilia. Open daily; closed major holidays. Fee. (219) 925–1444; www.acd.museum.org.

WHERE TO STAY

Auburn Inn. 225 Touring Drive, Auburn, IN 46706. Although it is not glamourous, this inn is tidy, with attractive rooms and plenty of amenities, including a continental breakfast buffet, evening cookies and milk, and an outdoor pool. Kids stay free. $$. (800) 44-LODGE or (219) 925–6363; www.focus.com.

FOR MORE INFORMATION

Fort Wayne/Allen County Convention and Visitors Bureau. 1021 South Calhoun Street, Fort Wayne, IN 46802; (800) 767–7752 or (219) 424–3700; www.fwcvb.org; www.visitfortwayne.com.

Carmel · Westfield · Atlanta

Hamilton County, one of the fastest-growing counties around, offers a multitude of attractions to visitors. In Carmel's many restaurants alone, you could eat out every meal for a week, all offering superior dining, and never at the same place twice. Shopping, too, is a popular pastime in this part of town, with two large shopping plazas, one on Keystone at 116th Street and the other on U.S. 31, just around 146th Street. Because Hamilton County is so easily accessible, never mind the traffic, you can make frequent forays, eventually covering it all. (See Northeast Day Trip 1 for the rest of the county.)

CARMEL

To get to Carmel you can either head north on Meridian Street (State Road 31) and then east on 116th to Range Line Road; north on Westfield Boulevard, which turns into Range Line Road north of Eighty-sixth Street; or north on Keystone Avenue and then west on 116th Street to Range Line Road. Once a sleepy town with a single main intersection (Range Line Road and Main Street), Carmel grew as Indianapolis boomed beyond its borders and urbanites sought the pleasures of newly created suburbia. Today Carmel is a city in its own right with beautiful homes, office towers, some grand shopping, and more.

WHERE TO GO

Museum of Miniature Houses and Other Collections. 111 East Main Street, Carmel, IN 46032. The museum is 1 block east of Range Line Road. You don't have to be a little girl to be fascinated by the miniature houses and rooms collected here. There are mansions, modest dwellings, and a museum. One house is a replica of its owner's home; another dollhouse has a miniature of itself in the playroom; and in another, a wedding is about to be held. Exquisite in detail, these homes are little museums all by themselves. The small gift shop sells hard-to-find items for the well-appointed dollhouse. Open Wednesday through Sunday; closed some holidays and the first two schoolweeks of January. Free; donation requested. (317) 575-9466; www.museumofminiatures.org.

    Prairie View Golf Club. 7000 Longest Drive, Carmel, IN 46033. Take Keystone north to Main Street, which is also 131st Street, and turn right. Drive 4 miles east, go around through the first circle and take the second right on the second circle, which is Longest Drive. Hamilton County is building a reputation for great golfing, fueled by its tremendous growth. Prairie View, the only Robert Trent Jones Jr.-designed course in the state has gained a reputation that has drawn golfers from around the state and beyond, including Michael Jordan. In addition to the fine links, there's an attractive club house and grill. (317) 816-3100; www.prairieviewgc.com.

WHERE TO SHOP

Acorn Farm Country Store. 15466 Oak Road, Carmel, IN 46033. From U.S. 31, turn east on 151st Street and north on Oak Road to the second drive on the left. Some antiques and some new items fill several rooms of an old home set in a woods, once a camp for children. Lamps, wardrobes, clocks, quilts, candles, and more make up the delightful mix. You're sure to walk away with a treasure, large or small, old or new. Open Wednesday through Sunday. (317) 846-6257.

    The Foolery. 10 South Range Line Road, Carmel, IN 46032. For young boys, this is the must-stop shop. Home to all manner of collectibles but mainly cards—baseball, Pokemon, whatever is hot—this shop has devotees all around the state. When no one else stocks your dream card, you'll find it here. Open Monday through Saturday. (317) 574-9876.

541 Salon. 541 North Range Line Road, Carmel, IN 46032. This sunny little shop combines an upscale hair salon with an upscale home decor and accessories shop, along with jewelry, hair products, and a few gourmet items. You could line up a perm and a massage in the morning and walk out a few hours later with a new do, a lamp, gourmet soups, earrings, and an afghan. Open Tuesday through Saturday. (317) 580-0541.

Vine & Branch. 4721 East 146th Street, Carmel, IN 46033. Travel north on U.S. Highway 31 to the large shopping plaza. Turn right (east) at the Galyans entrance. Follow the road as it bends to the right and you will come out on 146th Street. The shop is located in an historic home on the south side of the street, just west of Gray Road. For garden lovers there is a large selection of antiques and high-fashion accessories sure to please. Open Monday through Saturday. (317) 571-0527.

WHERE TO EAT

The Glass Chimney Restaurant. 12901 North Old Meridian Street, Carmel, IN 46032. One of Carmel's first gourmet restaurants, the Glass Chimney still goes strong, with an ever-changing menu of Continental cuisine, white-linen dining, and a reserved waitstaff. Steaks are premium quality and most all entrees issue forth from the chefs looking like works of art. Open for dinner Monday through Saturday. $$$. (317) 844-0921.

Helios Gifts & Tea Room. 220 East Main Street, Carmel, IN 46032. Carmel seems to combine concepts nicely. This spot is a ladies tearoom and gift shop, with an emphasis on seasonal offerings. Located in an old house, the rooms are crammed with bears and bowls, jellies and jams, linens and lotions, books and baubles, and so much more. Open only for lunch, Helios offers a set-price menu, including soups, salads, and sandwiches. Reservations are recommended. Open for lunch Monday through Saturday. $-$$. (317) 844-4606.

Mangia. 2340 East 116th Street, Carmel, IN 46032. Drive north on Keystone to the Merchants Square Plaza on the northwest corner of 116th and Keystone. Created by one of Indianapolis's most-noted restaurateurs, Gino Pizzi, Mangia satisfies the Italian-loving appetite with a Tuscan-style bistro. Any dish with the chef's delicious marinara sauce is sure to be a winner. Open for lunch Monday through Friday and for dinner Monday through Saturday. $$. (317) 581-1910.

Panache Bistro. 12237 North Meridian Street, Carmel IN 46032. This stylish restaurant is tucked in an upscale strip mall on the east side of Meridian. A hit as soon as it opened in late 2000, Panache Bistro serves an ever-changing array of delicious dishes. Whether you order tuna tartare, roasted quail, or warm goat cheese salad, you can be sure that the flavors will be delightful. Superb soups, conjured up daily by a chef dubbed the Soup Dragon, can be ordered at noon in sixteen-ounce bowls, a meal unto themselves. Give this restaurant a gold star for creating an easy-to-read wine list that allows even wine neophytes to order with confidence. Open for lunch and dinner Tuesday through Saturday. $$$. (317) 706–3463; www.panachebistro.com.

Restaurant 210. 210 North Range Line Road, Carmel, IN 46032. Situated in a charming old Victorian with a back deck for dining outside in pleasant weather, this cheerful restaurant offers a varied menu, changing each month. Soups are always good, as are desserts. This is an inviting choice for a special occasion of any sort. Open for lunch Monday through Saturday and for dinner Tuesday through Saturday. $$$. (317) 582–1414.

Ye Olde Library. 40 East Main Street, Carmel, IN 46032. This actually is the old Carmel library, and the owners have carried out the theme delightfully, with menus inside books at dinner and well-stocked bookshelves within easy reach of tables. Luncheon salads, such as caesar and spinach, are good, and there are tasty soups at every meal. Dinners include a variety of entrees, which change periodically. You may wish to dawdle over dessert, so you can finish one more chapter of the novel you picked up after you placed your order! Open for lunch and dinner Tuesday through Saturday. $$$. (317) 573–4444.

WESTFIELD

WHERE TO SHOP

Beauchamps Antiques. 16405 Westfield Boulevard, Westfield, IN 46074. Among antiques lovers, the name Beauchamps is spoken in reverential tones. The selection of high-quality antiques is simply the best in central Indiana, and it's the place to go if you have a specific need, such as a white-marble fireplace, preferably from a European castle, or an eighteenth-century bulls-eye mirror, preferably from some former senator's home. The shop, in the woods on the east side of the street, isn't visible from the road. Watch carefully for the sign. Open Tuesday through Saturday. (317) 896-3717.

WHERE TO EAT

Pickett's Cafeteria. 102 South Union Street, Westfield, IN 46074. A cozy and homey cafeteria, Pickett's is best known for its fried chicken, offered daily, even though there are four other main dishes served at each meal. Mashed potatoes, green beans, stuffing, and pies (made fresh daily) are all popular accompaniments. Open for lunch Monday through Friday; for dinner Tuesday through Friday; and for brunch on Sunday. $-$$ (317) 867-5492.

ATLANTA

Head north on U.S. Highway 31 and turn east on 296th Street, which will take you into Atlanta. Atlanta is a quiet hamlet where the action takes place on Saturday night, when the music hall lights up and a six-piece band plays. Fletcher's is the big draw.

WHERE TO EAT

Fletcher's of Atlanta. 185 West Main Street, Atlanta, IN 46031. Once you've crossed State Road 19, go a couple of blocks to Walnut Street. Turn right and go 2 blocks to the intersection of Walnut and Main, which is where the restaurant is located. Fresh ingredients and distinctive blendings of flavors characterize this menu, which changes regularly and is supplemented by about as many daily specials as you'll find entrees on the printed menu. Owner Fletcher Boyd calls it "contemporary Hoosier eclectic," which translates as exquisite. Open for dinner Tuesday through Saturday. $$$. (765) 292-2777.

WHERE TO STAY

Asher Walton House Bed and Breakfast. 100 East Main Street, Atlanta, IN 46031. Built in 1868 this house features antique hardwoods, beautiful wood trims, and stained glass throughout. Rooms are finished with some antiques and Victorian trappings. There are three guest bedrooms, which share two bathrooms. Your stay includes a four-course breakfast tailored to your wishes. Not wheelchair accessible. $$. (765) 292–2422; www.asherwaltonhouse. com.

FOR MORE INFORMATION

Carmel-Clay Chamber of Commerce. 40 East Main Street, Carmel, IN 46032; (317) 846–1049; www.carmelchamber.com.

    Hamilton County Convention and Visitors Bureau. 11601 Municipal Drive, Fishers, IN 46038; (800) 776–TOUR or (317) 598–4444; www.visitcentralindiana.org; www.hccvb.org.

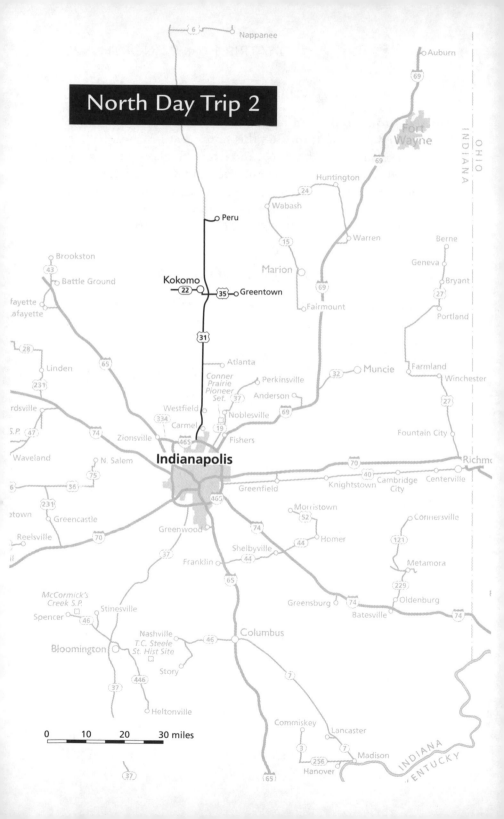

NORTH DAY TRIP 2

Kokomo · Greentown · Peru

Although some travelers find U.S. 31 north of Indianapolis a long, straight, dull stretch, it actually has many interesting sites, including round barns, a giant rocking chair, turnoffs for Denver and Mexico, and an ostrich farm.

KOKOMO

From U.S. 31, Kokomo puts on a bleak face: a swathe of chain restaurants, car dealerships, and factories. So foraging west from the highway brings a pleasant surprise: tree-lined streets, a tidy downtown, and two historic homes to tour.

WHERE TO GO

Automotive Heritage Museum. 1500 North Reed Road, Kokomo, IN 46901. Chief among Kokomo's claim as the City of Firsts is America's first car, the Pioneer, which Elwood Haynes first drove in 1894. While that car is not on display, the 1895 Pioneer II is, as well as a 1902 Haynes-Apperson, a 1932 Chrysler Imperial, and other cars. A thirties gas station, a fifties diner, and other old facades help evoke bygone eras. Open daily; closed major holidays. Fee. (765) 454–9999; www.kokomo.org.

    Elwood Haynes Museum. 1915 South Webster Street, Kokomo, IN 46902. This museum sits on the eastern edge of Kokomo's loveliest park, Highland Park (home to two curiosities: a gigantic stump and an equally large stuffed bull). Elwood Haynes, an energetic inventor, and his wife moved into this sturdy brick home in 1915. Display cases chronicle Haynes's many inventions, including stainless steel and stellite, a tough alloy; other exhibits are devoted to his personal life, including his childhood in Portland. There are items owned by the family, including clothing, furniture, and documents. A garage displays some of his automobiles. Open Tuesday through Sunday afternoons. Free. (765) 456–7500.

Seiberling Mansion/Howard County Historical Museum. 1200 West Sycamore Street, Kokomo, IN 46901. This Neo-Jacobean gem looks like something out of a movie set, with its sweeping porches, cupolas, and fanciful windows. The inside is first a county history museum with displays of items such as old swimsuits and the history of the local police force. Second, it is a house museum, with charming Victorian rooms, such as the children's bedroom with its elegant Art Nouveau window. Take note of the fabulous woodwork and fireplaces. The stairwell displays clippings and a history of how the house was brought back from near ruin. The museum regularly hosts such events as mock weddings and mystery evenings. Open Tuesday through Sunday; closed January and major holidays. Fee. (765) 452–4314; www.howardcountymuseum.org.

WHERE TO SHOP

Op Shop. 1310 South Market Street, Kokomo, IN 46904. Stained-glass windows, decorations, plates, lamp shades, and more are available at this factory shop, which prides itself in shipping its sheet glass to artists around the world. Tours of the factory, the Kokomo Opalescent Glass Company, which has been in operation since 1888, are available on Wednesday and Friday mornings. Open Monday through Friday; closed major holidays. (765) 457–1829; www. kog.com.

GREENTOWN

To reach Greentown travel east from Kokomo on East Markland Avenue/State Road 22/U.S. 35 for about 8 miles.

WHERE TO GO

Greentown Glass Museum. 112 North Meridian Street, Green-town, IN 46936. To reach the museum, turn south at the only traffic light in Greentown; the museum is in the old city hall. Although Greentown Glass was manufactured only from 1894 until 1903, it was widely popular and its creations, including rose agate and chocolate glass, are wildly popular with collectors, who travel from around the country to see the pieces on display here. Open Tuesday through Sunday mid-May through the end of October; open Saturday and Sunday during November, December, March, and April though mid-May; closed January, February, and holidays. Free. (765) 628–6206.

WHERE TO EAT

Country Cook-Inn. 10531 East 180 South, Greentown, IN 46936. Take U.S. 35/State Road 22 east of Greentown until you reach County Road 1100 East (there is a large electrical substation), where you turn south. Take that route to County Road 180 South; turn west and travel for about ½ mile, where you will see the parking lot on the south side of the road. The restaurant itself, an energy-efficient structure, actually appears to be buried in a hillside, although you would not know that once inside the sunny dining room. The Voorhis family has been serving Hoosier home cooking in the midst of their own nature preserve since 1979. Baked ham, roast beef, and baked cod are among the dinner staples; at lunch, soups and sandwiches are the fare. About a half dozen homemade pies, cooked daily on site, are available for dessert. Open for lunch Tuesday through Friday and for dinner Tuesday through Saturday. Dinner by reservation only. $$. (765) 628–7676.

PERU

Peru has two principle claims to fame: Cole Porter was born here, and for decades major circuses wintered here, prompting the town to bill itself as the Circus Capital of the World. At the chamber of commerce you can pick up some brochures with suggested walking and driving tours. One is dedicated to Porter and highlights such spots as the church where he was baptized, his grandfather's brewery, and the cemetery where he is buried. The Miami County Museum has a Porter display and a selection of circus memorabilia. Each July a youth circus festival is held here—eight days of performances by area children. Miami County, of which Peru is the county seat, was an important site for the Miami Indian Nation. A driving tour points out interesting sites, including the cemetery where Francis Slocum, a Quaker child carried off and raised by the Indians, is buried.

To get to Peru from Greentown, travel west on State Road 22/U.S. 35 to Kokomo. Then head north on U.S. 31 toward Peru and follow the signs.

WHERE TO GO

International Circus Hall of Fame. Wallace Circus Winter Quarters, 3076 East Circus Lane, Peru, IN 46970. To reach the Hall of Fame, take State Road 124 east of Peru about 3 miles. As soon as you cross the bridge over the Mississinewa River, turn left and follow the clown signs to the parking lot. Once an enormous complex that housed up to seven circuses in the winter, the Wallace site is now a National Historic Landmark and museum, which has improved its offerings each year since it opened in 1994. On the grounds there are old circus wagons and concession stands. Inside one of the vintage barns, there are displays dedicated to the memories of great performers, including brief biographies, photographs, and memorabilia, such as old costumes and posters. There are also large models of old circuses. For ten weeks beginning in late June and ending Labor Day, there are daily performances under the Big Top. In addition to the concession stands, which operate during the performance season, there is a gift shop. The museum is open daily May through October. Fee. (800) 771–0241 or (765) 472–7553; www.circushalloffame.com.

Grissom Air Museum. 6500 Hoosier Boulevard, Peru, IN 46970. The museum is on U.S. 31, 60 miles north of Indianapolis, adjacent to Grissom Air Reserve Base. Grissom is a trip into the world of the Air Force from World War II until the present. Until recently this site was part of the Grissom Air Force Base. Now there is an outdoor display with a B-17 Flying Fortress, a B-58 Hustler, and an A-10 Warhog, along with more than a score of other planes. Inside, you can sit in the cockpit of a Phantom jet, view "aviation armaments," view a movie in the theater, and stop in the gift shop for aviation-related souvenirs and more. Open Tuesday through Saturday; closed January and holidays; outdoor exhibits open daily. Free. (765) 688-2654; www.grissomairmuseum.com.

Rock Hollow Golf Club. County Road 250 West, Peru, IN 46970. The course lies west of Peru and east of U.S. 31, just north of State Road 24, also known as Business 24. (Don't confuse this road with U.S. 24, which runs on the north edge of Peru.) Winner of numerous awards, this public course, built in 1994, is considered one of the best courses in Indiana and one of the best public courses in the Midwest. Created from a former rock quarry by Indiana course designer Tim Liddy, Rock Hollow has unusual and interesting terrain. The clubhouse has a snack bar. Open March through December. Fee. (765) 473-6100; www.rockhollowgolf.com.

WHERE TO SHOP

Billie's Homemade Pie Shoppe. 21 West Third Street, Peru, IN 46970. Located in the first block west of Broadway, Peru's main north-south street, this tiny little shop sells pies—and more pies. The most popular flavors are Dutch apple, black raspberry, and sugar cream, but there is a wonderful selection every day. You can even buy pies made especially for diabetics. Open Monday through Saturday; closed holidays. (765) 473-3760.

WHERE TO EAT

Grant Street Bar & Grill. 26 North Grant Street, Peru, IN 46970. Although the exterior hasn't much to recommend it, the interior offers some of the city's best cooking. You might begin with steamed mussels and mixed baby greens, then move on to trout, filet of beef, lamb, or tuna steak. Preparations are innovative and enticing, such as brandy cream mushroom sauce over the filet. In addition to the main dining room, there is a bar where you can order from the main menu. Dinner Tuesday through Saturday. $$. (765) 472-3997.

The Siding Restaurant. 8 West Tenth Street, Peru, IN 46970. Tenth Street is immediately north of the train viaduct, and the restaurant is in the first block west of Broadway. There is a reason the Siding has been in business for more than thirty years: It has good food and a delightful setting. The space is a converted grocery store, expanded to include two old train cars and all decorated handsomely with a cross between old-time-train and Victorian decor. There are daily specials, and the most popular dishes tend to be hearty home-style fare, such as beef filets and catfish. The Friday night seafood buffet is always popular. Soups are homemade. (Ladies: You are welcome to try on the hats in the bathroom.) Open for lunch and dinner Tuesday through Friday; dinner on Saturday; and brunch on Sunday. Reservations recommended. $$. (765) 473-4041.

WHERE TO STAY

Rosewood Mansion Inn. 54 North Hood Street, Peru, IN 46970. The home itself—the woodwork, stained-glass windows, the sweeping staircase, the oak-paneled library—are opulent, but the furnishings are a bit disappointing. Nonetheless, the Rosewood makes a pleasant perch for the night. There are eleven rooms, all with private baths, and most are large and attractive. $$. (765) 472-7151; www.rosewoodmansion.com.

FOR MORE INFORMATION

Kokomo Visitor's Bureau. 1504 North Reed Road, U.S. 31, Kokomo, IN 46901; (800) 837-0971 or (765) 457-6802; www.kokomo-in.org.

   Peru/Miami County Chamber of Commerce. 2 North Broadway, Peru, IN 46970; (765) 472-1923; www.miamicochamber.com.

There is no easy way to get to Amish country, and it is undeniably farther than two hours—even from the most northeastern corner of Indianapolis. My favorite route is to take U.S. 31 north to U.S. 6 east to Nappanee and begin the tour there. Alternately, you can take U.S. 31 north to South Bend, then U.S. 20 east to Elkhart. Either way, the trip is close to three hours. Although I recommend an overnight in Amish country, you can make it a day trip by going just to Shipshewana and Middlebury or to Nappanee.

Indiana lays claim to roughly 17 percent of all Amish in North America. There are many different sects of Amish, all of which may hold slightly differing beliefs. Essentially, though, the Amish choose to live plain lives, unfettered by modern conveniences, including electricity and gasoline-powered equipment. They choose modest clothing, which looks old-fashioned to visitors, and avoid outsiders. This is part of what makes visiting Amish country so picturesque. Here you'll see farmers plowing with old-fashioned horse-drawn plows, laundry hangs on clothes lines, and no electrical lines run to the properties.

The Amish travel on foot and by bicycle and horse and buggy. This requires that automobile drivers take special precautions. On the narrow county roads that sew these communities together, cars traveling at 55 miles per hour can come flying up on buggies in just seconds, and roads are often too narrow for much maneuvering. It is particularly treacherous at night, because the buggies are so difficult to see along dark roads. Proceed with caution!

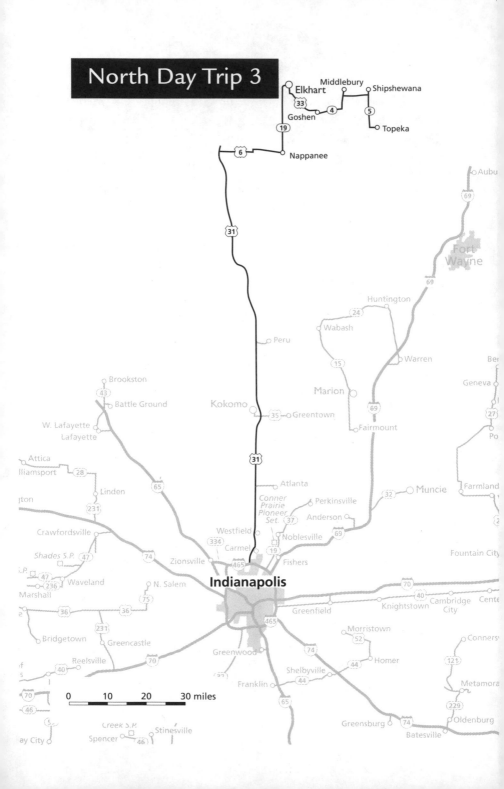

North Day Trip 3

Elkhart
Middlebury
Shipshewana
33
Goshen
4
5
19
Topeka
6
Nappanee

Aubu
69

Fort
Wayne

69

Huntington
24
Wabash
Peru
15
Warren
Ber
Marion
Geneva
69
27
Brookston
Po
43
Battle Ground
Kokomo
W. Lafayette
35
Greentown
Lafayette
Fairmount
Attica
Iliamsport
28
Atlanta
Muncie
Farmland
Linden
Conner
32
65
Prairie
231
Pioneer
Perkinsville
Set.
37
Crawfordsville
Anderson
Po
Westfield
69
Shades S.P.
47
74
334
Noblesville
Fountain City
.P.
47
Zionsville
Carmel
19
236
Waveland
N. Salem
465
Fishers
Marshall
Indianapolis
75
70
Cambridge
Cente
36
36
40
Knightstown
City
231
Greenfield
Bridgetown
Greencastle
Morristown
Conners
52
Greenwood
121
Reelsville
74
Homer
40
Shelbyville
44
Metamora
f
Greenwood
44
S
Franklin
229
65
70
Creek S.P.
Stinesville
Greensburg
74
Oldenburg
46
Spencer
46
Batesville
ay City
5

0   10   20   30 miles

The Amish and Mennonites are known for their high-quality craftsmanship, which makes shopping one of the major draws to this part of Indiana, although not all the items sold here are made by the Amish. Amish-made furniture, kitchen cabinets, and quilts are particularly sought after. Each fall there is an internationally known quilt auction in Goshen. You will notice that some of the store listings do not have telephone numbers, because Amish do not own phones. Also remember that Amish have religious objections to being photographed, so do not ask them to pose for pictures.

Do not, however, devote your entire time in Amish country to shopping, no matter how tempting. Visit Menno-Hof or one of the other sites, which will help you understand the Amish lifestyle. At the Elkhart Visitors Center you can get tapes for 90-mile tours of Amish country. The Heritage Trail focuses on the Amish and Mennonite communities. The furniture-crafters tour directs you to businesses and craftspeople.

Many stores and attractions are closed on Sunday, because this is also a religious community and most of the inhabitants are in church. Sunday is a good day for driving and enjoying the country-side or touring one of the non-Amish-related museums in Elkhart. Some businesses are not open in the winter.

NAPPANEE

Of the communities in Amish Country, Nappanee is the closest to Indianapolis. You can reach it by taking U.S. 31 North all the way to U.S. 6 East, which is north of Plymouth.

WHERE TO GO

Amish Acres. 1600 West Market (U.S. 6), Nappanee, IN 46550. You could easily spend two days at Amish Acres alone, with its variety of activities and shops. The historic section is the Stahly-Nissley-Kuhns farm, a preserved and restored Amish farm, which is listed on the National Register of Historic Places. You'll discover how the Amish made soap, kept flies from getting in the house, and stored cold foods. There's also a *grossdaadi haus*, where the grandparents lived. Guided tours (fee) take you through the farm. There is no charge to enter Amish Acres itself, with its multitude of shops—more than 400 booths featuring a broad range of items: candles, soaps, dolls, quilts, furniture, and more. The School Belfry and the Cow Shed are the places to stop for antiques on site. Plus there are several places on site to grab a bite, including a spot to buy Amish cheese, fudge, and ice cream. For a full meal head for the Restaurant Barn, where meals are served family style, including heaping platters of potatoes, vegetables, and chicken.

For entertainment there is the Round Barn Theatre, which produces musicals year-round. You can see as many as three different shows a week during the summer season, often including the quintessential Amish musical: *Plain and Fancy*. (800) 800-4942 or (219) 773-4188; www.amishacres.com.

ELKHART

While the surrounding countryside is bucolic, Elkhart has always been a business center, beginning as a shipping port on the St. Joseph River. It is known as a center for making musical instruments and recreational vehicles, but it is also the place where Alka-Seltzer and One-A-Day vitamins were created.

WHERE TO GO

Midwest Museum of American Art. 429 South Main Street, Elkhart, IN 46516. Located in an old bank building, this museum surveys nineteenth- and twentieth-century American art, including Grandma Moses, Norman Rockwell, and Grant Wood. In addition to the originals, the museum has the largest Norman Rockwell print collection in the Midwest. The gift shop sells books, original art by regional artists, Native American jewelry, cards, stationery, and more. Fee. (219) 293-6660.

Ruthmere House Museum. 302 East Beardsley Avenue, Elkhart, IN 46514. You may have seen this home on A&E, featured in the series *America's Castles*. Built by a student of Frank Lloyd Wright between 1908 and 1910, the mansion combines Beaux Art and Prairie School architecture and uses predominately American-made materials. Each room is like a little jewel box with ornate frieze, intricate paneling, silk and satin draperies, and exquisite furnishings. The dining room walls are covered with scenes of Italy painted on velvet. Guided tours take about an hour. The small gift shop sells books, small porcelain boxes, and things that evoke the heyday of the home, which the Beardsley family occupied until 1944. Open Tuesday through Saturday beginning the first Tuesday in April through December. Open on Sunday afternoon during July and August. Fee. (888) 287-7696 or (219) 264-0330; www.ruthmere.com.

S. Ray Miller Auto Museum. 2130 Middlebury Street, Elkhart, IN 46516. Swanky cars, such as the 1909 Sterling Brass once owned by Al Capone's lawyer, Jackie Hughes, fill this museum. Most of the cars are Hoosier made: Cords, Studebakers, Marmons, and Dusenbergs. There are about forty cars, plus a variety of period memorabilia. Open Monday through Friday and the last complete weekend of each month. (888) 260-8566; www.millerautomuseum.org.

GOSHEN

The odd little octagonal building on the northwest corner of Main Street and Lincoln Avenue by the county courthouse was a police booth, built in 1939 to give police a vantage point to watch for bank robbers, such as John Dillinger, an Indiana boy. The town is nationally known for its Michiana Mennonite Relief Sale, which is held the fourth Saturday of September each year, when hundreds of quilts and related items go on the auction block.

WHERE TO SHOP

Old Bag Factory. 1100 Chicago Avenue, Goshen, IN 46528. Coming into town on U.S. 33, take that road until you come to Chicago Avenue; turn north on Chicago and follow it as it curves west, where you will find the Old Bag Factory on the corner of Chicago and Indiana Avenues. Built in 1896, this sturdy three-story brick building was once a bag factory and, before that, a soap company. Today it is a shopping center with about twenty different stores featuring hand-thrown pottery, quilts, chocolates, gifts, and more. Open Monday through Saturday. (219) 534-2502; www.oldbagfactory.com.

WHERE TO EAT AND STAY

Checkerberry Inn. 62644 County Road 37, Goshen, IN 46528. For a splurge, this is tops in Amish Country and beyond. The restaurant, open only for dinner, is nouvelle American cuisine with first-rate service and an extensive wine list. The menu changes frequently but you might have cashew-encrusted lamb with merlot sauce or chicken breast stuffed with pistachios and Brie. The rooms are beautiful, each one a little different and all with spacious bathrooms and good views of the surrounding farmland. There are some suites. Outside there's a pool, croquet lawn, and plenty of comfy rockers on the broad front porch. Inside there's a large gathering room with board games, a TV, and books. Breakfast is included. $$$. (219) 642-4445; www.checkerberryinn.com.

MIDDLEBURY

The road between Middlebury and Shipshewana is one of the most scenic in Amish Country because it is bustling with buggies, bicycles. and pedestrians. Remember to drive slowly! Downtown Middlebury is easy to navigate on foot.

WHERE TO GO

Sunshine Animal Farm and Miniature Golf. 240 U.S. 20, Middlebury, IN 46540. For families with youngsters, this is a pleasant diversion, part of the Das Dutchman Essenhaus complex. There's a farm tour, with opportunities to pet the animals, ride a pony, and play miniature golf. Open Monday through Saturday, with more-limited days in winter. Fee. (800) 455-9471; www.essenhaus.com.

WHERE TO SHOP

Amish Heritage Furniture. 52886-A State Road 13, Middlebury, IN 46540. Although only some of the furniture here is crafted by the Amish, the company was founded by an Amish family and continues to uphold the standards of building set by the family in the mid-1800s. All furniture is solid wood, with no particle board or veneers, and each piece is bench-built by a single craftsman, who signs and dates his work. The company accepts custom orders in addition to offering more than 150 different styles. Open Monday through Saturday year-round. (800) 870-2524 or (219) 825-1185; www.ahfurniture.com.

Essenhaus Village Shops. 240 U.S. 20, Middlebury, IN 46540. Part of Das Dutchman Essenhaus this complex includes a range of shops where you can by food, clothes, gifts, and more. After a filling meal at the restaurant, you can walk off a few calories roaming from store to store. There is playground equipment outside for the children. Open Monday through Saturday. (800) 455-9471; www.essenhaus.com.

WHERE TO EAT

Amish Country Kitchen. 240 U.S. 20, Middlebury, IN 46540. Part of the Das Dutchman Essenhaus complex, this enormous restaurant serves traditional Amish meals. Chicken, fried ham, baked steak, roasted potatoes, and homemade desserts and breads are all part of this meal. Pies are spectacular. As you arrive, you may be overwhelmed by the crowd, but the restaurant is so large that all lines move quickly. Open Monday through Saturday. $-$$. (800) 455-9471; www.essenhaus.com.

WHERE TO STAY

Essenhaus Country Inn. 240 U.S. 20, Middlebury, IN 46540. Adjacent to the Amish Country Kitchen, this new lodge brings the outside into its atrium, with picket-fence railings, window boxes with posies, and plenty of light. Rooms are comfy and all are decorated differently. A continental breakfast is included. $$. (800) 455-9471; www.essenhaus.com.

WHERE TO STAY AND EAT

Patchwork Quilt Country Inn. 11748 County Road 2, Middlebury, IN 46540. In Amish country style, the Patchwork Quilt Country Inn serves a feast at every meal. Roast beef and buttermilk pecan chicken are favorites, and the homemade breads are irresistible. Leave a bit of room for dessert. Accommodations are crisply clean and attractive, with quilts on every bed. $$. The restaurant is open February through December; the inn is open year-round. No smoking; no alcohol served. $$. (219) 825-2417.

SHIPSHEWANA

There are lots of spots to shop in Shipshewana, along with one of the areas most edifying cultural sites.

WHERE TO GO

Menno-Hof. 510 South Van Buren Street (State Road 5), Shipshewana, IN 46565. Although the Amish themselves shun "the English," as nonbelievers are called, you can get an introduction to their culture and beliefs, as well as those of the Hutterites and the Mennonites. A variety of interactive exhibits, including movies, tell the tale. The brave will be thrilled by the "tornado" room, which simulates the experience of being in one. Youngsters play happily with sturdy wooden blocks in a large play area. The gift shop is operated by Ten Thousand Villages, which promotes the works of native craftspeople around the world, with profits going back to the creators. Open Monday through Saturday. Free; donation requested. (219) 768–4117; www.mennohof.com.

WHERE TO SHOP

Shipshewana Flea Market and Auction. Considered one of the largest flea markets in the country, this event, held Tuesday and Wednesday May through October, draws buyers and sellers from several states. The auction, held Wednesday year-round, features antiques and gently used items. At the Wednesday livestock auction, held in a barn, you can take home a pig or a goat. (219) 768–4129.

Yoder's Department Store. State Road 5, Shipshewana, IN 46565. If you have a hankering to stitch a quilt yourself, this is one of the best places to get a start. Famous for its fabrics, the store carries more than 10,000 bolts—from burlap to silk to felt and cotton. There are also other items, most with a practical bent for the area farmers: work clothes and hats. The same shopping plaza has a hardware store that will make any do-it-yourselfer salivate. (219) 768–4887; www.shipshewana.com/fabrics.

WHERE TO EAT

Blue Gate Restaurant. Riegsecker Marketplace, 195 North Van Buren Street, Shipshewana, IN 46565. Meals feature hearty Amish food, such as chicken and noodles; thick, rich soups; home-baked pies; and more. Here you order from the menu, but just 2 blocks north is another Blue Gate, owned by the same people and serving the same food, only family style, where big bowls and platters of food are brought to your table. There is always a crowd, so be prepared to wait, but the landscaping around the market, with little water mills and a stream running through a little garden, is charming to look at. Open for breakfast, lunch, and dinner Monday through Saturday year-round. $–$$. (219) 768–4725.

WHERE TO STAY

Green Meadow Ranch. 7905 West 450 North (State Road 5), Shipshewana, IN 46565. Travel north of Shipshewana about 2 miles, where you'll see the white picket fence on the east side. Around since 1984, this bed-and-breakfast offers a pastoral retreat where miniature horses and other animals dot the pasture and guests lounge on the large sunny porch, stroll the lawn, relax in the gazebo, or gather around the player piano. Rooms are large, light, and accented with antiques, but not all have private baths. $$. Call for open times in winter. (219) 768–4221; www.greenmeadowranch.com.

TOPEKA

There isn't so much a downtown Topeka as there is a scattering of shops with Topeka mailing addresses, all south of Shipshewana along and shooting off State Road 5.

WHERE TO GO

Hoosier Buggy Shop. 5345 West 600 South, Topeka, IN 46571. Although you may not want to take home a buggy, which can cost $3,000 to $6,000 or more, you will enjoy watching the Hochstetler family craft and repair carriages and buggies. Their work not only supplies the Amish, who travel by buggy, but also places that offer carriage rides, such as Disney World. Fee.

WHERE TO SHOP

Fern's Country Foods. 7970 West 400 South, Topeka, IN 46571. To reach Fern's, take State Road 5 south of Shipshewana; you'll see Fern's on the northeast corner of the intersection of that road and County Road 400 South. If you've enjoyed your Amish meals, this is the place to find the ingredients to re-create them at home. You'll find rivels, which are a type of Amish noodle, loads of jellies and jams, potato soup mixes, and more. You can watch the Amish women in the back roll out the sheets of noodles or have a sandwich on the spot. (219) 593-2222.

Red Geranium. 9440 West 400 South, Topeka, IN 46571. Once a general store, the Red Geranium is now stocked with antiques and accessories with a bent toward a European country look. It's a sister shop to the White Swan across the street. Both are delightful. (219) 593-3398.

White Swan. 9440 West 400 South, Topeka, IN 46571. With antiques, gifts, cards, and accessories, the White Swan has a grand mix of items. The main focus, though, is on traditional European furniture and china. There are several rooms to explore. (219) 593-3851.

Yoder Popcorn. 7680 West 200 South, Topeka, IN 46571. Drive south on State Road 5 about 4 miles to County Road 200 South, where you turn left, or east. You'll see the sign for Yoder's about ¼ mile on the right. You've probably seen Yoder's Popcorn in grocery stores, but this is home base. In the store you'll find popcorn of every variety, more than you imagined there might be. There are samples as well as popcorn poppers, popcorn seasoning, and other accoutrements. Open Monday through Saturday, May through December, and Wednesday, Friday, and Saturday, March through April. (800) 892-2170.

FOR MORE INFORMATION

Elkhart County Convention & Visitors Bureau. 219 Caravan Drive, Elkhart, IN 46514. In addition to brochures this center has tapes you can rent, guiding you through Amish Country mile by mile. (800) 262–8161 or (219) 262–8161; www.amishcountry.org.

Helen Wernie O'Guinn began her journalism career in the late 1970s, working for *The Saturday Evening Post*. Her interests and opportunities led her to travel journalism, a field to which she has devoted most of her time since then, working as a magazine editor and freelance author. O'Guinn, a member of the Society of American Travel Writers, has spoken on travel and journalism at seminars, on television and radio, and to classrooms.

O'Guinn lives in Indianapolis with her husband and son. A grown daughter in Los Angeles, an older son on the move, and a brother in London offer the author regular reasons to pack her bags.